The Muggletonian Works of Laurence Clarkson: The Onely True Bishop

Edited by Mike Pettit

Visit us online at www.muggletonianpress.com **and view our entire range of Muggletonian Literature**

A Muggletonian Press Book

Copyright © Mike Pettit 2009

All rights reserved. No portion of this publication may be reproduced, stored in a retrieval system, or transmitted in any form or by any means, electronic, mechanical, photocopy, recording or otherwise, without prior written permission of the copyright owner. While many of the original texts which form the basis of this publication are to be found in the public domain the texts found herein have been typographically modernised and reformatted at great expense. Please respect the resulting copyright that such work has created.

ISBN 978-1-907466-02-1

Cover Image: plate 7 from Isaac Frost's "Two Systems of Astronomy" published in 1846, depicting Muggletonian cosmology.

Published by:
Muggletonian Press
129 Hebdon Road
London SW17 7NL
England

I would like to make it clear that in editing and publishing this volume I am not seeking to advocate any element of *Muggletonian* theology. I fully subscribe to historic orthodox Christianity as expressed in the Reformed Confessions of Faith and would plead with all the readers of this work to consider the claims of the triune God.

From the Heidelberg Catechism

Question 3. Whence knowest thou thy misery?

Answer: Out of the law of God.

Question 4. What does the law of God require of us?

Answer: Christ teaches us that briefly, Matt. 22:37-40, "Thou shalt love the Lord thy God with all thy heart, with all thy soul, and with all thy mind, and with all thy strength. This is the first and the great commandment; and the second is like unto it, Thou shalt love thy neighbour as thyself. On these two commandments hang all the law and the prophets."

Question 5. Canst thou keep all these things perfectly?

Answer: In no wise; for I am prone by nature to hate God and my neighbour.

Mike Pettit

CONTENTS

Introduction v
The Dictionary Of National Biography 1
The Right Devil Unfolded 5
   The Epistle 6
   The Index 7
   Introduction 8
   CAP. I. 11
   CAP. II. 37
   CAP. III 41
   CAP. IV 52
The Quakers Downfal 59
   Rom. 15.4 60
   Phil. 2.6 72
   Rom. 9.11 98
A Paradisical Dialogue Betwixt Faith & Reason 111
   CHAP. 1. 114
   CHAP. 2. 121
   CHAP. 3. 126
   CHAP. 4. 130
   CHAP. 5. 135
   CHAP. 6. 138
   CHAP. 7. 142
   CHAP. 8. 149
   CHAP. 9. 154
   CHAP. 10. 159
   CHAP. 11. 162
   CHAP. 12. 166
   CHAP. 13. 175
   CHAP. 15. 182
   CHAP. 16. 185
   Divine Prospect 196
The Lost Sheep Found 203
   An Epistle left upon Record for the Believers 245

INTRODUCTION

Laurence Clarkson is without doubt one of the most fascinating characters to emerge from the seventeenth century. Clarkson's autobiography "The Lost Sheep Found" represents one of the finest insights we have into what is arguably the most interesting chapter of English history.

Clarkson is chiefly remembered by history as a "Ranter", with his later devotion to Muggletonianism being largely forgotten. There has been much scholarly debate as to whether the Ranters actually formed a popular movement, or whether they played a more mythic role, much akin to witchcraft in the popular imagination. Even Ranter skeptics admit that "Laurence Clarkson in 1650 came closest to the Ranter stereotype*".

Laurence Clarkson (or as he often referred to himself "Lawrence Claxton") passed through the established Church, the Puritans, the Presbyterians, the Baptists, the Seekers, the Ranters and finally he found his journey's end as a Muggletonian.

Clarkson's first works were the 1646 "Truth released from prison to its former liberty" and the now lost "The Pilgrimage of Saints, by church cast out, in Christ found, seeking truth", followed by the 1647 "A Generall Charge or, Impeachment of High-treason, in the Name of Justice Equity, Against the Communality of England". In 1650 came the Ranter classic "A Single Eye, All Light, No Darkness; or Light and Darkness One".

In 1658 Clarkson met John Reeve and converted to Muggletonianism, writing "The Right Devil Unfolded" and "The Quakers Downfal" in 1659. John Harwood responded to "The Quakers Downfal" in "The Lying Prophet Discovered And Reproved: In An Answer To Several Particulars in a Book Called The Quakers Downfall Said To Be Written By Lawrence Claxton". Harwood records a meeting between himself, Clarkson and Lodowick Muggleton where Clarkson rather surprisingly appears to dominate Muggleton.

Clarkson went on to write the autobiographical "The Lost Sheep Found" and "A Paradisical Dialogue Betwixt Faith and Reason" in 1660, his final work "A Wonder of Wonders" has now been lost.

---

* Davis, J. C., "Fear, Myth and Furore: Reappraising the "Ranters" (*Past and Present*, No. 129. [November, 1990], 79-103), 95.

These works record Clarkson's belief that he was:

> "the onely true Bishop and faithful Messenger of Christ Jesus"*

> "the alone, true and faithful Messenger of Christ Jesus"†

> "the onely true converted Messenger of Christ Jesus"‡

It is not surprising therefore that following John Reeve's death in 1658 Clarkson sought to take leadership of the movement, a development that was strongly resisted by Muggleton, who Clarkson was effectively seeking to exclude from the commission. Soon after he had claimed exclusive authority Clarkson recanted in the face of Muggleton's opposition and lack of support within the Church.

What is surprising is that Clarkson, for all his spiritual wandering, accepted Muggleton's 1661 terms for his excommunication to be lifted by ceasing his writing and losing the financial support that he had been receiving from the Church. Clarkson eventually went to his sad, lonely death in debtor's prison in 1667.

Muggleton recorded the latter years and death of his old adversary in Chapter Six of his autobiography "The Acts of the Witnesses of Spirit":

"He continued thus, four Years after John Reeve Died, until the Year 1661, and in a while after Laurance Claxton humbled himself to me, and acknowledged his Fault, and I forgave him, and took him into my Favour, but ty'd him not to Write any more. So he continued several Years afterwards, justifying his Faith and Confidence, in this Commission of the Spirit. But it came to pass, when the Fire destroyed the City of London, he, to get a Livelyhood, did engage to help Persons of Quality to borrow Money, to build their Houses again. But the Persons that had the Money did run a way, and left Claxton in the Lurch; the Debt was one Hundred Pounds. So he only was Arrested, and put in Ludgate Goal, for this Money: He lay there a whole Year, and Died there. But he gave a very good Testimony of his Faith in the true God, and in this Commission of the Spirit, and of that full assurance of eternal Happiness he should enjoy to Eternity, after his Death. Insomuch that all the Prisoners marvelled, and were sorry they had opposed him so when he was alive."

---

* "The Right Devil Unfolded" title page
† "The Quakers Downfal" title page
‡ "The Lost Sheep Found" title page

THE DICTIONARY OF NATIONAL BIOGRAPHY

From pages five to seven of Volume XI of "The Dictionary of National Biography" (1887). The contribution being written by Charles William Sutton (1848-1920).

CLAXTON or CLARKSON, LAURENCE (1615-1667), sectary, was born at Preston, Lancashire, in 1615. He was brought up in the faith of the church of England. In an age of puritanism his conscience was afflicted, among other things, with the 'toleration of maypoles, dancing, and rioting,' with which the Lord's day was profaned in Lancashire. He started on a strange pilgrimage through various sects, beginning, as a layman, with the presbyterians, with whose system he quarrelled after a time. He then made a brief trial of the independents, joined the antinomians, became a preacher among them, and in his own opinion was 'not inferior to any priest in those days.' After this time he held for six months a 'benefice' of the value of about 50*l.* per annum. The name of the place at which he was 'parish priest' is called by him Pulom. There is little doubt that Pulham Market in Norfolk is meant, although his name does not occur in the registers. In the course of a rambling life which he afterwards led he became a dipper or anabaptist (immersed 6 Nov. 1644, exercised his ministry till 24 Jan. 1645), and his practices brought upon him a prosecution, when he was cast into prison at Bury St. Edmunds. He was released from confinement 15 July 1645, having procured his liberty by formally renouncing the practice of dipping. He is found shortly after among the seekers, and we have the first of his tracts, entitled 'The Pilgrimage of Saints by Church cast out, in Christ found, seeking Truth' (Lond. 1646, 4to). Edwards (*Gangræna*) states that as a seeker Claxton preached one Sunday at Bow Church before a large and distinguished congregation. He was appointed minister of Sandridge in Hertfordshire, where he 'continued not a year.' To this date belongs another tract, 'Truth released from Prison to its former Libertie; or a True Discovery who are the Troublers of True Israel; the Disturbers of England's Peace' (London, 1646, 8vo, pp. 26). It is dedicated to the 'mayor, aldermen, and inhabitants of Preston.' Soon after this he wrote a tract against the parliament, called 'A General Charge or Impeachment of High Treason, in the name of Justice Equity, against the Communality of England' (1647, 4to). He was presented to a small parish in Lincolnshire, but soon grew weary of it. On 19 Dec. 1648, according to a record in the manuscript minutes of the Fourth London Classis (now in Dr. Williams's library), 'Mr. Laurence Claxton presented himselfe, brought certeine papers as testimonials wch the presbyterie returned, as not satisfactorie.' After the rejection of these overtures he became a ranter. His extravagant and extremely licentious conduct brought again upon him the displeasure of the authorities. For publishing 'an impious and blasphemous' tract called 'A Single Eye all Light no Darkness, or Light and Darkness One' (1650, 4to, pp. 16), he was condemned by the House of Commons to be sent to prison for one month, and from that time 'to be banished out of the commonwealth and the territories thereof, and not to return upon pain of death.' The book itself was burned by the common hangman. Somehow its author escaped the penalty of banishment, and for a while he travelled about as a professor of astrology and physic, and even aspired to the art of magic. He states that he was afterwards 'beneficed' at Terrington St. John parish in Marshland, Norfolk, and was 'by all the town received' at Snettisham in the same county. In 1658 he came to London from the eastern counties and made the acquaintance of John Reeve and Ludowick Muggleton, to whose doctrines he became a convert. On the death of Reeve about the latter end of July 1658 he applied for and obtained 'leave to write in the vindication and justification of this commission of the spirit.' The treatises he wrote are entitled: 1. 'The Right Devil discovered, in his Descent, Form, Education, Qualification, Place and Nature of Torment,' 1659, small 8vo. Muggleton in enumerating Claxton's books states that the first he wrote (as a Mugggletonian) was styled 'Look about you, for the Devil that you fear is in you,' but this may have been the title of the above work while yet in manuscript. It is, however, given by Claxton himself in 'Lost Sheep found,' p. 33. 2. 'The Quakers Downfal, with all other Dispensations, their inside turn'd outward,' 1659, 4to. On the title-page of this work he styled himself 'the alone, true, and faithful messenger of Christ Jesus, the Lord of Glory.' It was answered by John Harwood, a quaker, in a tract entitled 'The Lying Prophet discovered and reproved,' 1659, 4to. 3. 'A Paradisical Dialogue betwixt Faith and Reason: disputing the high mysterious Secrets of Eternity, the like never extant in our Revelation,' 1660, 4to. 4. 'Wonder of Wonders,' 1660. 6. 'The Lost Sheep found, or the Prodigal returned to his Father's House, after many a sad and weary journey through many religious countreys,' 1660, 4to. pp. 64. The last work, which is really an autobiography, was used by Scott in 'Woodstock;' the author's weaknesses are displayed in it with extraordinary frankness. 'He had grown so proud as to say that nobody could write in the vindication of the commission, now John Reeve was dead, but he.' Muggleton was highly offended at the work, and at once discountenanced the author. Before this time there had, however, been a difference between them on another business. For twelve months (till 1661) he sought in vain for followers, but finding Muggleton's power too strong for him he humbled himself to the prophet and acknowledged his fault. Thereupon he was taken again into favour, but undertook not to write any more. His subsequent conduct seems to have been exemplary, as he gained credit from Muggleton as a faithful disciple. His later publications contain much practical moral teaching, especially against uncleanness, as is characteristic of Muggletonian writings. He is supposed to have been twice married, first to the daughter of R. Marchant, by whom he had five children. He probably got his living while in London by trading. At an earlier date, according to Edwards, he was a tailor. His last speculation was disastrous. After the fire of London he undertook to obtain money at interest to help sufferers to rebuild their houses, but he was left in the lurch by some persons who had procured 100*l.* through him, and for this debt he was put in Ludgate gaol, where after lingering a year he died in 1667.

The name is written Clarkson in his earlier tracts and Claxton in the later ones. It was no doubt originally Clarkson. In that form the name is still common about Preston, where it is pronounced Clackson.

[Claxton's Lost Sheep found; Edwards's Gangræna, 3rd edit. part i. 15, 19 (second pagination), 103, ii. 6, 23, 29, 42, 136; Commons' Journals, vi. 427, 444, 475-6; Hart's Index Expurgatorius Anglicanus, 1872, p. 166; Sir W. Scott's Prose Works, xviii. 86-9; the same article in Quart. Rev. xliii. 475-8; Rev. Alex. Gordon in Proc. Liverpool Literary and Phil. Soc., 1869-70, xxiv. 199-201; additional information and suggestions given by Mr. Gordon privately; Notes and Queries, 4th series, xi. 278, 350, 487, xii. 17; Jos. Smith's Biblioth. Anti-Quakeriana, pp. 124-6; Muggleton's Acts of the Witnesses of the Spirit (as quoted by A. Gordon, ubi supra, and in Notes and Queries).]

C. W. S.

Look about you,
For the Devil that you fear is in you:
OR, THE RIGHT
D E V I L
UNFOLDED:

1.		*Descent*
2.		*Form*
3.	*In his*	*Education*
4.		*Qualification*
5.		*Place and nature of Torment.*

With many other Divine Secrets, never from the beginning yet extant till this Last Witness, so beneficial both for the Seed of *Cain,* and the Seed of Faith.

Written by *Laur. Claxton.*

John 8.44. *Ye are of your father the devil, and the lusts of your father ye will do,* &c.
   He that committeth sin, is of the devil, &c.
I John 3.8,9. *Whosoever is born of God, doth not commit sin, for his seed remaineth in him, and he cannot sin, because he is born of God.*

LONDON:
Printed for the Author, and are to be sold by *William Learner,* at the *Blackmoor* near Fleet-bridge. 1659.

THE EPISTLE.

To you the Seed of Faith, the onely beloved Family of the Lord of Glory, your poor despised Brother, yet heir with you of that immortal endless kingdom, saluteth you as followeth:

In this Treatise I have brought to publique view your grand Opposite *Cain,* the father of all the devils children, in which you may take full sight of his majestical person in this his kingdom, with all his glory appertaining to him; therefore you that are not onely verbally, but really the Seed of *Adam,* sing praises to Christ your Savior, that your treasure is not laid up in this kingdom that shall perish and have an end; and because of poverty here, rejoyce that your riches is in your kingdom yet to come, mourn not because of hatred here, for this kingdom loves its own; let this rejoyce your souls, that every day you are nearer your Journeys end, and let this elevate your spirits, that before you be aware, the Lord whom ye love & have long looked for, is a coming, and will wipe away all tears from your eyes, and sorrows from your hearts; for believe it, the Lord hath recorded all your enemies in his brest, and will execute vengeance upon them; therefore fear not the credit of this world, nor the loss of thy life for thy God, but rejoyce thou hast power over thy corruptions, I say rejoyce for evermore, for our God doth love an upright innocent soul; therefore take heed of hypocrisie, and deceive not thy self in acknowledging a personal God, and hatest to be reformed, for it is life eternal, not onely to be a professor, but a possessor; this is the *White Stone* and *Hidden Manna,* that hath so few, and no name, you know what I say; therefore forget not that first of *John 3.17.* I say remember upon what account, and to whom I speak it, otherwise at the last day thou shalt finde those sayings in *Matthew 25.34* &c. fall heavy upon thee.

Now who ever shall peruse this Epistle, and hath a desire to read one thing more then another, then cast thy eye upon this ensuing *Index,* and there from Page 1 to 20, and so on, thou shalt finde by the Figures, what thou most delightest in; and the Lord give thee understanding in it, and faith to observe it.   *Vale.*

THE INDEX

I.   *You have the Introduction of the miraculous Convert.*

CAP. I.

II.   *The first descent and true form of the right Devil discovered.*
III.   *Certain notable Queries answered.*
IV.   *The Righteous Rule, by which you shall finde few rich men saved, and that very few, if any of the Seed of Faith shall be rich in this world.*
V.   *The difference of rich men.*
VI.   *The right devil proved by Scripture.*
VII.   *The devil that tempted Christ interpreted.*
VIII. *None but the Seed of Faith understand the Scripture.*

CAP. II.

IX.   *No Saint educated like the devil.*
X.   *Not onely a rich, but a poor devil.*

CAP. III.

XI.   *The light ranting devils quality.*
XII.   *The dark ranting devils quality.*
XIII. *The covetous devils quality.*
XIV. *The vast differences of the two seeds in death.*

CAP. IV.

XV.   *The Saint-like moderate devils quality.*
XVI. *The maner of Christs coming to judgement.*
XVII. *The place where the devils shall be tormented.*
XVIII. *The nature of the devils torment.*

THE INTRODUCTION.

About the first of February 1657. *I took my journey for* London, *for the accomplishing of a place then in agitation, and at my arrival there, I was informed that the two Witnesses that I had often read of in* Revelation *the* 11th, *was now to be seen and spoken withal, unto whom I forthwith applied my self to hear what they could say for themselves; then thinking in my self, there was none in mortal flesh able to maintain an argument with me, as to those fundamentals by them published to the world, viz. God, Devil, Heaven, Hell, Angels, and the mortality of the Soul; but, alas! when I came to* John Reeve, *so styled the Prophet of the Lord, which at that time I could not believe, and observed his position then stated unto me, which was this, Did I know the form, nature, and essence of God? Instead of cavelling or improving the weapons of reason, with which I was well guarded, I was admiring the word* Form, *how it was possible God should admit of a Form: to which I replyed, desiring to know what maner of Form he had. His answer was, God was in the Form of a man, clearer then Chrystal, brighter then the Sun, swifter then thought: Then was my soul the more troubled, that God being a man, should be swifter then thought; This I concluded, it was requisite God should be swifter then thought, but God having a Form, I could not understand how he should be swifter then thought; well notwithstanding I was not satisfied, yet at that time little did I say, onely took his book along with me, and to my Chamber I went, perusing his writing, in which I found such heavenly Mysteries, that the eyes nor ears of mortal flesh had never writ, seen, or heard the like before; so that now began the travel of my soul, how I should own this unparallel'd truth, and hold my Benefice, which was the onely livelihood of my self and five children, consulting with my reason, it would be well if I could injoy both; and to that end I endeavored my self, and to my Benefice went again, improving my parts as formerly, but the more I labored to preserve my self under that goard of above an hundred pounds* per annum, *the more the beams of the eternal God did scorch and wither my shadow of rest.*

Yea, presently after there came in me a mighty conflict which did sift, turn, yea, search the whole man in me, insomuch that I was as it were in a warlike posture, whether I had best yeeld up my Benefice, or hold it at a venture; but then, even then, was I summoned to give an account of my Stewardship, how I had spent my life this forty years, and what I did think would become of my Soul, and what would thy riches and glory here avail thee in the grave, but especially at the great day of account?

Now friends, I would have you understand that I was in a strait betwixt two, so that out of hand the spirit of Faith pleaded thus in me, That I had no Commission to preach, and forthwith must cease, though it was to the loss of my hundred pound a year; then stept in the spirit of reason, and pleaded, How shall my self, with five children subsist, when as this Benefice would comfortably and honorably provide for us during life. Then, even then, was death and life before me, and the spirit of Faith pleaded thus within me, That whether I had rather injoy my Benefice, and therein live honorably in this world, and so be damned to all eternity in the world to come, or whether I would hearken to that call within me, to forsake my preaching with the benefit thereof, and trust the Lord with my self and the children? this lay hard upon me, and so narrowly pursued me, that for the space of three weeks I could not be at quiet sleeping nor waking, going nor riding, in which time I had no little conflict to disown the glory of this world, for the glory of God, supposing my condition to be safe and secure as any man or Parish Priest in the world whatsoever; and for my doctrine, I was not inferior to any, but more able to declare the truth which I apprehended to be truth, then the best of them.

Notwithstanding, all this would do me no good, nor in the least silence this combate within me, but I must cease my trade of preaching, lest a worse thing befall me; and at that instant it came in my thoughts, Remember me, how here in this world where now thou livest, I was a poor despised Saviour, though now a rich immortal glorious God; and therefore take no care, I will provide for thee and thine, so far as is requisite for such a one as thou art to be; and withal remember when thou wast in thy wickedness, not knowing me, then I provided for thee, How much more now shall I be mindful of thee so far as shall concern thy good: Many of these refreshings did arise from my seed spring within me, that I was made willing to disown all, that not long before I had taken great pains to perfect, and so in submitting to the true light, darkness fled, and the Lord freely forgave me all that was past, present, and to come, and hath every week more and more enabled me to walk obedient and upright before him, mortifying sin continually within me, to the onely praise of my God be it spoken, that my calling and election is so firm and sure, that I weigh not the censure of men nor Angels, but as sure as Christ is the eternal God, I shall at his appearance reign eternally with him in the heavens; and though in my journey to my bed of sleep, the grave, instead of riches, I shall meet with poverty; instead of fullness, want; instead of honor, dishonor; instead of love, hatred; instead of a good name, all maner of evil tearms; instead of friends, foes; yea, may be such as will persecute me to the graves mouth, yet now all this I matter not; in that sin is my servant, and Christ is my Master, whom my soul earnestly craves more *knowledge of himself, with assistance of his power to withstand the despisers of thy person so glorious in my eyes.*

Now since the Lord in his own time, hath in his free mercy called and chosen me according to his eternal purpose of old, that I should redeem the time, I have lost forty years, and for the future, the short time I have to stay in this present evil world, my God, I doubt not, will enable me to walk holy and without blame before him till I be called to sleep, or the day of his appearance change this my poor mortal, to that immortal like himself, either of which it shall please my God of mercy in his own time and pleasure to call me unto, I had rather enjoy, then now at this present [mark what I say] then now at this present, enjoy all the riches and wisdom that ever God gave to Solomon; *so that I can boldly say, Happy, yea, thrice happy am I that the seed of* Cain, *that lying murthering devil, who captivated my soul many years a servant of sin, and all maner of evil, is now disarmed and silent in me, and in room thereof the seed of* Abraham *that blessed seed of Faith, hath got the victory, by which I am delivered from the power of the fruits of flesh, and translated to the fruits of the spirit of Faith, in the person of Christ the onely true and everliving God.*

After this remarkable change, being at home, silent and quiet in this my mortal tabernacle, I was powerfully commanded, yea my seed-spring hath certain times invited me to demonstrate to publike view, that point concerning the Devil; which very title or name Devil, doth fright the Devil himself, and the ground of this his fear doth arise from the non-knowledge of his first rise, the description of his form, as also his education and qualification, with the place and nature of his torment: thy ignorance in these things, hath produced matter sufficient for my Genius to recal thy thoughts, as touching thy mistake of the right Devil, and so according as the true onely wise God hath revealed in me, I shall make known these in their order, which hath not yet been branched forth as aforesaid.

CAP. I.

The first descent and true Form of the right Devil, discovered.

First, as touching the Devil, his rise and originality, I shall infallibly make known unto thee, and from inspiration shew, that subtile beast or Serpent there spoken of, was no horned beast or creeping Serpent, as the Priests vainly teach; neither was it any Pippin or Pearmain, or any other sort of Apple that was so pleasant in *Eves* eye, or delightful to her taste: No, no, it was that reprobate glorious Angel, that was far more pleasant and sweeter to *Eves* taste then the sweetest fruit whatsoever: therefore I shall demand of the proudest of his seed now living, what was, or which now of all creatures or things in this world, is most pleasant in thy eyes, or most in thy soul desiring to taste? Art thou a man, then is not a woman beautified and richly attired, most pleasant in thy eyes, and sweetest to thy taste? Art thou a woman, what saith thou, is not a man beautified and richly attired with subtile and sophistical expressions, most pleasant in thy eyes, and soonest deceived by him?

Even so that reprobate Angelical man, was that subtile Serpent or beast of the field; minde what you read, that angel-man was so pleasant to her taste, that she took it, and did eat, which is no more then this, That proud, beautiful, glorious angel-man, did by his seeming divine wisdom and Angelical person, bewitch *Eves* innocent soul to hearken unto him, and her eyes to dote upon him, that she admitted him enterance into her body, in which, and by which she found so much delight (that after that) she iniced her husband, who had copulation with *Eve,* as man with woman in these days; so her innocent soul and body being defiled by that reprobate Dragon-angel, after which her husband *Adam* going in unto her, was also defiled, as a sound woman should receive into her body a diseased man, not onely her womb is defiled, but she pollutes her husband also; as the Pox or Gangreen doth eat throughout the whole man, so *Eves* soul and body being defiled, did putrifie the seed of *Adam*: From hence it was there came two seeds, the one pure, the other impure, the one righteous, the other wicked; Instance, from the womb of *Rebecca* came two seeds at one travel, blessed *Jacob,* and cursed *Esau;* thus in plainness of termes, I have in short writ to plain sober-hearted men.

But now from the words of the Scripture, I must speak to the seed of Faith, that innocent soul-saved generation, and that because the learned of this perishing world cannot believe, though an Angel should speak from heaven, as you the seed of the Lord shall hear that seed of this Serpent will hiss, yea, if possible, sting from his venomous tongue, this infallible interpretation of these ensuing words; *But of the tree of knowledge of good and evil thou shalt not eat of it, for in the day that thou eatest thereof, thou shalt surely dye:* Now if you look into the third of *Genes.* with an eye of Faith, then you may clearly see what the Tree of Knowledge of good and evil did signifie: The words are these, *And the Serpent said to the Woman, ye shall not surely die, for God doth know that in the day ye eat thereof, then your eyes shall be opened and ye shall be as Gods knowing good and evil: And when the Woman saw that the Tree was good for food, and that it was pleasant to the eyes, and a Tree to be desired to make one wise, she took of the fruit thereof, and did eat, and gave also unto her husband, and he did eat.* Oh my spiritual brethren, in that my soul desireth your perfection as my own, therefore I would gladly have you possessed with an infallible understanding between *Michael* and his Angels, and the Dragon and his Angels, or between the seed of the woman, and the seed of the Serpent: Why? because in the knowledge of these two distinct seeds, sons or generations, depends a general understanding of the spirit of the Scriptures; therefore let thy ear wait on thy eye, and thy heart on both, for now I shall unlock that secret Cabinet that hath not been opened since the creation till this last Witness; therefore attend and take notice that it is a general opinion amongst learned men, that the Serpent which appeared unto *Eve,* was one of the beasts of the field which the Lord God had made, and that the devil was an invisible spirit which entred into the body of the Serpent, and spake those subtile speeches through his mouth, and so caused the woman to eat of the fruit of the natural Tree which the Lord God had forbidden, and tempting her husband to eat of that fruit with her, it operated that venomous evil in them, and all mankind. [Note] Oh the gross darkness that possesseth the learned men of this perishing world, you know that the Scriptures are generally expressed in natural terms, for the manifestation of spiritual things to the weak comprehension of sinful mortals, and yet notwithstanding, the natural wisdom of this world would perswade men to understand them exactly in the letter, because they measure the glorious things of eternity by their rational learning onely, as aforesaid; but to enlighten thy understanding, minde Scripture-records, how that Christ is called a Lyon, a Lamb, a Stone, a Door, a Way, a Vine, a green Tree, and such like expressions in reference unto spiritual meanings; also you may read evil-minded men are sometimes called by the names of Devils, Dragons, Vipers, Serpents, Dogs, Swines, fruitless Trees, and such like, according to that of *John* the Baptist, when he said, *Now the ax is laid to the root of the Tree, every Tree therefore that bringeth not forth good fruit, is hewn down and cast into the fire:* So likewise you that are spiritual, may know that, yea, that Angelical reprobate, by whom *Eve* was deceived, was called a Dragon, an old Serpent, the Devil and Satan, a Deceiver, or the Tree of knowledge of good and evil; and such like names suteable unto his cursed nature; so that the naked truth is this, that Serpent that tempted *Eve,* was that Angelical Dragon-devil beforesaid, which the Lord God from the highest heavens cast down to the lowest earth, where there, as beforesaid, he bewitched *Eves* innocent soul; for if you know what you read, you shall finde three prevalent arguments perswading her to consent unto the Serpents language:

1. *The Tree was good for meat.*
2. *It was pleasant to the eyes.*
3. *It was to be desired to make one wise.*

But before I write of the three secrets hid in the Angelical temptation, give me leave to speak a little of the dispensation of the secret wisdom of God to his chosen ones: You that are of the seed of Faith, and none but you, doth know that in the Divine will of the infinite Majesty, there is a twofold operation, which is this, minde what thou readest, this is a great mystery, When the wisdom of God seeth fit to reveal a Divine secret to his own seed, then his holy Spirit is all active, and when he seeth fit to obsure it from them, then his Divine Spirit is all passive: Why? because for the manifestation of his infinite power and wisdom, that he can create light out of darkness, yea life out of death with a glorious advantage: For understand this, that if the glorious Creator, for the tryal of his creature, should leave the most experimental man that is, to his own inspired light, and suffer him to be tempted to that evil of murther or adultery, & overcome thereby, he must of necessity lose that former joy and peace of the divine light or love of God in him, and in the room thereof, both see and feel nothing but spiritual darkness, with a secret fear of eternal death, until the light of life appears again, with a new assurance of a glorious deliverance from that sinful darkness and fearful death, as aforesaid; truly whatever man shall imagine to the contrary, as sure as there is a God, this was the condition of both *Adam* and *Eve* when they were defiled with unlawful lust one towards another, by that subtile temptation of that Serpents counsel, called the Tree of knowledge of good and evil.

Again, though it is said, It was a Tree to be desired to make one wise, yet you may know that the soul of *Eve* was not of a desiring nature after wisdom in her creation, because she was all divine satisfaction in her self, therefore that desire of tasting of the fruit of a Tree, to make her wise as Gods, to know both good and evil, proceeded onely from the rational nature of an unsatisfied spirit of the Angelical Serpent; for this I would have you to understand, that at that time when *Eve* was tempted to evil by the Serpent, she was wholly left to her own strength, & it was the seeming glory of his Angelical language that over-topped her present light, and begot that desire in her understanding, through which her soul was moved with a powerful desire to make tryal of his Serpentine counsel, and to taste of his spiritual meat, so highly exalted by him: Why? because to her received new thoughts, she had not heard so glorious a language before. *Also the Tree was pleasant for sight;* yet before that glittering Serpent appeared, *Eve* wanted no satisfaction in beholding the man *Adam*, but she was looking a little too long upon the comeliness of his form, through his infused Witchcraft, her soul was ravisht through his Angelical person.

Again, *it was a Tree whose fruit was to be desired to make one wise as Gods, to know both good and evil:* Now minde the pretended meaning of the serpent in those words, was this, If she did but taste of the fruit of that Tree, it was so full of divine vertue, that she could not only be like unto God, but she would be as a God to her self, also to know all that was to be known, whether good or evil, within her own soul; but the truth is, the Serpents secret intent was this, that when she has tasted of that forbidden fruit, she should with him both know and feel in her own spirit, the difference between light and darkness, life and death, love and envy, peace and war, good and evil, or God and devil; likewise observe since *Eve,* the natural mother of all man-kinde, was overcome by lust, through the subtilty of the Serpent, hath not many a poor innocent virgin, or virgin-wife in like maner been deceived through the comeliness of mens persons, and their Serpentine languages, by perswading them that they loved them above their own lives, and of giving them such content they know not of; or if they deny them, it will be their death, yea, telling them, All men are but one man, and all women are but one woman, and therefore it is purity to be free unto all, and that they are in the greatest bondage which are united unto one onely; I say, hath not these, and such like cursed counsels, occasioned many innocent soul to betray their virginity, or virgin-bed unto their perpetual sorrow and shame afterwards; Just thus was it with the virgin-wife *Eve,* though it may seem strange at the first unto many that shall read this Epistle; yet you know the Scripture saith, *That she seeing the Tree good for meat, and pleasant to the eyes, and a tree to be desired to make one wise, took of the fruit thereof, and did eat;* that is, When the innocent soul of *Eve* was overpowered with the Serpents subtile language, as beforesaid, her spirit did consent unto him to come in unto her, and take full possession of her, to be her God and guide in stead of her Creator: Truly in this case the Virgin *Eve's* condition may fitly be compared unto the Virgin *Mary,* for you know after the Angel had told her, that without knowing of man, she should be with childe, through the power of the most High overshadowing of her, how easily was she intreated, not onely to have it so, but also how exceedingly did her soul rejoyce with the very tidings thereof? Again, if men look with a spiritual eye between their Angelical salutations, you may see more seeming glorious injoyments in the unclean angel greeting of Eve, then in the holy Angels saluting of *Mary:* Again, though men or Angels should gainsay it, from the spirit of truth it self, I shall declare the very sense of this secret in plainness of speech [which was this] As soon as ever Eves innocent soul, through the permissive power of God was overcome to consent to the Serpents cursed councel, his Angelical person entered into her womb through her secret parts, and being united to her soul and body, his serpentine nature dissolved it self into her pure seed, and defiled her throughout, and so became essentially one with her; through which naturally she conceived a Serpent Dragon devil, into a man child of flesh, blood and bone; and brought forth her first begotten son of the Devil, yea the very Dragon, serpent, devil himself, and called his name, according to his nature *Cain*, or cursed, though ignorantly she said she had received a man from the Lord: So likewise on the contrary, the womb of the Virgin-wife *Mary* was honored with the onely wise Angelical God himself, through which her polluted nature was not onely cleansed whilst he was in her womb, but also by vertue of the Divine power, she was enabled to conceive his glorious majesty of her seed, into a holy Babe of unspotted flesh, blood and bone, and in his season to bring forth her first begotten Son of God, and call his name, according to his nature, *Emmanuel, Jesus,* or *Blessed;* so that you which are truly and inwardly baptized with the true knowledge of the holy One of Israel, may see in some measure what is meant by the two Scripture-seeds, the Angelical devil first became a man-child, and the Angelical God afterwards became a man-child: thus the most holy God abased himself in the very womb of a woman, that he might first or last destroy the power of that serpentine reason, or lying imagination in all his elect Israelites.

Thus, if you be not stone-blind, you may clearly see that the serpentine angel when he tempted *Eve*, was no homely beast, as men vainly imagine from the beastly reason, but he was a spiritual body, and appeared unto *Eve* in form like unto a glorious God or man. Now if you be unsatisfied as touching the Angelical serpent, consisting of as large a compass as the person of a man, and yet could enter into the womb of Eve through so narrow a passage, as is declared by me; I shall answer these in those sayings of *Nicodemus* to Christ, *John* the third, where he saith, *How can a man be born when he is old, can he enter the second time into his mothers womb, and be born again?* As our Lord answered *Nicodemus* unto his fleshly question, so likewise from his own light in like maner, I shall make answer unto this: Though the body of the Angelical Serpent in his length or breadth was as a man is, yet you may know it was not of a gross substance as man is, but it was a spiritual body created in another world, for though the bodies of the mightly Angels are in forms like men, yet you may know that they shine like unto the Sun or a flame of fire, being formed in a Region of a more higher nature then this, therefore they are of motion more swifter then though, & of a pure, thin, or bright fiery nature; so that with great ease they pierce through a narrow passage, at the divine pleasure of the Creator: So likewise it was with the Serpent-tree of knowledge of good and evil, for though his created purity was become all maner of imaginary impurities, through his outcast condition, yet you may know that his form was of a more fiery brightness then that of *Adam,* or else *Eve* could not possibly have been deceived by him, as aforesaid; also his body being spiritual, though his nature was carnal, there was no let to hinder this descending into her womb, to bring forth the Creators secret purpose of two generations, coming through the loins of one woman, to make an everlasting distinction between the transcendent glory of respection, and shame of rejection.

Again, though the Angelical Serpent descended into the womb of *Eve,* yet you may know that his ascending nature was utterly lost; so that in stead of his ascending upward into that habitation of ravishing glory, from whence he was cast, he was ignorant of it, and of that God and his mighty Angels, as if he had never known them in the least; therefore he imagined his serpentine subtilty, to be the onely wisdom then in being, and this world to be the onely heaven: Thus all the seed of Faith may be satisfied, that the Devil that was, is, or at the resurrection shall so rise, is in the form of a man, and this *Cain,* man-devil, in process of time, married and begat sons and daughters, so that there shall not onely be a male, but female devils also; yea, since there hath been, and now is legions, yea millions of legions of his seed, in the forms of men and women, and that as comely persons as ever were born of a woman. O then ye seed of *Cain* look about you, and seriously lay to heart, how rashly it hath, and now at this day is preached, and by you believed, that the devil was long before man was created, as also that the devil had never the form or shape of a man, but as it pleased Master Painter to draw him forth in such a form, that when the devil knows himself to be a devil, thou wilt see the cheat of both the Limner and his Picture.

Notwithstanding it hath been infallibly proved, that there is no other devil but what is in men and women, yet it is made known unto me the various pleas and excuses (why, or wherefore) the generation of *Cain* have endeavored to finde out a devil before, and without man: First, because that which is a devil, is in antipathy to God, so a professed enemy to his glorious person; also the very name devil, is a frightful cursed name, a name that is a terror to all sober-minded men; therefore to cloke their cursed devilish actions, and that they may not be noted by the righteous *Abels* to be devils, this devilish generation attribute it to a devil without them.

First, It is by them supposed, the devil is a deformed creature, of an ugly shape, with a cloven foot, &c. and therefore, say they, it cannot be a man or woman, for they are comely, beautiful creatures.

Secondly, It is by them believed, that the devil can transform himself into any form, and appear, where, how and when he pleaseth; therefore it cannot be that man should be the devil, in that man can do none of these things.

Thirdly, say they, The devil is in hell tormented, and torments all that he can captivate in his bounds, but we are upon the earth, not tormented, neither torment we any man.

Fourthly, say they, The devil is a wicked cursed blasphemer against God and all that is good, yea the devil is a lying, murthering persecutor of the children of God; therefore it cannot be that man should be this devil, in that he is a true worshipper of God, and is reverent of his name, no blasphemer, or persecutor of his people.

Fifthly and lastly, The greatest Appeal the seed of *Cain* can make for himself, is this, If there be no other devil but what is in men and women, then, say they, Kings may be devils, Magistrates devils, Merchants devils, Lawyers devils, Soldiers devils, Doctors devils, and Preachers devils, and so in conclusion there may be few other in this world that at the day of judgement shall be raised, but devils.

From these and such like, hath that proud spirit of Reason in them corruptly imagined a Devil after their own fancy, and have christened him *Devil,* yea, and given him a place of abode, either under the earth, in the hollow of the earth, in the depth of the waters, or in the air, or some place they know not where; and all this is because they would not have God nor his people take notice that they are his seed: These and such like, are in some measure satisfactory to the spirit of Reason, that there is a devil without them, besides them, and contrary to mans form.

Notwithstanding, it hath been sufficiently maintained, nay, against all Gain-sayers proved, what the first descent or rise of the Devil was, which never any since the foundation of the world could reveal till this Last Witness; yet for thy further satisfaction, I shall in short answer those thy frivolous Pleas and Excuses.

First thou pleasest, *The devil is a deformed creature, of an ugly shape, with a cloven foot, &c.*

Answer. This is one of the imagined whimsies of the ignorant and learned in these days; this is one of the Scar-crows and Bug-bears believed, and so reported by his own seed, that the devil cannot be a man, in that he is a deformed beast; and yet not any of you dare avouch unto me where, when, and in what shape thou sawest him, but in that thy soul is clothed with that ignorant dark devil within thee, thou apprehendest and imaginest strange appearances without thee, insomuch that an old Tree in the night is supposed a devil unto thee: where this ignorance of a true God and a right devil hath taken place, oh how fearful is that soul of something without it, when the rise of thy fear is really within thee! As consider, what is the cause that a soul cries out, *The devil, the devil stands before me, waiting to carry me away from him,* and all that are with thee beholds nothing but thy self frighted and tormented by the devil within thee? for my seed-spring declares unto thee, there is no such things as is supposed by thee; but that devil that ever was, is, or shall be, is for the most part as comely a creature as walks in *London* streets, and hath as neat a foot and a hand as any Lady in the land, which shall appear more at large in that Chapter that treats of the seed of *Cain,* his education or bringing up.

Again, It is by the Seed of *Cain* believed man is not the devil, *in that,* saith thou, *the devil can transform himself into any form, and appear how, where, and when he pleaseth.*

Answer. If this were true, as it is not, it were nothing advantageous unto thee, in that I can in truth and reality instance one remarkable Devil-man now living, whose name is *John Robins,* that did more devilish exployts then any conceited devil without thee: Sometimes he did present the form of his person riding upon the wings of the winde, like unto a flame of fire; also he did present unto some in their beds a great light, like unto a flame of fire over all the room, that they have been compelled to hide their faces in their beds, fearing they should be burned; but when they hid their faces in their beds, the light did appear more brighter then before: also he would present unto them Half-moon and Stars, and sometimes thick Darkness, darker then any natural darkness whatsoever: also he did present in the day time his head onely without a body to a Gentlewoman in her chamber, presenting unto her, to deceive her, the forms of strange beasts, as namely dragons, and such like: much more might be spoken of his deceits in this kind, how many great lying signs and wonders this prince of devils was acted forth far beyond all his cursed seed, though a great many more hath assumed to raise various appearances, yet notwithstanding all this the fundamental was in themselves; as thus, A real devil within them, but an imagined devil without them; and thus their consciences being seared, they seek to make others in faith with them, that can raise a devil without them, which at the great day they shall finde it to be a cheat that shall burn in their souls and bodies more hotter then any fire and brimstone.

Again, thou sayest, *The devil is in hell tormented, and torments all that he can captivate in his bounds, but we are on the earth not tormented, &c.*

Answ. This thy plea thou hast received from others as wise as thy self that knows no more of a hell without man, then of a heaven within man; for alas poor deceived soul, thou apprehendest a devil thou knows not what, and a hell thou knows not where, for the learned or the proudest of his seed little think or can believe, that their body shall be their hell, shut up close prisoners on this earth tormented to all eternity? neither shall you the seed of *Cain* believe that your cheats, oppression, adultery, swearing, drunkenness, and persecuting this infallible truth, with all other of your filthiness, shall be that fuel that shall burn more hotter then any natural fire in this world? And as toucing that, whereas thou saith, *We are upon the earth not tormented.* Alas pititous soul! though all the seed of *Cain* are not tormented alike, by reason of long habit and custom, through which thy conscience is seared, that no small sin will torment thee, but there are thousands of thy brood that have an earnest-peny of that they shall be hereafter; otherwise what causeth the hideous, doleful sighs, groans and cries of many of your seed in health, but much more on thy bed of sickness, concluding in thy self, I am damned, I am damned to all eternity, finding in thy self no peace, in that thou knows not the God of peace, neither hast thou walked uprightly in doing to others as thou would they should do to thee, but have either publickly or privately transgressed the Law, by which thy sin is strengthened, for the strength of sin is the law; and so death which is the sting of sin, arraigns thee at the bar of thy own conscience, reading within thy own soul, all thy private evils against God and man, nay from my seed-spring I speak it, many of this cursed seed are seemingly Saints, and do live as a people that doth righteous things, and in gifts of nature, heaven-like praying and preaching, to the admiration of all that hears them, and yet they find in themselves, if they would speak the truth, what sad torments they undergo while they live on this earth, yea so great in some, that their torment cannot cease till the soul make away it self: As touching this I shall remind you of remarkable accident, which many in *London* this day can witness the truth of what I write, *Thomas Gun* by name was the man, who for gifts and parts in the Ministry, as also for a civil life, did equalize all the teachers of the Baptists, if not excell them, and yet at that very same instant was guilty of adultery, and that for a long time deceived his own soul and the poor woman, his torment for which could not be satisfied till he took a Pistol and shot himself to death: thus it was with him, and so with many more little or much, are in hell, yea on this earth tormented, though nothing comparable to what thou shalt be at the day of Christs next appearance.

Again, thou sayest, *The devil is a wicked cursed blasphemer against God and all that is good, yea the devil is a lying murthering persecutor of the people of God, therefore man is not the devil, because he is a true worshipper of God, &c.*

Ans. If thou understoodst what thou sayest, I could set to my seal, that whosoever is a true worshipper of God, is no devil, for indeed none can worship him, or be reverent of his name, but those that are of the seed of Faith, those that are eternally preserved in peace here, and glory hereafter; for it is life eternal to know thee the onely true God, without which knowledge, none can worship him, or be reverent of his name; thus far I agree and set to my seal, that this man is no devil: but alas, how many of these are in this perishing world, though millions of thousand thousands make a show and a talk of a God, yet very few there are that knows him as he is, a glorious personal God, so that true was that saying from the Lord in *Isaiah 10.22. For though my people be as the sand of the sea, yet a remnant of them shall be saved: Fear not little flock, it is your fathers pleasure to give you a Kingdom: One of a tribe, two of a City;* so few are those that knows the true God, that they are but a handful to them that knows him not. But now to the Query in hand, *The devil,* saith thou, *is a wicked cursed blasphemer against God and all that is good;* from whence thou concludes man cannot be this devil, in that man is not so wicked as to curse and blaspheme God; what if I can find out such men that hath, and at this day will curse God to his face? is not this sufficient to convince thee there is no other devil but what is in man? for I'le assure thee there is some this day in *London,* and Country also, that in my hearing hath said, God is a devil, and that he hath done that he cannot make good; that God is a tyrant, a Cock and Bull, a Horse, and all such like cursed terms; also that devil man hath said, *That is God did damn him, he would damn God;* nay, it hath been spoken, *That God durst not damn him, and that God was more beholding to him, then he was to God;* Also a man hath said, *That the blood of Christ was of no more value then the blood of a dog,* if these be not the seed of *Cain,* and at the great and terrible day shall be raysed devils, then let them say the Lord spoke not by me; nay, there is a swarm or brood of this cursed seed of *Cain,* that deny a God, or at least they make him a cloak for all their lascivious lust, running after the steps of their father *Cain* in all manner of wickedness: And what is their saying, If I can but have my Money-god, let it come right or wrong its all but one to me, I will not put it forth to usury, but I will spend it freely upon my lust; and as for this glorious personal God, I own no such God, for what say they, Our God is an infinite formless spirit, or an infinite nothing, or an infinite all; that is to say, all in beasts, all in fish, all in fowls, all in herbs, trees, and plants, all in men and their wickedness too; even thus this cursed seed do believe that just, holy, glorious God, to be the Author of all their uncleanness, so that true is that saying *Psal. 50.21. Thou thoughtest I was altogether such a one as thy self;* but at the mighty day of my account, thou shalt then have all thy sins set in order before thee, and the sentence of this despised God, pass upon thee.

And whereas thou saith, *The devil is a murthering persecutor of Gods precious ones:* Well, what devil was that, think you, that from the beginning to this day persecuted the people of God? was it a devil without man or in man? Surely the Scripture with our experience, can to any sober man make it appear, it was no other devil but man: As instance, who persecuted the Prophets of the Lord of old, was it not the Priests and Elders of *Israel?* Who was it that persecuted Christ Jesus? was it not their children the holy devout Jews, that murthered the Lord of glory? Who persecuted the Apostles? was it not the same generation of the cursed seed of *Cain?* Who put the Martyrs to the fires? was it a devil without a form, or was it not a devil in Queen *Marys* form? Who is it now that persecutes the substantial light or life of the seed of faith? is it not the devil in man, or man-devil? Nay had it not been for the late Lord Protector, whose soul was merciful to tender consciences: O had it not been that God had honored him before and above all, in wisdom to go in and out before Parliaments, and the Priests of this Nation; what a bloody persecuting day had here been in *England?* and yet you cry out of the devil for a persecutor, when it is the devil in you; so that you see there is no other devil but what is that cursed seed of *Cain.* O therefore look about you, for the devil that you fear, is in you.

Now to the last and greatest appeal the seed of *Cain* can make for himself, is this, *If there be no other Devil but what is in man or woman, then Kings may be devils, Magistrates devils, Lawyers devils, Merchants devils, Soldiers devils, Doctors devils, and Preachers devils, and so at the day of judgement, few other but devils shall arise.*

Answ. What a Catalogue of great men is here recorded, thou supposing such men as these, its pity to damn them, or at least God will have more mercy on them, then on the poor ragged seed of *Cain,* [and that because] of their greatness: Surely, if possible, thou wouldst turn God from being God, and that because he saith, *He will have mercy on whom he will have mercy: And with our God there is no respect of persons;* So that mark what is said, What is a King? what is a Magistrate? what is a Doctor? what is a Lawyer? what is a Soldier? what is a Merchant? what is a Preacher? though their houses be full of gold and silver, and their body richly clad with Jewels and raiment? What is all this to the Judge of Justice? its but as filthy raggs, no nor the persons of such men are no more esteemd then the dunghil begger; Nay what doth the Lord say, *Not many wise, not many mighty, not many noble men shall be saved,* but the poor persecuted for his names sake, are his beloved: Again, he saith, *It is easier for a Camel to go through the eye of a needle, then for a rich man to enter into the kingdom of heaven:* Do you hear, will ye believe, or understand that these sayings needs no interpretation, however you may slight it, take notice that what I now say, you shall finde it, that since God became flesh, there is no promise in Scripture to those that truly knows him, and so professeth him, shall be rich in this world; As find me out ten among ten thousand, from the first of *Matthew,* to the last of the *Revelation,* that were true believers, so living and so dying; I say thou canst not find out half that number that were really of the seed of faith, and rich in this world, so few they were then, and so few now, that I think it should make the rich of this world to tremble, for though you can pass the Scripture, with some evations of your own, and defer the application of them as concerning your selves, yet from my Seed-spring, this you shall know, that those sayings, *It is easier for a Camel to go through the eye of a needle, then for a rich man to enjoy in his own souls the external truth,* there being such antipathy betwixt them, that they accord like two contrary elements, *viz.* fire and water, no society till one hath conquered the other: As instance, the riches and glory of this world, it elevates the soul beyond its bounds, it finds so much content here, that that truth that will not maintain this perishing fleshly glory, with all its lust and pride, Oh it is as hard a saying as that of Christ to the young man in the Gospel, when truth presents it self to a rich worldly man, and yet this man a great professor of the letter, and makes a great flutter in vain repetition to a God thou knows not; yet I say, when the eternal truth tenders it self to thy soul, in a poor persecuted distressed condition, and tells thee I the Lord of glory had not a bed to lay my head on; and those that will raign with me in that endles glory to come, must forsake all, & take me for their pattern; and as for the riches here, make as good shift as thou canst, provided thou doth as thou would be done to. Oh saith the rich soul, This is a hard saying indeed, for let me be of what Art or Calling soever, if in that Art or Calling I do righteous things, I shall be poor enough in this world, for I finde in my Art and Trading, that all men that grows rich, hath got it by cheat and deceiving those they have to deal with; for if a man deal justly, he shall have much ado to maintain his family; therefore well might the God of all knowledge say, *Not many rich, not many noble, but the poor shall enter in at the straight gate;* for the way, the path, the gate, to the possession of the real durable truth is so narrow, that the soul with its body must enter in pure and undefiled, not laden with cheats and deceits, as thousands at this day strives to enter in, and are not able for want of their certificate, that golden Rule, *In doing to others as thou would other should do to thee:* Now if thou say, *Where is that man, or how is it possible for any man to perform this?* I answer, I can both show thee the man and affirm it is possible, for since I have known the true God, and been made obedient to the rule thereof, mark what I say, I have not to my knowledge, done that to another, which I would not the same party should do to me, and for the possibility thereof, it lieth in thy power to do, minde what I say, It is as possible for thee to do justly as unjustly: As instance, thou having a friend that reposeth confidence in thee, and declareth the truth of his business unto thee, concerning which he entrusteth thee to do for him, as if occasion require, thou would have him do the like for thee; now the occasion upon which thou art imployed, is a business of great advantage, as a bargain of Land, Merchandize or otherways, which if thou deal with him as for thy self, sufficient benefit will acrue thereby; but now in the managing of this his affairs, thou findst thou canst gain for thy self twenty pound more or less, and yet thy friend shall accomplish his desire, cheaper then if he had aggitated the business himself, and as touching this thy pretended plain-dealing, and seeming honesty, thou hast contrived a way that he shall never know of it, but account himself as much obliged to thee for this thy great kindness and just dealing with him, as if it were really so. Now speak for thy self, was it not in thy power to give him all or no, and deal plainly? was this any kindeness or just dealing in the least? or hath it any relation to that Golden saying of Christ, *Matth. 7.12. Therefore all things whatsoever ye would that men should do to you, do ye even so to them, for this the Law and the Prophets:* No, no, thou wouldst never imploy him no more, but judge him, and so look upon him as the ungratefullest man living upon the earth; therefore look to thy own soul, how it stands related to that golden rule aforesaid, that whether thou finds in thy self a desire of revenge towards him, or if ever occasion of such an account be tendered to thee, thou wilt serve him the like; I say be thou what thou wilt, thou maist shake hands like *Simeon* and *Levi,* brethren in cheat and deceit; as thou may call to minde one remarkable cursed rule betwixt buyer and seller, as thus, Suppose thou be the seller, and I the buyer, I come for such a Commodity which thou hast, I ask thee the price that thou canst afford it to live by, thou doth protest, as thou intends to be saved, it cost thee so much, I having no experience, and believing thee, gives thee thy price, when thou knows, thou hast cheated me both in the goodness of the Commodity, and the price; now judge thou if this be as thou would have another serve thee? or dost thou think for all thy long prayers and heaven-like carriage, that these ill gotten riches, by which thou art grown great on the earth, that such as thou shalt enter the straight gate, or that thou shalt rise a rich, glorious Saint at the day of judgement? then I may say in vain was it for me, to forsake a hundredth pound a year, and expose my self and children to strayts, because I could not cheat; for I tell thee, if to do just and unjust be all one, then I say with *Paul, Of all men we are most miserable,* when we might be rich, to live poor here, and be damned hereafter. Oh no, no, as sure as God is God, thou shalt know, that so continuing and so dying a cheat, shall have all thy heaven here, and everlasting torment hereafter; therefore wonder not why it is a hard thing for Kings or great men to be saved: As take account from *Saul* the first King of *Israel*, to the coming of Christ, and observe seriously how many of them shall arise Saints; also take notice from Christ, to the raign of the Lord Protector, thou shalt find it is a hard thing to deal justly and be rich in this world; certain it is, from experience I find it so far different, yea, so contradictory, that from the seed of Faith I speak it, to deal justly thou cannot be rich, but poor in this world, and yet what striving here is to be rich, yea wise and great in this perishing world, not in the least laying to heart that saying of *James 5.1 &c. Go to now ye rich men, weep and howl for your miseries that shall come upon you; your riches are corrupted, and your garments moth eaten; your gold and silver is cankered, and the rust of them shall be a witness against you, and shall eat your flesh as it were fire; ye have heaped treasure together for the last dayes; ye have lived in pleasure on the earth and been wanton, ye have nourished your hearts as in a day of slaughter, ye have condemned and killed the just, and he doth not resist you.*

Now look about you the seed of *Cain*, and tell me to whom was this spoken, or whom doth it concern, if not the great men of the earth, or rich men of this world; and yet how few of you do consider that destruction will be the end of this thy fleshly perishing glory? Alas, what though thou live thirty, fourty, fifty, or eighty years, this know, thy glass is a running, thy brave time will have an end, and to thy bed of sickness thou must be brought, when then all thy rich robes and precious Jewels may hange by thee, but thou canst not make use of them, and in room of them death prepares a garment for thee. O then, even then, is a believers joy, which now is thy sorrow; for instead of speaking peace to thee, they will be a witness against thee, yea a declaration of dreadful things concerning thee, reminding thee of all thy proud thoughts and lofty looks; as also how thou hast spent thy time in pleasure on this earth, and been wanton in the day of judgement; yea, cruel in the day of mercy in condemning, yea, killing the Just, that blessed seed of Faith; now if these men shall be saved, and if those works shall be justified, that is recorded in *Mic. 3.11. viz.* abhorring judgement, perverting all equity, judging for reward, teaching for hire, divining for mony, grinding the faces of the poor, enriching themselves in the ruine of others; I say, if such great men as these, that have here enjoyed all the pleasure and glory of this perishing world, shall enjoy that immortal ravishing glory in the world to come, then minde what will follow, then in vain were the Scriptures written, and to no purpose was those great sufferings of our Lord Jesus, who saith, *Mat. 19.29. And every one that hath forsaken houses, or brethren, or sisters, or father, or mother, or wife, or children, or lands for my names sake, shall receive an hundred fold, and shall inherit everlasting life;* and then in the same Chapter, Christ shews from the young mans going away sorrowful, *How hard a thing it is for a rich man to enter,* yea, saith Christ, *A rich man shall hardly enter into the Kingdom of glory:* and in *vers. 27.* when *Peter* said, *Behold we have forsaken all and followed thee, what shall we have therefore;* now you may read his answer was this, *That ye which have followed me in the regeneration, when the Son of man shall sit in the throne of his glory, ye also shall sit upon twelve thrones, &c.*

Now in all these words, expound, or interpret which way ye can to stile your fears of death, and your dreadful portion at the great day, I say from the Lord of glory you cannot find any colour or title in the least that doth encourage or give any admittance to a worldly minded rich man, for if you minde what you read, you shall find all the promises here, or in Scripture elsewhere, doth onely appertain to such that hath forsaken all false worships and false Christs, and hath renounced all unjust ways or means whereby he hath enriched himself, yea he that hath slighted a good name with the credit of this world, and is not onely ready to persecute, but be persecuted for that glorious, yet despised man Jesus; I say from the spirit of Faith, all the promises of the Lord in Scripture doth onely belong to these poor despised scum of the earth, as in these words, Thou *Peter,* or ye my disciples, or any other of my precious ones, that hath lost all for me, you are those that shall have all gain by me, you shall have everlasting life, and be with me in my Kingdom, yea in glory like my self, as mind that saying of *James* the second chapter and fifth verse,

The Right Devil Unfolded

Hearken my beloved brethren, hath not God chosen the poor of this world rich in faith, and heirs of the kingdom, which he hath promised to them that love him?

Now what can be said more, or what more wouldest thou have God do for thee? wouldst thou have him unjust, or contradict his own word? then be content with thy rich glory here, and let us have our glory with our God; we grudge not at thy greatness in this world, no nor thou shalt not hinder us, or detain us from our portion of glory to come, thine is almost at an end, ours is yet to come; and shall never end; therefore be not deceived, thou canst not live the life of the devil here, and live eternally with the Lord hereafter: then, as I said before, so against men and angels I should say again, that such as I had better never been born to deprive my self of such a livelihood, as I might not have been inferior to many, and all to live upright and justly in this my strange country, which now I am deprived of all; Surely, if it were so as some of *Cains* cursed brood doth say, and binde it with an oath, That all shall be saved, the poor *Paul,* and the poor Prophets, and we in these days, have made a sad exchange, but as sure as God is God, whosoever thou art, be thou Ranter or Quaker, King or Beggar, thou shalt finde at the day of our Saviours appearance, that thou so dying, shall never be saved; and then if it were possible, thou wouldst say what I here write, is truth, and such as thou art found lyers.

Now one word more to this last plea of the seed of *Cain*, and so touching this point I have done, which is this: If there be no other devil but what is in man or woman, then thou sayest, Kings may rise devils, Magistrates devils, Lawyers devils, Soldiers devils, Merchants devils, Doctors devils, yea and Preachers Devils, these being for the most part the richest men of this world, and the Scripture in many places extends it language onely against such men, may cause not onely a supposition in the seed of faith, to judge according to the tenor of the inspired Writ; but also a terror upon the souls of rich men, in that Christ compareth riches to bryers and thorns, as in that parable of the sower, *Mat. 13.22.* where he saith, *And the cares of this world, and the deceitfulness of riches choak the word, and he becometh unfruitful,* riches being such a snare and deceiver of the soul, may justly, and that not without suspicion, cause a serious examination, whether riches be not the onely instrument, why or wherefore the true God nor his word doth not take root within thee, where there is so much fulness of the treasure of this world, there can be no admittance for the treasure of God, ye cannot serve two masters, and that because the riches of this world is in antipathy to the riches of heaven, in that one is perishing, the other everlasting, the one clouds or draws the soul from God, the other expells mists, and draws the soul to God; so that Christ knowing it was the greatest tryal and snare to the soul, doth declare it a hard thing to enter, yea so difficult, that since he took upon him the form of flesh, there hath not, nor now is, not one of ten thousand knowing the true God, that shall be much troubled with the riches of this world; for where riches is, there must be a mighty power of faith keeping the soul in obedience to its God, and that because where there is riches, it requires the creatures whole attendance, to give all care and diligence that possible may be, to augment it, or at least to uphold the stock or principle, in so much that it makes him uncapable to cast his whole care upon the God of endless riches. Now to conclude, there is one thing more of great concernment to be seriously laid to heart by these rich men, which is this.

First, How thou camest to this thy greatness, whether it was by birthright, or inheritance, as the eldest son.

Secondly, Whether it came by thy acute subtile wit and ripe ingenuity, in improving thy Art or Calling, by which thou wert capable of, by which fleshly wisdom of thine thou art possest in thy riches?

Ans. I shall from my seed-spring give thee the result of my thoughts as touching thee, and as sure as God is God, thou shalt finde what I write is truth.

I. For the first, Suppose in my condition, as I am, kindered or friend, should unexpected by me, give me a thousand pound a year more or less, now it is just in me to receive it, and possibly as justly I improve it, onely here consists the danger, that if by these riches my soul is drawn from God, and more delighted in the pleasure of my riches then God, so that I think my self a great man, and now am grown lofty, hard-hearted, and such like corruption attends me, in so much that not onely my self, but likewise my neighbors, takes notice that I am not like the man I was before.

So that now thou that hath thy greatness successively, is not by Scripture condemned, provided it prove not a snare or a thorn, to choak thy soul, by having such a deep impression in thy heart, that the infallible truth cannot take root in thee, onely here is the hazard as aforesaid, if thou use it as though thou use it not, which is no easie thing, yet if thou canst make use of it to the glory of our God, by feeding the hungry, and clothing the naked in the name of a Prophet or a righteous man; so said, and so done, thou shalt have a Prophets or righteous mans reward, which is eternal life in the world to come; I say if these things, in the enjoyment of thy riches, are performed by them, then it may be thou art one of those few of the rich and noble that shall be saved: But,

2. Thou that has got thy riches by thy subtil wit, is much different from the other, in that the first was freely given, so that he came justly by it; but as for thee, thou best knows how thou came to thy greatness; for thou hast heard, as aforesaid, it is a wonder for a man to do just and upright things, and yet grow rich; therefore the Scripture calls thee to account, and that the more thou mayest remember not many years ago thou wast but a poor Journy-man of

thy Trade, not worth a groat, but in debt, and now in these years thou art worth thousands.

O friend, deal plainly with thy soul, though thou may hide it from man, thou canst not hide it from God, for thy ways are naked to his glorious piercing eye, that although thou may blind man with thy fair carriage and sugared pretenses, seemingly gilt over with holiness and purity of life, yet for all this our glorious personal God doth know, and in thy conscience will read, how many thou hast cheated and murthered to make thy self great by undoing of others; in this thing are not most of your Doctors over shoes and boots in this crying sin, in taking a crown for that which cost but six pence, and onely so, but for want of judgement and mercy, destroys the poor creature, to the utter ruin of his family, so that thou art of that number that treadeth in the broad way, that at last will lead thee to the destruction of thy soul eternally, yea world without end; and therefore take notice, that God is not afraid to call thee to account, or that he will be more merciful to thee then a beggar, because of thy greatness, or that thy white hand or fair face adorned with Silk, Gold or Silver, shall cause an eye of compassion more to thee because of that, then to a black deformed creature; No, no, our God thou shalt finde, seeth not as man seeth, neither is his thoughts as mans, if he were, then had the fair, neat, rich, proud daughters of *Sion* been respected, but in stead of a blessing, he blasted all their glory and bravery, as you may read at large, *Isaiah 3*. from the 16 to the end, first repeating how they walked with stretched-out necks and wanton eyes, walking and mincing as you go, and making a tinkling with your feet, therefore the Lord in stead of shewing mercy, did smit with a scab the crowns of the heads of the daughters of *Sion,* yea, the Lord did discover their secret parts, and took away all their bravery of tinkling ornaments about their feet, their cauls and round tires like the Moon, the chains, bracelets & mufflers, the bonnets, tablets, ear-rings, and nose-jewels, wimples, and crisping pins, the glasses and fine linen, the vails, with the changeable suits of apparel.

O if God were a respector of persons, here was invitations plenty: but you may read, *that in stead of a sweet smell, he gave them a stink, and in stead of a girdle, a rent, in stead of well-set hair, baldness: in stead of beauty, burning;* yea, and that with eternal burnings, shall all proud despisers of this infallible truth undergo, at the great and terrible day of our Saviors appearance; concerning which I shall open at large in the last Chapter. Thus much in answer to your Pleas, now I shall prove from Scripture the seed of *Cain* to be of the devil.

The devil or Seed of Cain *infallibly proved from experience in Scripture.*

II. Because of the great opposition that may arise up against this glorious Truth, through the exceeding pride and unbelieve in the hearts of most men, give me leave to cite a few Scriptures in confirmation of this work in hand: In the first Epistle of *John,* the third Chapter, you shall find it thus written, *Not as* Cain *which was of that wicked one, and slew his brother:* Also in the 13th chapter of *Matthew* it is thus written, *He that soweth the good seed is the Son of man, and the field is the world; the good seed are the children of the kingdom, and the tares are the children of the wicked one, and the enemy that soweth them is the devil.* Moreover, in the 8th chapter of S.*John,* Christ Jesus the God of Truth speaketh thus, *Ye are of your father the devil, and the lusts of your father ye will do: he hath been a murtherer from the beginning and abode not in the truth, because there was no truth in him; when he speaketh a lie, then he speaketh of his own, for he is a liar, and the father thereof.*

My spiritual and rational friends which are sober, was not *Cain* the first murthering lying man that ever was born of a woman, seeing no true Christian can gain-say it? was not that cursed *Cain* from the beginning, that murthering devil and father of lies, spoken of by Christ aforesaid, in answer to those carnal Jews which boasted themselves to be of *Abrahams* seed? and were not those lustful murthering-minded Jews or Gentiles which our Lord branded with titles of serpents, vipers, children of the devil, and such like filthy Canaanites, which proceeded out of the spirit of cursed *Cain* that old serpent, dragon-devil, and father of all the damned in this world, and not from the spirit of *Abraham,* though they might proceed from his loins according to the flesh, through mixtures of seeds in marriages: *the sons of God saw the daughters of men to be fair, and they took of them to be their wives.* Again, though the blessed Israelites and cursed Canaanites are mixed together by carnal copulation, since the prince of devils became flesh, yet you that are spiritual may know, that the Lord Jesus that made them both, knew how to separate them for all their close union, and to call them by names answerable to their own natures.

As consider, did not the glorious Creator and blessed Redeemer himself, make a clear distinction between two worlds or generations, when he said, *I pray not for the world, but for them that thou hast given me out of the world;* can you therefore that are sober, imagine or think, that there is any spiritual salvation for these men or women, which the Saviour of the world excludes in his petition: Moreover, it is written, that the Apostles said, *We know that we are of God, and the whole world lyeth in wickedness:* Behold, ye redeemed ones of the most high God, it it not as clear as the light it self, that there is two distinct whole worlds, according to that saying, *Then all Israel shall be saved:* a redeemed world of elect Israelties, and an unredeemed world of reprobate Canaanites, that were never truly lost in themselves, and therefore never capable of being found in Christ, according to that in the Epistle of *Jude*, where it is thus written *For there are certain men crept in, which were of old ordained to this condemnation, ungodly men, which turn the grace of God into wantonness, and denying Christ the onely Lord, wo unto them, for they have followed the way of* Cain, *and are cast away by the deceit of Balaams wages, and perish in the gain-saying of* Core: Thus is it not clear unto all such that have in them any faith in the truth of the Scripture, that there is two distinct whole worlds, to distinguish between the divine glory of Election, and everlasting shame of Rejection? a cursed *Cain*, a blessed *Abel,*, a suble serpent, and a simple Saint; a scoffing carnal *Ishmael*, and a spiritual *Isaac;* a bloody minded *Esau,* and a merciful minded *Jacob;* a persecuting *Saul,* and a prophetical *David;* a treacherous *Judas,* and a gracious and glorious *Jesus,* from the beginning of the world unto the end thereof; yea, and a blessed *Seth* born in the stead of righteous *Abel,* to bring forth the generation of the just, that the Lord of eternal glory, might according to the flesh, as well as the spirit, spring from a spiritual line of his own light of life eternal, and not from a rational or carnal line of eternal death in chains of utter darkness; which if it had power, according to its cursed desire, it would destroy God, elect men and angels, heaven and earth, and all in them, and it self also, rather then by subject to any, or might not onely it self bear rule over all.

But now to the matter in hand, and withal consider what you read, for it highly concerns you to look about you, that if there should be any evil angels, or devils living in the air, and a devil amongst them, called *BeelZebub* the prince of devils, then I say, what need any man trouble himself with the least fear of eternal death, what wickedness soever is committed by thee; why? because if a man is tempted by any devil but what is in his own nature onely, that evil spirit is to be eternally damned, and the man set free; nay moreover, if sin or evil issued not from mans unclean reason or lying imagination within him, is it possible, think you, that any man should be tormented, as some men are, with an inward burning through a secret fear of eternal sufferings rising in them, from the guilt of former evils committed against the light of their own consciences; furthermore, seeing all men which live after the flesh, must die or perish, and that mans own lust is that imaginary devil from whence proceeds all sin or evil.

Without controversie though men or angels should gainsay it, there are no other evil spirits, angels, or devils, but unmerciful men and women onely: Again, if envy, pride, covetousness hypocrisie, lust, and such like, be the devil in man, then are not men and women those devils that are under the power of those evils? I would fain know from the learned men of this world, whether there are any other evil angels or devils besides mankind, that lust after women, or silver, or honor, or revenge, or any kinde of evil whatsoever? truly if those supposed wise men that talk so much of the subtilty of the prince of the air, that rules in the children of disobedience, could possibly know that their own imaginary Reason was the evill spirit or prince of all their airy disputes concerning God, angels, devils, Heaven, hell, eternal glory or shame to come, which they know not of according to truth, then in stead of their rejoycing in the approbation of many men in relation unto their natural gifts, their own spirits would immediately become the principle of all those howling, groaning serpent-devils spoken of in Holy Writ, even in the sight of elect men and angels in this mortal life.

Again, is it not against all spiritual or rational sense, that any man, angel or devil should suffer eternal damnation for the sin of another, or for anothers tempting him to sin or evil? Moreover, doth it stand to very good sense, that, yea that creature that is left to himself to be tempted unto sin or evil, and overcome thereby, and remains under the power of it to their lives end? its requisite at the great day he should suffer for his own sin, and not for anothers iniquity: wherefore, judge you, is it not one of the vainest things in the world, for any man to think that there is any other evil spirit, angel, or devil that tempts him to any motion, imagination, thought, desire, word, or action of rebellion against God or man, but the proud, lying, envious devil living in his whole man, as aforesaid?

Therefore let no man that professeth spiritual light or life in him, for very shame say, that God can be tempted, or tempt any man unto sin or evil, neither let him say, that any evil spirit, angel, or devil in the air, or earth, or in the water, or in the fire, tempts him to commit any sin or evil, but that airy, watery, fiery, lustful, fleshly devil dwelling in his own body; I say, let him know [that, yea, that] is the prince of the air, which thorow the absenting vertue of the holy Spirit, begets those legions of devils, or lusts in the soul of man; and it is the true light of the Lord Jesus Christ in all his new born babes, that crusheth the Cockatrice eggs before they become serpent-devils, to sting the whole man with fear of eternal death.

So that, understand what I say, those devils which by the powerful word of the Lord Jesus were cast out of *Mary Magdalene,* or any other creature spoken of in Holy Writ, were onely all maner of filthy diseases, or violent fiery distempers in man, that hurried him about any desperate wickedness whatsoever, oftentimes increasing so powerfully, as you may read in *Mark* the fifth, that it did not onely occasion him to rend his own body, and break iron chains, but also he is ready to tear any one in pieces, until the Lord of Glory shined into his distempered soul, with that golden Grace of true Faith, through which that imaginary devil is chained up, whereby all his fleshly goods were spoiled of ever having power in him as formerly, and being now in his right minde at the glorious feet of Christ Jesus, through his own pure light, leading him into heavenly raptures, in reference unto his eternal glory, at his visible appearing in the clouds with all his mighty Angels.

Therefore seriously consider, that if *Cain* or *Abel* were both begotten by *Adam* upon the body of *Eve,* as for the most part all men vainly imagine, from one bare Scripture-record which they understand not, I would know of that man that is offended with me concerning this point, why *Cain* was not nominated in Holy Writ to be of that wicked one aforesaid, and branded as an out-cast, fugitive, vagabond, and cursed from the divine presence of the Creator, and cast out of the natural presence of his parents for ever, and condemned with *Balaam* and *Core* as a perishing cast-away? This I am sure of, that no spiritual rational man that is sober, dare say that either *Adam* or *Eve* was that wicked one from whence the cursed spirit of *Cain* sprang, why? because there is no such opprobrious names attributed unto them through the sacred Scriptures; Moreover, you may know that, yea that wicked one from whence *Cains* spirit proceeded, could not possibly have any relation to *Adam* or *Eve,* though *Cain* was conceived in her womb, and born of her body, and that because there was an absolute curse denounced upon the Angelical Serpent and his seed in her womb, as aforesaid, without any after-promise in Holy Writ, for ever being redeemed by the Creator, but on the contrary, you know there was a gracious promise by the Creator himself of the Redemption of *Adam* and *Eve,* after their fallen estate, with their whole generation of righteous *Abels, Seths,* or *Abrahams,* in that glorious hidden saying, *The Seed of the woman shall break the serpents head.*

Now one Scripture more, which shall be against all gainsayers interpreted, which is this, *Matthew* the fourth, beginning at the first verse: *Then was Jesus led up of the spirit into the wilderness to be tempted of the devil, and when he had fasted forty days and forty nights, he was afterward an hungred; and when the tempter came to him, he said, If thou be the Son of God, command that these stones be made bread: then he answered, Man shall not live by bread onely, but by every word of God, or that word that proceedeth out of the mouth of God: then the devil taketh him up into the holy City, and setteth him on a pinnacle of the temple, and saith unto him, If thou be the Son of God, cast thy self down, for it is written, He hath given his angels charge concerning thee, &c.*

Again, the devil taketh him up into an exceeding high mountain, and sheweth him all the kingdoms of the world, and the glory thereof, and saith unto him, All these things will I give thee, if thou wilt fall down and worship me, &c.

In that these hidden sayings hath their dependence on the precedent Chapter, I must from thence make way to this divine Secret: As if thou couldst but understand what thou readest, thou shalt finde, that as soon as ever Christ was baptized by *John,* the Holy

Ghost fell upon him, that did impower him to encounter with the devil; in which Dispute we must observe these two particulars.

1. *Who this tempter or devil was.*
2. *The nature of this temptation.*

First, take notice that this tempter was one of the wisest and soberest, yet subtilest Disputant amongst the Pharisees and Sadduces, and therefore appointed by them to have conference with Christ, as by and by you shall read; for if you cast your eyes on *John* the third, the fifth, sixth and seventh verses you shall finde, *there went out to him* Jerusalem *and all* Judea, *and all the region round about* Jordan, *and were baptized of him in* Jordan, *confessing their sins;* as touching these *John* used no words of reproof or dislike in the least, but when he saw many of the Pharisees and Sadduces come to his baptism, he forthwith upbraided them with a sad, yet just sentence, saying, *O generation of vipers, who hath forewarned you to flee from the wrath to come? &c.* as if he should have said, Ye are the children of that wicked one, that onely comes to dispute and to cavel, therefore *John* cuts them short with these words, *Bring forth fruits meet for repentance, and think not to say within your selves, we have* Abraham *to our father:* Then *John* proceeds further, and tells them, *I indeed baptize you with water unto repentance, but he that cometh after me, is mightier then I, whose shoes I am not worthy to bare, he shall baptize you with the holy Ghost and with fire.*

Now when the Pharisees and Sadduces heard this, they forthwith commissionated one of the wisest and subtilest devil amongst them, which by experience they found was best versed in Scripture, to see if this man-devil could perswade the Lord Jesus to baptize them with the Holy Ghost and with fire: Now that you may no longer doubt, but that this tempter or devil was onely a man, as aforesaid, cast thy eye into *Deuteronomy* 6. and the sixth verse, where it is thus written, *Ye shall not tempt the Lord your God as ye tempted him in Massah,* so read *Heb.* 3.9 Now tell me friend, who those were that tempted the Lord, were they not the people of *Israel*, men and women? So this tempter or devil that I am now treating of, was onely a wise subtile man, as you have already heard, and will in this temptation be made more apparent.

2. To the nature of the temptation, beginning at these words: *Then was Jesus led up of the Spirit into the wilderness to be tempted of the devil.* First minde, the Spirit that led Jesus up into the wilderness, was the Holy Ghost which came upon him at the baptism of *John*, a little before the tempter came, as you may read in the last verse of the third of *Matthew*. I have found it true by experience, that whosoever hath received the Holy Spirit, cannot be free from the temptation of the devil, that is, the cavelling, contentious disputes of unreasonable and unmerciful men: But,

Secondly, in the next place I shall give you to understand, that this wilderness here spoken of, was not a wilderness yielding fruit for the supporting of life, where nothing but wilde beasts void of reason doth inhabit, as the seed of *Cain* doth imagine, and the learned of that seed do vainly teach: though this wilderness was the same that *John* quotes in *Mat. 3.13.* saying, *The voice of one crying in the wilderness, prepare ye the way of the Lord, &c.* Now let any sober man judge the black darkness that is over the learned, to think that *John* should cry the message of the Lord to a wilderness of wood and wilde beasts, that hath no understanding to receive it! and as great a darkness it is for thee to think that any devil without man, or devil-man, could so far overcome Christ, as to lead him into such a wilderness, no, no: therefore take notice that wilderness *John* preached in, and this wilderness Christ was lead up into, was onely the wilderness of mans heart, whose hearts are as barren as a natural wilderness that beareth no fruit, as unto the true knowledge of things appertaining unto eternal life: O minde what you read, it was the wilderness of mans heart, and not such a wilderness as *Moses* led the people of Israel through; for neither did *John* preach, nor was in any such wilderness.

3. Its said, Christ fasted forty days and forty nights, but from what he fasted is not in the least mentioned, therefore I affirm, that as *Moses* fasted forty days and forty nights in the mount from natural food, so did Christ fast forty days and forty nights in the spiritual, that is, Christ did baptize none with the Holy Ghost nor with fire, neither did he do any miracle for the space of six weeks, and the original of this was, that he might be tempted of the subtile serpentine devil-man, as aforesaid, which made that devil-man say, *If thou be the Son of God, command that these stones be made bread;* however thou that readest mayest not apprehend this, yet let me tell thee that man-devil did not mean the hard stones that we tread upon, no more then *John* when he said, *God is able of these stones to raise up children unto Abraham.* Oh what absurdity is it in any man to think that God would of natural dead stones, raise them up spiritual living children, no, no: when the devil-man said, *Command that these stones be made bread* [which was this] Command this stony heart of mine, and the stony hearts of the Pharisees and Sadduces that sent me, command them to be made hearts of flesh, by baptizing of us with the Holy Ghost and with fire, whereby I and others may so believe, that we may become true bread unto Christ; for in *John 4.32,34.* there saith Christ, *I have meat to eat that ye know not of,* meaning his dispute with the woman of *Samaria;* as touching this, it was his meat and drink to do the will of his Father, which will was to baptize his Elect with the Holy Ghost and with fire, without which no man could have eternal life abiding in him.

4. *Then the devil taketh Jesus up into the holy City, and setteth him on a pinnacle of the temple:* Observe that the City and pinnacle of the

Temple, were both in the self same place, yet understand that the Temple and the City signifie one and the same thing, as from the words of *Paul, Defile not the temple of God, whose temple ye are; yea, ye are the temples of the holy Ghost, and the city of the living God,* as is recorded in the *Corinthians* and *Hebrews,* and yet you shall finde, though the Saints are the City and Temple of God, that the Scripture calls the Nation of the Jews the holy City; so that I know that was the holy City that the devil-man took Christ up into, and there in the most eminent or highest place of the Temple, stated his temptation in the pinacle, that is nothing else but the high temptation that this devil used out of his own high spirit of reason, saying, *Cast thy self down,* that is, submit unto this people which in *Moses* time were the onely Nation or City of God, do but submit to be Governor or King, in condescending to us, there can no harm befal thee, in that he hath given his angels charge concerning thee, thou being the Son of God and our King, we shall conquer the whole world; but Christs kingdom not being of this world, he tells them, as at other times, *Thou shalt not tempt the Lord thy God:* It might well be called the high temptation of the devil, that if it had been possible to unthrone Christ of his immortal Crown and Kingdom, and crowned him King over a mortal, bloody and perishing kingdom, I say, as in relation to the strength and subtilty of this temptation, a man might well be called devil.

5. *Again the devil taketh him up into an exceeding high mountain, and sheweth him all the kingdoms of the world, and the glory thereof, and saith. All these will I give thee, if thou wilt fall down and worship me.*

Answ. If you could understand the Scriptures, you shall read it calleth rich wicked men *Mountains,* and poor believing men *Valleys,* as saith *Isaiah* chap.40 verse 4. *Every valley shall be exalted, and every mountain shall be made low:* there is very little of the New Testament to be understood in the letter, but spirit onely; therefore saith Christ, *My words are spirit and life,* so that if thou couldest see with an eye of Faith, then thou couldest with me acknowledge that this exceeding high mountain which the devil shewed Christ, and all the kingdoms of the world with the glory of them, were all in the devils own heart; for if you minde the Chief Priests and Rulers, from whence this devil-man was sent, they in their Councel instructed him, that if that Christ to whom he was sent, would but come and submit, yea, side with them; for submitting you must understand, is no less then to worship, that if Christ Jesus would but submit to be their king and governor, then thy would assure him he should have all the kingdoms of the world; for thou being the Son of God, no earthly king can stand before thee, for in so doing we shall have the rule and government of the whole world, and the glory thereof, which if thou wouldst but condescend to this, we could make our words truth, that *Herod, Pilate* and *Cesar* would give place to thy crown and dignity, by which we should become a greater people then ever we were: these and such like thoughts was in the Priests and Rulers, which they thought they had so wisely compacted together, as a mountain not onely strong and great, but a high mountain over-topping all other mountains whatsoever.

So that now you have the interpretation of that Scripture, which till this last Witness could never be rightly understood, that the high mountain there spoken of, was the moderate, wise, and high read Consultations in the breasts of the Rulers, given into a particular, moderate, wise, high, learned man, much read in the Law and the Prophets, to tempt, and if possible, to perswade Christ to yield to this his high and learned Position; but you may read this man-devils mountain was too weak, and too low, for the high immortal God to rest or cast himself down upon; for to that end he came not into this kingdom to be King, but to fulfil his own determined will, in destroying him that had the power of death even the devil, yea, that devil-man that would, if possible, have deceived God himself, and so returns his positive Answer, *Get thee hence, Satan, for it is written, Thou shalt worship the Lord thy God, and him onely shalt thou serve,* that is, thou oughtest to be ruled by me, and not I by thee, therefore depart, my kingdom is not of this world, but of that world which is everlasting, immortal, and to all eternity. Upon which that man-devil leaveth him, tormented for not prevailing, and Christ refreshed by his Messenger from his glorious Kingdom above the stars.

Question. *If this be infallible what you have here written, then may you ask me, How comes it the Learned of this world could not, as well as this Witness, make known this hidden divine Secret, seeing they give themselves wholly to finde out the true interpretation of the Scriptures?*

Answ. What ever the Learned of this world dream of finding out the invisible things of Eternity, by searching into Scripture Records, and comparing them together, yet know this, the Divine Majesty hath locked up all the principal Secrets of the Scriptures in his own spiritual breast, that he by an immediate inspiration may dispose of them into the spirits of elect men and angels, most advantageous for his own glory, and their consolation; therefore minde what you read, and seriously observe, that the Scriptures runs not in the line of Reason, but in the line of Faith, Inspiration, or Revelation, according to those sayings in the *Hebrews* and other Records: By Faith the divine Work of Creation, and wonderful Mystery of Redemption was, and is known, with the immortal eternal Glory, and everlasting shame of mens persons in the end of the world: but of the contrary you shall never read in any place of Scripture, that any man in the least knew the things of eternal Glory by any kinde of rational comprehension whatsoever; I confess the natural Reason of man is a very good handmaid, if it be well qualified with the spiritual dame of divine Faith, for illustrating of the things of God unto weak comprehensions; but as for truly understanding the invisible things of God by the highest reason that ever was in man or angel, it is utterly impossible, as beforesaid, and that because though the spirit of reason were never so pure, yet you may know reasons nature is but a desire after the knowledge of the divine nature of the Spirit from whence reason had its living being: but of the contrary, spiritual Truth or Faith, is of the divine nature of God himself, and therefore in what soul soever that Heavenly Seed is sown, it springeth up in that spirit all variety of divine knowledge, with glorious raptures in reference unto life eternal, by vertue of an intercourse with the eternal Spirit from whence it came. Moreover, I confess a man that is indued with a *Solomon*-like gift of natural reason, may be able to comprehend all words, whether they are spoken in a good form, sense or language, or no; yea, and such a man may be mighty in disputes about the glorious things of Eternity; but as for thy real understanding, whether there were, or be any such eternal things or no, thou hast no certain knowledge of that at all, but thy bare thoughts onely, which if equally weighed in that balance, it may be true, or it may be false, and all this is for want of an infallibility of Truth it self; therefore though the divine things of the eternal Majesty be nothing else but spiritual purity, of an infallible truth in themselves, yet unto that rational wise man, they are nothing but non-sensical blasphemy or lying tales, till his reason is confounded in him by a true and heavenly Faith.

Now thou that hast perused this Epistle, if thou understandest what thou readest, mayest behold how infallibly I have proved both by Reason, Faith and Scripture, that there is no other devil but what is in man and woman; also how this devil came to be a devil; so that if thou wilt not, because thou canst not believe, much good may that imaginary devil do thee, yet by the way let me tell thee one word, which is irrevocable, that thou canst not now really, nor at thy resurrection shalt finde, or in thy self feel any other devil, but thy soul onely, which if it were possible for thee then to utter thy self, thou wouldest tell me what now I write to thee, was the naked truth; but then, even then I shall be far enough from thee, in that I shall be with the Lord above the Stars; this thou shalt finde, and this I shall be (as sure as God is God) for believe me whether thou wilt or no, I do not write now as formerly I have done, *viz.* hab nab, as a man onely indued with reason, but take notice I write from that revealed Seed-spring within me. Now to the seed of *Cain* his Education.

CAP. II

*The Seed of Cain his Education or bringing
up, undeniably proved against any
of his tribe that shall oppose it.*

As touching this I shall not need to spend much ink or paper, and that because not onely Scripture, but likewise experience doth confirm, that there is none of the Seed of Faith so honorably educated as the rich sort of the seed of *Cain;* for indeed to whom doth this wisdom and government of this world belong to, but to them? and therefore nothing that in the bounds of reason can be attained unto, but his seed enjoys it, nay, they are so exactly educated in the affairs of this world, that by their reason they are able to comprehend all words whether they are spoken in a Philosophical form, sense, or language; nay, many of them are not onely mighty in disputes as touching the Government of this their kingdom, but they are also able in dispute about the glorious things of Eternity, though they understand not the matter disputed of in the least; for as *Paul* saith, *I Cor. 2.14. Neither can they know them because they are spiritually discerned;* for their education in the greatest knowledge is but natural, and therein they are able to dictate unto the unlearned of their seed, laws and rules to preserve this their kingdom in peace among themselves; for you must understand what wisdom Learning can teach them shall not be wanting, and the wisdom they attain unto, is not that spiritual or divine Wisdom, for this onely belongs to the Seed of Faith; As read but *I Cor. 2.4,5,* and *6* verses, and there you shall hear *Paul* shew the vast difference of the wisdom of Faith, from the wisdom of flesh; for the wisdom of *Cain* is a meer cheat, yea, leads him forth to nothing but pride, oppression and cruelty, for by that wisdom they put the Lord of Life to death, as in the eighth verse: therefore you that have eyes may see what this learning and knowledge is the seed of *Cain* are tutored in, that it is no other but the wisdom of this world, which is foolishness with God, and that is the cause they come to tempt or dispute with the Seed of Faith, whose wisdom is given him by inspiration or revelation, in the demonstration of the Spirit; I say, because the wisdom of *Cain* cannot receive the things of the Spirit of God given this precious soul, O how they rayl with tearms of a fool, an ass, a dunce, a coxcomb, a heretical blasphemer, an ignoramus, one that hath no sense, these and such like tearms this cursed Brood will brand the Seed of Faith with, the onely wise men in Christ; for which cause the Lord in *I Cor. 1.19.* saith, *I will destroy the wisdom of the wise, and will bring to nothing the understanding of the prudent. Where is the Wise? Where is the Scribe? Where is the Disputer of this world? hath not God made foolish the wisdom of this world?* and all because the foolishness of God in the Seed of Faith, is wiser then that great knowledge in the seed of *Cain*: for take this infallible truth along with you, which is this, that the Scriptures in the life and power of them were never given to the learned men in those days; *For,* saith Christ, *to you it is given to know the mystery,* to you my Disciples, or elected Seed of Faith, to you, and for your sakes did I speak this: and therefore it was the wise, learned Priests and Rulers did imprison and put to death, not onely the Disciples, but Christ also, as Blasphemers, for publishing this Scripture, which now their wise children do make a Trade of, and will not onely imprison, but, if possible, put to death the onely Witnessed and true Interpreters of this Holy Writ which was given by inspiration, for the proper use of his blessed Seed of Faith.

Again, the seed of *Cain* are educated in the fulness and plenty of this world, insomuch that there is no novelty, delicate or dainty, that by the spirit of reason can be invented, but for their belly it is prepared; as also no new antick fashion can be imagined, either of silk, gold, or silver, but their backs are adorned with it, nay, there is no attendance of men and maid-servants that this their kingdom can afford, but the seed of *Cain* enjoys it; yea, they are so tenderly and princely brought up at home and abroad, and so hurried in their Coaches and Sedans, that if possible the cold wind should not blow on them, nor the glorious Sun with his beams should scorch them, so careful are they of their beauty and comely, streight, proper persons, that if possible, there shall not be a wrinckle on their hands, nor a spot on their faces, unless it be of their own making, for the more grace of their comely persons; thus what by art in their wisdom can be invented, shall not in the least be wanting, if it can be had for gold or silver; and whatever Science, Pastime or Pleasure their soul can desire, as Hawking, Hunting, Bowling, Shooting, Gaming, at Dice, Cards, or Tables, or any other delight of Musick, Dancing, Courting of Ladies, with the satisfaction of the greatest lust, and that with the greatest pomp and state this their heaven can afford; and then in the last place for carriage and behavior none in this world like unto them, as observe how proud, and *Lucifer*-like, their father, they carry their heads, insomuch that they know not what fashion or coloured Perriwig to hang upon it: and when they meet any of their brethren, O what congeying and bowing with Cap in hand to the ground, saluting each other with these and such like complementary tearms, as *Your servant, Sir,* or, *Your servants servant, Sir,* or *Madam,* and *fair Lady, I am yours to command by night or by day,* and that with so much stateliness and comely behavior, that I wonder thou shouldest be affrighted at the name or person of the devil, considering what a glorious, proud, majestical creature the devil is, as aforesaid.

But now you ask me, *Are all the seed of* Cain *thus educated?*

Answ. No: for you may understand some are brought up to one Calling or another, that some of them do undergo hard labor and great pains, to maintain themselves with their families, in this their perishing kingdom, so that they have neither gold nor silver [the dust of this earth] to mannage such a fleshly glorious education, as aforesaid.

And others there are that are educated, yea, brought up servants, yea slaves, to the great Rabbies of their seed, which none of them have that attendance, fulness, delights & pleasures as aforesaid; but on the contrary, are deprived of all that their happiness the other enjoy, insomuch that in stead of giving relief, they beg relief; in stead of a Bed of Doun, they lye on a bed of straw; in stead of being clothed with silk, they are clad with rags, yea many times ready to starve for want of food; so that you may behold there is not onely rich, but poor, miserable, ragged devils, that shall rise at the day of our eternal Gods appearance, so that I say these of all the tribe or generation are to be pitied, if pity did belong to them, to consider what affliction they undergo in this their heaven, and yet be eternally damned hereafter.

Question. But now you may say unto me, and that seemingly affirm, both from my writing and the Scripture, in that I have before treated much of the rich men of this world, how hard a thing it is for them to walk in the way of God, they being so educated in the pomp and glory of this world; which I say, and your experience findes it is the greatest thief that steals away the heart of man, and so makes that soul as difficult, as a woman in travail, to enter into the life and power of the Gospel; therefore we being poor, and the Scripture saith, the poor receives the Gospel, we much marvel how your writing will be found truth in Scripture, that any poor should rise devils, when the Scripture saith, it is onely the poor that receives the Gospel.

Answer. From this thy curious Query I shall answer thee in those words of *James 2.5.* where it is thus written, *Hearken my beloved brethren, hath not God chosen the poor of this world, rich in Faith, and heirs of the kingdom which he hath promised to them that love him?* Now if you intend these poor, I affirm what you say, yea, from my Seed-spring I declare, not one of these poor shall rise devils, in that these are the Seed of Faith, and educated in the knowledge of eternal Truth, yea, tutored by the spirit of divine Wisdom: But now tell me how many of these poor you can find among the poor seed of *Cain,* for if thou understandest what thou readest, thou shalt finde, though the Seed of Faith for the most part are but poor in this world, *viz.* your kingdom, yet minde what the Holy Writ saith, though poor in estate, yet they are rich in faith, so that these poor by Faith receives the Gospel; therefore take notice of this, it is not poverty in the outward man that makes thee rich in the inward man; for if you could discern, by the spirit of Faith you shall finde, that the major part of the poor in this world, are poor in faith, yea so poor, that they cannot give thee the least account of what God is, or what a rich treasure it is to believe in God, therefore in stead of loving God, they hate God; as if it were but recorded how many times in a day at *Billings-gate,* as also in the Streets of *London;* thou shalt hear they are educated in little else but to blaspheme the name of our glorious personal God, as shall be seen more at large in the devil his qualification; so that deceive not your selves, and that because of your beauty or greatness, no nor for your poverty, unless you be richly clad with that rich Jewel of Faith, for that will manifest who was thy tutor, and the nature of thy education.

CAP. III

The devil or seed of Cain *his Qualification, and how he is acted forth.*

For your better understanding of what I shall now write, you shall finde this matter ensuing divides it self into several branches, and not onely as touching his thoughts, words and actions, but there are several distinct actings forth of this wicked seed in matter of qualification, and yet all makes up but one seed as unto its original, even the seed of *Cain* their father: as,

First, some of this seed you shall hear are acted forth to all maner of uncleanness, yea such as is spoken of in *Romans* the first, from verse 21. to the end of the Chapter, *For this cause God gave them up unto vile affections, for even their women did change their natural use into that which is against nature, and likewise also the men leaving the natural use of the woman, burned in their lust one towards another, men with men working that which is unseemly:* Of these sorts of devils we have among us at this day, and that not onely such that doth take shame for what they have done, but rather will maintain such gross, foul, filthy acts, and that because, say they, there is nothing that I can think, speak, or do, but God is the Author of it; so what if I lye with another mans wife, what harm can be in that? I know no evil in so doing, for to me all women are but one woman, and this woman, a man, and that man, I man eternity; and therefore if I lye with twenty, they are but all one to me, and there being a free consent, what sin can be in this? for what hath some in *London* said, that it is no more sin for a man to lye with any woman, then a Cock to tread a Hen, or a Bull to serve a Cowe? nay this ranting devil is qualified and acted forth, saying, till a man can act sin as no sin, he cannot be free from sin; for thinking this, it is impossible for any man to be free from these sins, unless he can steal, murther and commit adultery as no sin, then, and not till then, say they, thou hast no power over sin, and so thou encourages thy self in all thy impurity, in that saith thou, *to the pure all things are pure,* so that nothing is unclean of it self, but to him that esteemeth it so, not in the least considering as unto what the Apostle spake, that [*to the pure all things are pure]* from hence including all maner of filthy acts whatsoever: Now let any of the Seed of Faith judge, if thou art not given over to a reprobate minde to do those things that are not convenient? for as touching this, speak thy self, what convenience doth appear in any of these thy destructive actions? for indeed destructive they are, both to thy self, and them thou hast to deal with; witness the tears of many a poor virgin-wife, and the sad misery many an innocent virgin hath undergone by thy devilish temptation, to the loss of all her friends, the defilement of her own body, and the eternal hazard of her soul, yet all this is justifiable in thy reprobate minde, if thou canst but satisfie thy lust, and spend her money, that is all the love that she shall finde from thee; and when this pretty deluded creature comes and tells thee how the case is with her, I am with childe by thee, and thou hast spent all my money, what wilt thou do with me? wilt thou, according to thy promist, make me thy wife, and do thy best endeavor to satisfie me for this wrong thou hast done to me?

What is his answer, think you? even this he will reply: Alas, what can I do for thee? marry thee I cannot, in that I have a wife; and to maintain thee I cannot, in that I have it not for my self, so thou must provide for thy self as well as thou canst: Now if this poor deceived creature [should reply, and say] thou toldest me thou wast single, and it was nothing but pure love to me, and that thou lovedst me above all the world, so I did condescend to lie with thee, thinking thou wouldest make me thy wife, by which I have not onely brought my self to shame and beggery, but for ought I know, have damned my soul. Upon these words this Ranting devil breaks forth, saying, A pox take you for a whore, you are a dark devil, indeed, to say thou shalt be damned for thy love, the Scripture commands us to love our neighbor as our self, and therefore we are to love our neighbors wives, and how can our love be more exprest, then in kissing, sporting, and lying one with another? and thus they make *Solomon* and his writings their patern, nay, they will engage soul for soul that she shall not be damned, provided she do not look upon it as sin; for say they, to lye with a maid, widow, or our neighbors wife, is no more then to lye with that woman you call my wife; for I know none lawfully married in this world, but those onely that are one in flesh and spirit, and she that you call my wife, though I have had many children by her, she is but a whore, and the children bastards, for we were not contracted in this light and purity aforesaid.

Now let any sober man judge the quality of this kinde of devil, that his love and purity is to destroy and begger a poor innocent soul, and yet plead for it as the onely truth, saying, It is not I, but the Lord in me; of my self I can do nothing, and he is all in all, with many such like Scriptures they will produce, for to satisfie their devilish lust, perswading themselves that God is an infinite formless Spirit, and infinite Nothing, or an infinite All, in this their beastly reason, so that well comes in that saying of *David,* Psal. 50.21. *These things hast thou done, and kept silence, thou thoughtest I was altogether such a one as thy self;* as if he should have said, Thou thoughtest it was I that committed adultery, that did cozen and lye with the innocent, thou thoughtest it was I in thee that moved thee to swear, whore, and cheat thy fellow mortals; but thou shalt know that I am a God, that is not an infinite nothing, for out of nothing, comes nothing, as also thou shalt know, that I am not an infinite All in thy filthiness, for the day is at hand that I will reprove thee, and that god in thee, as in *Romans 1. thou hast changed the truth of God into a lye,* in supposing there is no other God but what is in thee, and so worship me as a God filled with all unrighteousness, fornication, wickedness, covetousness, maliciousness, envy, murther, debate, deceit, an inventor of all evil things.

Thus in part you have heard how this ranting devil is qualified and acted forth, and that not onely to all maner of women, but man burning in lust with man, and women with women, as before related; and the more it is to be observed, that what they do in this nature, they affirm it to be just, yea to do as they would be done unto, for you that knows them, as much as I, shall finde their tongues tipt with these and such like words, but in their actions, as you have heard, they have sold themselves to commit wickedness, and that with greediness, never finding themselves more happy then when they are a whoring or drinking, which to them is a pure truth as any sentence in Holy Writ; for they do not esteem that sin which the Scripture records for sin, in that they do not know what to make of that glorious personal God nor his writing, looking upon it as a History of mans invention; for, say they, the Scripture is a meer Map of Contradiction, so that such devils of this kinde in their hearts do not believe it no more then another writing, onely for fear of the Law they will say as you say, for what do they affirm, A lye and a truth all is one to us, and so whatsoever we do, is righteous, just and good, and when we die, we shall be swallowed up into the infinite Spirit, as a drop into the Ocean, and so be as we were, and if ever we be raised again, we shall rise a horse, a cow, a roote, a flower, and such like, and so turn the world round as before; as for hell or damnation it is all here, so if they can but escape prison, sickness, and want of money, they fear no other hell or torment hereafter whatsoever.

Now let any sober man consider the devils quality that acts forth this sort of this cursed seed, and as for language, if there were a devil without man, that had any dealings with man, if possible, they would curse and swear that the devil out of his name and wits; for some of this sort when they are in company with their cursed tribe, what oath or oaths was ever heard by the ear of man, but they have it, and that with authority from their father *Cain* they maintain it, and that seemingly from Scripture, and so will take oath against any one they have a revenge to, if the false oath will prevail, they will do it. Thus much of the white, light, ranting devil.

2. The next sort of this cursed seed are qualited and acted forth in most wickedness like unto the first, onely the difference is, the white ranting devil doth approve of all his wickedness to be righteousness, when this black ranting devil doth judge it a sin; and yet though his tongue will rayl on the white ranting devil, and in what company soever he comes he will speak against these cursed actions, and that because he doth not onely know them to be evil, but he is afraid his wife, husband, children, or parents should know of it, and not onely that, but he is afraid the Law will take hold of him, and so punish

him, if not put him to death for it; these and such like are the motives inducing him to speak against that with his tongue, which his heart burneth and lusteth after: but however all these outward fears attend him, yet this lust or devil is so desiring after a beautiful maid, or another mans wife, that though he will say it is a sin, and hath read the wrath of God due for it, yet he will hazard not onely his credit in the world, but the loss of his soul in the world to come; and the ground of this his dangerous attempt, ariseth from these and such like thoughts, I may escape as well as other, and I will be sure that none shall see me lye with any woman, neither doth any of my neighbors suspect me, so that I before I will the society of such a rare creature, in whom my soul is wholly ravish with the thoughts of what pleasures and delights I shall have with her, I will hazard both soul and body; for what faith such a sort of devil as this? as for the world I will play my cards wisely, that none shall hear or know of it; and though it be a sin, it is not the greatest, neither am I the first or shall be the last, and therefore I shall make as good shift as another, and besides that, I know that God is a merciful God, and though in my strength and youth of my body, I do now and then break forth a little, I hope the Lord, if I do but on my death-bed cry him mercy, he will forgive me.

Ah poor dark deluded soul, dost thou think that when the righteous, just, upright heart hath much ado to finde mercy, and yet thou wicked ungodly man thinkest it is easie for such as thou? no, no: thou shalt finde, that as in the strength of nature and health of body, thou hast spent thy time in satisfaction of thy lust, when all that thy pleasure is at an end, then is a small measure shall be presented unto thee what thou shalt be at the day of resurrection: for alas poor heart, thou thinkest the God of Truth, is like thee, a man of lies, and by thy corrupt petition to turn the will of God, as with a petition thou canst turn the will of man, but then to thy cost thou shalt finde he is a God that changes not; which in the last Chapter I shall shew thee at large.

Now to the matter in hand, as touching thy quality and acting forth, in thy Carriage and Language, that from my Seed-spring I speak it, if there were a devil without man, as there is not, that devil would tremble to behold thy carriage, and hear thy expressions; for pride doth so much attend thee, that thou knowest not how to fashion thy garment, nor which way to hang thy Cloak upon thee; now being richly clad, thou knowest not well what to think of thy self, that whether thou be a god or a man, thy garments so glitter, and thy heart so proud, and carriest thy head so high, that the poorer sort of thy seed stands cap in hand to thee, yea, gazing after thee, that thou art so puffed up with the thought of this, that thou thinkest in thy self none in the world like unto thee for beauty and proper person, so richly adorned with jewels of god and silver, that thou thinkest every one that looks upon thee, admires thee; from hence it is thy devil or soul is so ravisht with the vain glory of this perishing world, that thou art never better but when thou art abroad shewing thy bravery, with thy servants standing bare head before thee in the open streets; as also to your Church you go, and what is the load-stone drawing you thither? onely because you would be looked upon as a good Churchmen, and to have the praise of the world, also to shew your fine rags as aforesaid, and to see and be seen who outstrips thee in apparel, or what new fashion is invented, this, and onely this is the greatest loadstone inviting you; otherways if thou wentest to hear sin reproved, and thereby become humble for that thy rude carriage and corrupt behavior, then it would appear in they language, but thou art so much a stranger to sobriety of speech, that upon every occasion thou hast these and such like expressions, God damn me I will have my will, the devil take thee for thy pains, what are you mad you damn'd whore? I think the devil is in thee: the devil confound me body and soul if I be not revenged on thee: the devil rot thee, and the pox of God take thee for a pocky devilish whore, by his life, blood, heart and wounds, I will be the death of thee, with many such wretched blasphemous expressions, that the moderate devil doth even tremble to hear the language of this dark ranting devil: In these not excluding the light ranting devil, but as far over boots and shoes are they in these and such like cursed language, so that before I pass to the next sort of the seed of *Cain,* I shall parly a little with thee about these wicked tearms aforesaid.

Dost not thou desire to be saved? this I am sure thou wilt acknowledge, and yet thou callest upon God to damn thee, how canst thou think to be saved, when thy tongue will witness, that many times thou hast said, God damn me: and whereas thou saith, the devil take thee for thy pains, thou little thinkest that thou art that devil. Oh freind, time is coming that thou shalt finde, thou, and such as thou art, the onely devil and therefore for the time remember when ever thou saith the devil take thee, then thou must take her, or take him, to whom thou utterest those words, it is thou devil-man, thy self must take them, and when thou saith thou art mad, I think the devil is in thee, thou speakest truth not knowing it, and so when thou saith, If I be not revenged of thee, the devil confound me soul and body, now if thou be not revenged, as many times thou art not, then thou art justly confounded, and if thou do revenge thyself, thou art also confounded, in that thou shouldest leave that to the Lord; *For revenge is mine, saith the Lord* [I will, not thou] I will as I see cause revenge it, so that in this thou hast sealed thy condemnation; and whereas thou saith, the pox of God take thee: ah poor ignorant soul, thy tongue declares what a corrupt ulcerated humor doth run in the veins of thy soul and body, that thou thinkest God like thy self, when he declares himself a God all holiness and purity, glorious immortal, that no mortal corruption could in the least touch him; for it is written, *Thou wilt not suffer thy holy one to see corruption;* and that such a devil as thou shalt say, the pox of God, when it is really and truly the pox of thy devil lust within thee, as aforesaid: I told thee how thou wouldest hazard not thy credit and estate, but thy soul also, for a beautiful, yet pockey creature in whom, and for whom, thou has not onely beggered thy wife and children, but corrupted thy body, that thy nose or thy bowelts rot within thee, and yet thou so audaciously shalt say, the pox of God, when it is the pox of a whoring lustful devil thy self, and then in all thy discourse thou must swear by his life, when thou hast nothing to do with it, in that his life is death in thee and to thee, for thou hatest in thy life to be conformable to the life of Christ, and therefore take notice thou hast no share nor benefit in his heart, blood or wounds, it was never spilt nor wounded for them that are far better qualified then thou, yet the blood or wounds of the Lord was not for any of the seed of *Cain*, but he was onely wounded, and spilt his hearts blood for the seed of *Adam,* or *Abraham,* that blessed Seed of Faith; therefore thou wretched soul, let this my short parley with thee, be for ever a *Memento* to look into thy soul, and there thou shalt finde the devil that tempts or infuseth thee to utter all this diabolical language; but true is that saying in *John,* from the blessed tongue of Christ, *Ye are of your father the devil, and the lusts of your father ye will do;* for from him to you, comes cursing, oaths and lies, who is the father of it: As let but any sober man observe their quality in this, and you shall have them swear, and say, God forgive me whore, and cry, God forgive me: lye, and say, God forgive me; thus thou thinkest it is nothing, but with one and the same tongue say and unsay, to lye, cheat, whore, swear, and be drunk, and onely say, I have sinned, God forgive me, and so commit the like wickedness again and again, and thinkest this will serve thy turn; but alas for thee, the portion prepared shall at the great day lie heavy upon thee, as read *Matth. 12.36,37.* verses, *I say unto you, that every idle word that men shall speak, they shall give account thereof at the day of judgement; for by thy words thou shalt be justified, and by thy words thou shalt be condemned, for out of thy own mouth he will judge thee,* as thou shalt read at large in the next Chapter, that shall shew the place and nature of the devils torment.

3. The next sort of the seed of *Cain,* are qualited and acted forth to all maner of covetousness and worldly mindedness, insomuch that thou abhor a drunkard or any that is given to hospitality, and that because his quality is quite contrary to thine; for thou art all for toyling and moyling, rising early, and lying down late, neglecting no company wherein thou mayest enrich thyself, when as the other riseth up early, and lyeth down late in drunkenness, spending and making away that portion which was given thee, so that thou being covetous, he is no companion for thee; for thou hast so much care in thee, and upon thee, how to make thy self great on this earth, that unless thou canst advantage thy self, thou wilt not spend a penny; but when thou hast got five pounds, or more, or less, then whatsoever shift thou and thy family shall make, that shall not be diminished in the least, but to

usury it must go, and then thou pinchest thy belly, and the bellies of thy poor wife and children, by living so long upon small Beer and flet Cheese, and such like stuff, that thou increasest thy estate to a vast sum at last, that now the greatest care and thought of thy heart is, how thou shalt secure thy riches from some of thy seed, that if they should break into thy house, they may not plunder thee of it, and to that end thou inventest all maner of subtilty to deceive the deceived, that thou hidest some in the earth, and some on the house-top, and some in hollow trees, one place or another, that thy brother serpent may not steal it from thee, or the Law of this thy kingdom impose great Taxes upon thee; I say, thy care is so much upon this thy perishing earthly treasure, that thy heart, thy soul, is wholly wrapt up in it, insomuch that thy sleep and meat goes from thee; that now having what thy heart desireth after, thou art more tormented now then when thou hadst little or nothing; therefore remember that of Christ, *Luke 12.15.* where he saith, *Beware of covetousness, for a mans life consisteth not in the abundance of the things which he possesseth, and where thy treasure is, thy heart will be also;* so that what will all this thy greatness in this world, and plenty of gold or silver avail thee, when the tears of the poor are laid naked before thee, and starved for want of bread, which thou hadst in abundance? and not onely this, but it is read in thy soul, that thou hast enriched thy self in the ruine of others, and thy conscience tells thee, thou never got this justly, but by fraud and deceit, by grinding the faces of the poor, and keeping back the hire of the laborers. As touching this, look about you, ye Tradesmen of all sorts, yea, from the highest to the lowest, examine your own consciences how often ye have cheated; and remember this ye Landlords, that oppress the poor Tenents; as also ye Brokers that grinde the faces of the poor, in lending upon usury, or commodities, and that after forty or fifty pound in the Hundred; I say, remember this, that no cheater, oppressor, nor extortioner shall enter into the kingdom of Heaven, and therefore against you I cry wo, wo, wo: for this shall rise up a witness against thee, and shall eat thy flesh, as if it were fire, as it is in *James* the fifth, the first, second, third and fourth verses, and then, even then, when thou thinkest all is well, and that thou hast setled thy estate to thy hearts content, that now thou fearest no want, but canst without trouble cherish up thy soul with the fruits of thy wits and endeavors, and to take thy pleasure for the time to come, then comes the messenger of Death, and deprives thee of all the happiness of thy riches, and saith unto thee, *Ah fool, this night thy soul shall be required of thee, then whose shall those things be which thou hast provided?* Luke 12.20. Now thou hast brought thy covetous heart to perfect what it longeth after, and now must thou leave all, and knowest not what will become of thy soul on the other side of death, and so in terror and fear of death thou diest, and in torment thou shalt rise at the great day, as in the next Chapter thou shalt hear and read at large.

So that I cannot but admire the wonderful wisdom of my God, that notwithstanding the pleasure and pomp of this world belongs onely to the seed of *Cain,* yet he gives them a bitter cup to drink at last, which potion makes the devil afraid and to tremble at the thought of that day, by which they are not onely bridled from their great cruelty an tyranny they would impose upon the Seed of Faith, but also the thought of death doth in some measure out-top their pleasures and greatness, so that their life in this their onely heaven, is not much better then our life in this our onely hell; for though they have fulness, and such as we have want, yet we have peace, and they have war, yea oftentimes sad torment to think what will become of their souls, when as the Seed of Faith knoweth what he is here, what he shall be in the grave, and what he shall be at the resurrection, even glorified with his Savior.

So if you seriously lay to heart the vast difference of the Seed of Faith, and the seed of *Cain,* upon their bed of sickness or hour of death, it would cause admiration, as thus: The departure of the seed of *Cain* out of this world, is as much as if a Prince should depart, not onely from his loving wife and pretty children, but be banisht from his Crown and Kingdom, never to enjoy it more, and also where he is banisht, he is shut up prisoner all the the time of his life, even so is his death in this world; he must leave, not onely all his society, but the pleasure of this his kingdom, where he had delight as much as heart could wish, and in the grave his soul and body lyeth uncapable of either joy or sorrow, and then at the great day of our Saviors appearance, thou shalt be raised up thy body thy hell, thy soul thy devil, shut up close prisoner world without end.

Now death is unto the Seed of Faith as a Messenger of glad tidings, in that it frees him from the cruelty and oppression of the devill the seed of *Cain,* and take him from all his hardship and wants that he hath undergone, by living uprightly in this strange kingdom, and then he knowing, that all the time he is in the grave, there is no remembrance of good or evil, and as soone as ever his God comes, he shall be raised to meet him in the aire with his mighty angels, where he shall have a kingdom that one hours enjoyment of that, will be more then ten thousand times ten thousand the greatest substance of glory could be attained unto for ten millions of years in this perishing world. Thus in brief you have the difference of the two Seeds, what triumph the Seed of Faith have in death over the seed of *Cain:* Now to the last sort of this people.

4. The next and last sort of this seed of *Cain,* you cannot easily, neither for carriage nor action, finde them much different from the Seed of Faith, nay, in some things they outstrip some of the Seed of Faith, as by and by you shall hear: For carriage they are very sober, and much given to moderation, that they are very temperate both in meat and drink, and modest and decent apparel, and you shall not hear an oath from them, unless some small petty oath, as they call it,

by faith, or troth, and such like, and that very seldom, for thou art acted forth to be mindful of thy tongue, lest thou shouldest offend therewith; and for hospitality and benevolence, thou art no niggard, but free-hearted to them that thou respectest; and for private and publique duties thou art very observant, and in prayer and singing in Psalms, thou wilt many times shed tears, and sigh and groan if thou commit some crime against the Law, and very vigilant thou art to educate thy children in obedience to that God thou knowest, and for thy expressions, they are so seasoned with sugared heaven-like moderation, so affable and courteous, that thou wouldest, if possible, deceive God himself.

    Now if you say unto me, *How can this sort of people be any of the seed of* Cain? I answer: The moderate, hypocritical, Saint-like devil, is of all devils most to be suspected; for of this sort was that man-devil that came to tempt Christ; he was not onely moderate, as you have him related, but he was well read in the Scripture, and seemingly holy he behaved himself, otherwise he had not by the Priests and Rulers been sent to tempt Christ; so that I shall endeavor to satisfie thee in my Answer, both from experience and Scripture, which shall be made plain, that all that cryeth, Lord, Lord, shall not enter into the Knowledge of the onely Lord God; for of this sort of people are these, as is recorded *Matthew 15.8. This people draweth nigh unto me with their mouth, and honoreth me with their lips, but their heart is far from me,* however you may think it strange, that such a one that will not swear, whore, nor be drunk, nor take the name of God in vaine, but in stead of spending his time idly, he will be reading the Scripture, & in conference with good men about the things of God and in stead of walking in the fields on the Sabbath, he will be hearing the word preached, and then in the evening when others are sitting at door, to see and be seen, he will be in his chamber at prayer, and with his whole family singing of Psalms, or some such like exhortation, becoming the day, and if thou be an Officer in thy parish, *viz.* Constable, or Churchwarden, in stead of tipling in the Ale-house in the Sermon time, thou wilt rather lose the benefit of that word preached, and spend the time in searching and peeping into Ale-houses, to see if thou canst finde any of thy lewd brethren, to punish them for their drunken sins: this thou wilt do, and that with delight and pleasure.

    This sort of people you may admire should be the seed of *Cain,* so rise a devil at the last day, [what must be, must be] the Lord knoweth who are his, which with their whole heart walk without hypocrisie before him, for as touching this, you shall finde thy brother before thee was as careful to serve the Lord, as thou canst be; as read *Isaiah 58.2.* and so on, *Yet they seek me daily, and delight to know my ways, as a Nation that did righteousness, and forsook not the Ordinance of their God: they ask of me the ordinance of justice, they take delight in approaching to God.* Dost thou hear what a heaven-like character the

God of Truth gives of thy brethren? and if thou dost but mind what thou reads, thou shalt finde five special remarkable notes of a true Believer; and the first is, *they seek me daily,* not onely the Sabbath day, but every day. 2. *and delight to know my ways,* what my will and pleasure is. 3. *they ask of me the ordinance of justice,* as though they would do no unjust thing. 4. *It was their pleasure and delight in approaching to God.* 5. *Neither would they forsake the outward Ordinance of God:* But now one word cuts them out for hypocrites, and that because all this that thy do *[was but as a Nation] that did righteous things:* in plain tearms, they were not in their heart what was shewed by their tongues; for if you read the antecedent verses, you shall finde all this was but to be taken notice of by God; for if you minde the third verse, you shall there read their hypocrisie at large: and in the fourth and fifth verses, the all-knowing God reproving them for their cheating and deceiving in their hearts; and then in the sixth and seventh verses, tells them wherein there great error lay, saying, *This is the fast that I have chosen, to loose the bands of wickedness, to undo the heavy burthens, and to let the oppressed go free, and that ye break every yoke, is it not to deal with bread to the hungry? that thou bring the poor that are cast out, to thy house? when thou seest the naked, that thou cover him? and that thou hide not thy self from thy own flesh?*

These are the qualities of a true Believer, not to speak and prate, but to do; for behold, to obey is better then all thy hearing, praying and singing, as *James* saith, *Shew me thy faith by thy works:* Faith is of a doing and working nature; thou shalt not of such hear many vain boasting words, but many merciful actions; for if you minde that all the judgements that God denounced against the house of Israel, was for the non-performance of charitable actions; as read all the prophets, and where ever you finde the Lord contesting with strict, great professors, it was for neglecting the works of mercy, and therefore he saith in *Isa. 1.15. When ye spread forth your hands, I will hide mine eyes from you, yea, when you make many prayers, I will not hear:* and what is the cause, think you? alas, your hands are full of blood, ye do not seek judgement, nor rescue the oppressed, neither judge ye the fatherless, nor plead for the widow, with thousands of these and such like you shall finde, and yet thou makest no account of this: for what is thy thought? if I can but carry my self demure with a Saint- like countenance, and go Saint-like in apparel, and carry a heaven-like outside to the world, behaving my self civil and moderate in my words, I shall do well enough, though I do not those works of mercy so much spoken of: I say such as thou, this is thy thought, and this is thy practice, so to conclude, I shall refer the moderate seed of *Cain* to the three and twentieth Chapter of *Matthew,* where thou shalt read thy inward turn'd outward, yea, the hypocrisie and cheat of thy heart laid naked before thee, for what ever woes thou their readest against them, that wo concerns thy self: As wo unto thee moderate, heaven-like Saint, *for thou art like unto the whited sepulchers, which indeed appear beautiful outward, but within are full of dead mens bones, and of all uncleanness; even so ye also outwardly appear righteous unto men, but within ye are full of hypocrisie and iniquity:* wo unto thee, for now thou wilt make a trade of Christ, and his Apostles, yea, garnish the sepulchers of them as righteous men, and yet at this day will speak evil, imprison, if not put to death, the true prophets and righteous of the Lord, so that ye be witnesses to your selves, that ye are the children of them that murthered the Lord of glory. Ah wo, wo, as thou with the rest, in the next Chapter shalt hear thy doom and endless torment.

CAP. IV

The devil or seed of Cain, *the place and nature of his torment.*

In that the face of the Creation is vailed with darkness and ignorance of Christs coming to judge both the quick and the dead, therefore I shall treat of this most needful point, from certain sayings of himself, as read *Matth. 24* where you shall finde, *As the light cometh out of the east, and shineth even to the west, so shall also the coming of the Son of man be; and as it was in the days of* Noah, *so shall it be in the days of the Son of man, they ate, they drank, they bought, they sold, they married, and were given in marriage, until the day that* Noah *entred in the ark, and the flood came and destroyed them all: so in the days of* Lot, *they ate, they drank, &c but in the day that* Lot *went out of* Sodom, *it rained down fire and brimstone from Heaven, and destroyed them all; So the day of the Lord shall come as a thief in the night, in which the Heavens shall pass away with a great noise, and the Elements shall melt with fervent heat, the earth also and the works that are therein shall be burnt up,* then shall all the seed of *Cain* mourn, tremble and shake, when they see the Son of man in the clouds of Heaven with power and great glory, yea, at the sound of his coming, the devil or seed of *Cain* will cry to the rocks and mountains, *Fall on us,* yea, ye will run into Caves and Cellars to hide your selves from the presence of that glorious personal God, whom in your life time ye despised and rejected, yea, scoffing and walking after your own lusts, saying, *Where is the promise of his coming, for since the Fathers and the Apostles fell asleep, all things continue as they were from the beginning?* and so ye swear, whore and be drunk, yea, cheat, oppress, imprison and destroy the Seed of Faith, not in the least laying to heart that the day of Christ Jesus, that glorious God, is at hand, and will come as a thief in the night, yea, as swift as lightening in the air, insomuch that two shall be in the bed, two in the field, two in the mill, or wheresoever two or more are together, they shall not have time to separate themselves, till the Lord of glory take to him self the Seed of Faith from the seed of *Cain.*

As sure as the Lord liveth, thus it will be very suddenly with this proud, covetous, lustful, bloody world, that sport themselves about the resurrection of the dead, and the day of Judgement, saying it is already past, or there will never be any such day; I say, before ye be aware of it, Christ the King of Glory will open the firmament of Heaven, and stand in the air, with his mighty angels surrounding his person, and then by the power of his word speaking, as he raised *Lazarus* out of the grave, so will he raise all the Seed of Faith both dead and alive in the twinkling of an eye, as he did *Elias,* yea in a moment, changing our mortal bodies to immortal, like himself; for you read in that day that *Lot* departed out of *Sodom,* the same day it rained down fire and brimstone, and destroyed them all. Oh what a dreadful and sudden desolation fire maketh in a mortal world in one day! so swift the Lord will appear, that he will make a quick dispatch, and after all the Seed of Faith, that handful or little flock, are safely arrived with him in the air, then the Man Jesus with a flood of fire, will burn all the beauty and glory of this world to ashes or dry sand, leaving behind the souls and bodies of the seed of *Cain* then living, with the souls and bodies of their dead seed raised up, burning together like fire and brimstone upon this earth, in utter darkness. Having in brief, by Reason, Faith and Scripture, proved to all sober-minded men, that a day of Judgement will come, the maner and nature of his coming, now I shall shew thee the place where that seed of *Cain* shall be tormented, which yet from the beginning, till this last Witness could never be found out, nor any true, infallible description given, as touching the place called *Hell,* though most of the Learned have attempted, yea stretched the line of reason to the utmost, yet all to no purpose, for thy father before thee, and thou his learned son, art not in the least satisfied, and that because thou hast not the seed of Faith, which is the evidence of things not seen, therefore being out of the bounds of reason, thou writest of it thou knowest not where, and therefore it is by thee recorded, that place called *Hell* will be under the earth, in the sea, or in the bottom of it, if not, thou supposes *Hell* shall be in the air, or a place thou apprehendest not, therefore from my seed-spring I affirm, and that thy own experience shall finde, that place of thy torment shall be even there where thou tookest thy pleasure, that shall be the place of Hell, even here in this world, on this earth, where now thou walkest, shall be the place of thy endless misery.

For if you observe your own rule in the execution of your Law, when a malefactor is apprehended for wilful murther, or some such hideous crime, when he is brought to his Tryal, and by your Law found guilty, then the Judge of the Law passeth Sentence, that his body shall be burned or hanged, even in that place where he committed his bloody, filthy act, and that justly where he spilt blood, his blood should be required again; even so the Lord of Glory, Christ Jesus the Judge of the quick and dead, when he comes to Judgement, all you that have been guilty in the blood of the Prophets, Christ Jesus, and his Disciples, that have put to death, imprisoned, or any way persecuted the Witness and righteous of the Lord, that blessed Seed of Faith, I say, where you executed your oppression and cruelty against the sons of the most high God, even there will the righteous Judge execute his fury to take vengeance of all his bloody enemies in this world, in this earth, where thou committedst thy wickedness, thou shalt receive thy sad and dreadful portion, and that world without end; and therefore deceive not thy self with the vain imaginations of the spirit of reason, that though it be as I affirm, yet thou hopest it doth not belong to thee: but what is the cause of thy hopes? thou art neither satisfied in thy self, nor doth it appear to any other, onely thou hopest with the rest of thy seed, but hast no assurance in the least, and that because thou findest within thee that thou art guilty, if not of publick, yet of private filthiness; so that, mark what I say, believe it whether thou wilt or not, thou shalt by woful experience finde, that this beautiful world wherein now thou hast thy pleasure, shall at the day of Christs next appearance, be, as aforesaid, burnt to ashes or dry sand, where all the seed of *Cain,* which in his qualification I have branched forth into four particulars, shall not need to trouble themselves about Heaven, and how they shall come to it, for as sure as God is a chrystal, glorious, holy, righteous, personal God, thou that desirest with *Balaam* to die the death of the righteous, and not to live the life of the righteous, thou with all thy pretended holiness and unrighteousness, shalt be raised no higher then this earth that now thou treadest upon; for as here thou hast taken thy pleasure, so here shall be thy sorrow; as here thou hast been a persecutor of God and his people, so here thou shalt have the vengeance of God upon thee, and in thee; as here thou hast cheated, and burned in thy filthy lust towards woman, so here shall those lustful actions burn in thy soul and body for ever; as here thou hast sworn and been drunk, so here thou shalt have nothing to quench thy thirst, but even here upon this earth where now thou walkest, thou shalt howl, burn & fry to all eternity, when then none shall pity thee.

2. Having shewed thee the place where the seed of *Cain* shall be tormented, now I shall shew thee the maner and nature of thy torment, and therefore attend & give ear: That after our Redeemer hath called up the Seed of Faith, which are but few in comparison of what shal be left behind, yet I say, after he hath taken that little Flock to himself, then will our long looked for Christ Jesus, the God of Glory, immediately, yea in a few hours, burn all the riches, beauty and bravery of this world to dry sand, as aforesaid, insomuch that there shall not be left the least appearance of a house, herb, tree or plant; for the Stars, Moon and Sun that gave light and motion to the fruits of the earth, and moving of the sea, shall become nothing, yea, be put forth as the snuff of a Candle, and this world shall be as dark as the land of *Egypt* was for three days; for if you read *Exodus 10.22,23.* you shall finde there was a thick darkness in all the Land of *Egypt* three days, they saw not one another, neither rose any from his place for three days; so that after all is burnt to ashes, and that which gave life and motion to the earth and sea, is put forth, then shall the earth bring forth no more fruit, nor the waters run no more, but become a dark, standing, stinking pool, as it was in the beginning, and all the seed of *Cain* then both dead and living shall be left behinde with bodies as heavy as lead, and as black as pitch, which then their bodies shall be their hell, and their spirits or souls shall be the devil, shut up close prisoner together for ever and ever without end; and

that fire and brimstone that will burn, shall be those wicked thoughts, words and actions which in thy life time where now thou art, thou committedst against the Seed of Faith, yea with a great hand of pride acted against them, shall be the fuel, as wood and coal is fuel to the natural fire, so thy wicked lustful actions shall be the onely fuel that shall burn, yea flame more hotter then any natural fire in the hottest furnace whatsoever, and yet it shall give no light at all, but the flame thereof shall be of a durty, scalding, burning envious nature, which shall smoak and fry through thy mouth, thy nostrils, thy eyes, thy fundament, insomuch that there shall not from the crown of the head, to the sole of thy foot, be one part free, but tormented throughout thy whole soul and body. And no sooner hath our God caught up his blessed Seed of Faith, but this beautiful world becomes dark dust or sand, as aforesaid; but then, yea even then, begins thy kingdom of darkness, wherein thou must continue either sitting, lying, kneeling, or standing, not being able to move one foot from the place where thou art raised, but there being lockt up to all eternity, never to see thy own dreadful face, nor the frightful faces of others, their wailing and lamenting for ever: Considering,

First, as in relation, that thou hadst so many warnings by such poor despised ones as I, that hath hazared our estates, our liberty, yea life and all, by publishing such writings, and declarations from the Lord, that there was no other Devil but such as thou, as now to thy eternal wo, thou caust set to thy seal is too too true, that if thou hadst not shut thy eyes, and stopt thy ears, thou mightest have foreseen what now thou feelest, and not onely that, but thy remembrance shall flame, in that thou didst not onely slight, scoff and scorn such testimonies of truth, but thou persecutedst it to death, this is one thing that shall burn and never be put out.

Secondly, the remembrance how thou hast spent thy time in this perishing world, shall quicken, and rise afresh within thee, as though they were but then in doing, for from my seed-spring I speak it, as there is no remembrance of any thing in the dust, so there is no time to the dead in the grave, for the death of *Adam* to his resurrection, though it be thousands of years in respect to the living, yet to the dead, so long sleep, shall be but as one nights rest, I say when thou art awaked, it shall be unto thee as not time at all, for though thou hast lain in the grave a thousand years more or less, yet then it shall appear unto thee as though it was but the last night, and as thou in relation to thy thoughts, words, and actions died here, so afresh they shall rise with thee either to thy condemnation, or justification.

O then thou light ranting Devil, that died in the living lust of thy soul, to deceive the poor innocent virgin, or virgin-wife, and was never better, then when thou hadst opportunities to deceive thy own soul, in the undoing of other, perswading thy self and others it was no sin; but at this day thou shalt know it was a sin, and that personal God which thou in thy life time despises, will now leave thee to thy lustful dealing god within thee, where thou shalt be damned to all eternity.

O then thou dark ranting Devil, that died in the pride and ambition of thy heart, spending thy time in all wanton wicked sports and pastimes, thy eyes have stared with fatness of the earth, & thy belly swoln with drunken healths, yea thy tongue blisterd with cursed oaths, and yet thou knew it to be sin, but would not leave it till it was too late, where now God hath left thee to be damned to all eternity.

O then thou covetous worldly minded Devil, that regarded no other God but thy bags of gold & silver, and so died in the love and delight of thy riches, not in the least laying to heart, how many thou hast beggered to enrich thy self, how many thou hast murthered to make thy self great, all this thy oppression, by deceit and extortion, shall rise afresh with thee, yea flame as a hot fiery furnace, and shall eat your flesh, as if it were fire, where nothing shall quench it, and that world without end, yea damned to eternity.

O then thou moderate Saint-like Devil, that carried thy self so holy, and heaven-like, under which pretense, thou didst privately backbite, yea bear false witness against thy neighbor, through thy Pharasaical prayers, and large supplications, with reading and singing of Psalms, yea sighing, and groaning, and lifting up thy hands and eye to heaven, thou didst conzen cheat and defraud thy fellow creature, thinking by thy hypocrisie, to blind honest hearted simple souls, and so with thy cloak of Religion, thou didst privately and subtilly enrich thy self in this world, and yet got a name for a good chapman, and a great professor, when all this while, thou art ignorant of a true Church: and that glorious personal God, nay if thou be a Priest, or a Ruler, thou wilt persecute both God and his People, that knows him as he is, therefore then, thou, with thy seeming holiness, shall be damned to all eternity.

So to conclude, Let all the seed of *Cain* look about them, and while it is called to day, seriously lay to heart, and that because as sure as he will come, it will be very suddenly, and that such an hour that thou knowest not, therefore watch and be ready for such an hour as you think not, *for blessed is that servant whom his Lord when he cometh shall finde well doing;* which none shall be thus found, but onely the Seed of Faith: for as I have told you, all the seed of *Cain* shall be taken unawares, yea committing one sin or another, saying, This day will not be in my time, and therefore I will not leave the pleasure of this world, nor the lusts of my flesh, but I will one year more refer it, so that Christ will take thee in thy wickedness, and give thee thy portion with the hypocrites on this earth, clothed with darkness, in which thy soul and body shall remain with thy sin, kindling and flaming more and more of a dark envious nature, through which it shall burn perpetually as aforesaid, causing a howling, with hideous doleful sighs and groans, yea weeping, wailing and gnashing of teeth for evermore, crying, Wo, wo, wo, that ever I was born to see this black tormenting day, of which there is no

E N D .

THE
Quakers Downfal, With all other DISPENSATONS

Their inside turn'd outward:

Wherein you have it infallibly interpreted,

1. What Scripture is, what not.
2. By whom it was writ.
3. For whom it was writ.
4. The end wherefore it was writ.

ALSO,

A Brief Narration of the *Quakers Conference* with us the second of July, 1659. wherein we made appear, That all of their Sufferings in *New England,* or any other Nation, they suffer justly as evil doers, so that neither they nor their Persecutors, so living and so dying, shall escape Damnation.

With a clear Confutation of all *ARMENIANS,* [called FREE-WILLERS] that deny Gods Prerogative Power in matter of Damnation and Salvation.

Written by *Lawrence Claxton,* the alone, true and faithful Messenger of Christ Jesus the Lord of Glory.

LONDON:
Printed for the Authour, and are to be sold by *Wil. Learner* at the *Blackamoor* near Fleet-bridge. 1659.

Rom. 15.4.

For whatsoever things were written aforetime, were written for our learning, that we through patience and comfort of the Scriptures, might have hope.

The revelation of my Faith finding it requisite to give you the Seed of Faith, the true interpretation of this Scripture, in that you may understand why the same Spirit that was in them, now manifested more fully in me, doth in the first place pitch upon this saying, which is for these ensuing grounds following:

First, that you may know what Scripture is, and what not: As touching this, none can finde the nature of the Writer, and the language of what is written, but onely the Seed of Faith, so that take notice, that as Christ hath locked up all the principal Secrets of the Scripture in his own spiritual breast; so again observe, that the Scriptures are not interpreted by the light of reason, but the divine light of Faith, inspiration or revelation, unless the seed of reason would affirm that the Scriptures were written by the wisdom of flesh; if this could be made appear, then I should conclude with the learned of this world, that the interpretation of the Holy Writ belongeth onely to the light of reason, and learned in the wisdom of flesh, but in that we onely know by what light or learning the Scriptures were written, and have the experience of that saying, *All Scripture is given by inspiration of God;* I say, if I had not the spirit of inspiration or revelation in my own soul, not any part or portion of Scripture would belong unto me, no more then it doth to *Oxford* and *Cambridge;* but I assuredly know, and against men and angels affirm, that I write this by the same spirit of inspiration as the Prophets and Apostles did theirs; nay furthermore I affirm, that being called forth by virtue of this last Commission, infallibly to bear record to this last Witness of the Holy Ghost or Eternal Spirit, the knowledge of which doth interpret the mystery of the two former Commissions, which *Moses,* the Prophets and Apostles never rightly understood neither was it required of them to know Christ in their Commission any other but God the Father, neither was requisite for the Apostles in their Commission to know Christ any other but the Son of God; but now in this last Commission, it is revealed that Christ which died out of the gates of *Jerusalem,* was God the Father, God the Son, God the Spirit, in one single person glorified, as in the ensuing matter you shall finde, so that from the spirit of Faith in me, in opposition to all the seed of the Serpent, or seed of Reason in this world I affirm, that not any but this last Witness can give the true sense and meaning of any sentence in Holy Writ.

Although the Learned in their days did assume the interpretation to themselves, as now they do in this Witness or revelation of ours, yet you may understand none so much as the Learned did withstand *Moses,* and persecute the Prophets as the Priesthood and Elders of *Israel;* and you may finde *John 7.48.* the Learned of this perishing world, was those that persecuted Christ and his disciples, as mind what their learning directed them too, saying *Are ye also deceived, have any of the Rulers and Pharisees believed on him?* they judging it a dishonor to their wisdom to be ruled by him, supposing by their learning, they could onely interpret the wisdom of Faith in the Law, as minde the 52 verse, *Art thou also of Galilee? search and look, for out of Galilee ariseth no Prophet;* so that you may not question but the Rulers, Scribes and Pharisees did take great pains to finde out the true Christ, yet in that they did interpret or sought him by the wisdom of reason, and not with the wisdom of Faith, they could not know him when they saw him, and therefore *Paul* meets with them in the I of *Cor. 2.8* saying, *Which none of the Princes of this world knew, for had they known it, they would not have crucified the Lord of Glory,* and yet who but Princes, Priests, and Magistrates of this world do assume the interpretation of divine Revelation by their carnal wisdom that shall perish with them, so that as none of the Princes in the Apostles dayes knew Christ when he was among them so I know none, neither teacher or their hearer, that knows Christ clothed with three titles in one single person glorified.

And therefore it is the Preachers of our Nation know not what is Scripture, being unlearned in the language of the spirit of Faith, which knows and interprets that which is Scripture, but these wise men in our days take that for Scripture which is none; so wresting the Scripture to their own destruction, *2 Pet. 3.16;* as the wisdom of Reason takes the wisdom of *Solomon* to be as pure and heavenly as *David* or any of the Prophets whatsoever, when the beloved of the Lord can discern by the eye of faith in those sayings *I Kings 3.* from *9* to *12.* what wisdom it was *Solomon* was endued withal, was it not wisdom to discern between good and bad in the Affairs of his kingdom, *therefore give thy servant an understanding heart,* not to know thee as my father *David* did, but *to judge this great people,* so that according to this request, minde the words of the Eternal God, *I have done according to thy words, lo I have given thee a wise and understanding heart, so that there was none like before thee, neither after thee shall any arise like unto thee;* now let any of you the Seed of Faith judge, if this had been the wisdom of Faith, what a man of admiration had *Solomon* been, so that *Moses* before him, nor *Elijah* or any of the Prophets after him, had not been comparable to him; but alas his wisdom was but natural, and yet the highest pitch of reason that ever was, or shall be from *Cain* to the end of the world, for had his wisdom been divine as *Moses,* or the Prophets, or as his father *David,* then the Queen of *Sheba* or any of the heathen Kings would not have given *Solomon* a visit no more then *David* his father, but *Solomon* being endued with such a large measure of wisdom, as to finde out any difficult cause, and to give righteous judgement concerning it, and to speak a language above all the Princes, and to find out the secrets of Nature above all other men, that was the load-stone that drew the Princes of Reason to his Court, to behold his wisdom and glory, and ever since the greatest despisers in this world of the Lord Jesus and his heavenly wisdom, do embrace the wisdom of *Solomon*, even as eternal life it self, insomuch that the seed of *Solomons* body, *viz.* the wisdom of Reason, hath printed and bound up *Solomons* stories with the writings of *Moses*, the Prophets, and the Psalms, which were written by the divine wisdom of Faith, and at this day do preach it, and believe it as true Scripture, as those before mentioned, when you may finde it written *Luke 24.44. That all things must be fulfilled which were written in the Law of* Moses, *in the Prophets, and in the Psalms concerning me,* not in the least including, but absolutely excluding the writings of *Solomon*, as having no part or interest concerning him, as you may read the 27 verse, *And beginning at* Moses *and all the Prophets, he expounded unto them in all the Scripture the things concerning himself;* so that all, except those that are of the wisdom of *Solomon*, may undoubtedly believe that *Solomons* writings were no Scripture.

For you may remember when Christ was upon earth, he highly vindicates the writings of *Moses*, the Prophets, and *David*, but altogether takes no notice of the writings of *Solomon*, neither doth Christ give any applause to *Solomon* his wisdom or glory, but in *Matthew 12.* saith, *A greater then Solomon is here,* so that if the wisdom of *Solomon* had been divine, how had those sayings of God been true in the I of Kings 12? *I have given thee a wise and understanding heart, so that there was none like thee before, neither shall any be after thee,* so that Christ who is all divine wisdom, being upon the earth after *Solomon,* had been inferior to him, so that this will satisfie all but the seed of Reason, that *Solomons* wisdom was but natural, so his writings no Scripture, therefore not for our learning; and as for the glory *Solomon* possessed, was like his wisdom, not eternal, but perishing, as is all his children after him: And you may read another saying of Christ *Matthew 6.29. Consider the lilies of the field how they grow, they toyl not, neither do they spin, and yet I say unto you that* Solomon *in all his glory was not arrayed like one of these.* Ah may dear friends, you may clearly see that *Solomons* wisdom was not divine but humane, so perishing, yea more fading then the lilly of the field; and then in the last place you may read I *Kings 11.4. That* Solomon *when he was old, his wives turned away his heart after other gods, and his heart was not perfect with the Lord his God, as was the heart of* David *his father,* with such like vanity his wisdom directed him to, and his glory perished in, as is manifest at this day in his children after him, so that from hence forward all ye the faithful of the Lord take notice that *Solomon* nor *Job* their writings are no Scripture, though I judge *Job* a righteous man, who was a Caldean nigh a thousand yeares before *Moses:* But,

    2. For whom was the Scripture written? and that the letter saith, *By holy men of God, who spake as they were moved by the holy Ghost, 2 Peter* 1.21. So that from hence you may be confident, that it was none of the learned or great Rabbies of the seed of Reason for you must understand the Scriptures were not written by the wisdom of flesh, but the wisdom of faith, inspiration, or revelation; So then take notice they were poor trades-man, as shepherds, plow-men, and fisher-men, men of small account, and no reputation, as we are, no more regarded amongst rich and poor, nor taken notice, unless to be persecuted, then the dog; men that traveled up and down poor, weary, and hungry, glad of refreshment by friend or foe, and men subject to like infirmities as we the seed of faith are in these dayes, and so was the Prophets before them, as *James 5.17. Elias was a man subject to like passions as we are:* what such a Prophet as *Elijah* that was as God upon earth and represented the God-head above, yet this man was passionate, not as the seed of Reason, but the seed of faith, a man of like passions as we, *Paul* and the rest of the faithful, so that if you know us, even as we are, so were they, both in naturals and spirirtualls, these were the men that Christ did chuse for his Prophets and writers of Scripture, and if there were any of them is *Paul* that had been brought up at the feet of *Gamaliel,* for all his learning, till the seed of faith was lord over his Reason, he was not capable of being a messenger, or setting pen to write of Christ Jesus the Lord of Glory. So now you have heard they were the seed of faith which sprang in their souls revelations of the knowledge of the eternal God, men in their commission no more regarded then we are in our commission, till such time that they were dead, and all that knew them were also departed, then their writings was honorable, but whatever they writ in their time of life, was nothing so aceptable as it is now after their death: as touching this, I shall not need to trouble you what a catalogue of defamations reproaches, and terrible persecutions the prophets and Apostles underwent, for publishing and writing this Scripture, which now you, both teacher and hearer, their children and seed of their own body, makes a great Trade of, so that, [mind what you read, and observe] they were the knowing of the seed of faith that writ those letters in the first and second Commission.

    3. For whom was this written? *Paul* saith, it *was written for his learning, and all that was of the same faith with him,* therefore he speaks in the plural, *The Scriptures afore-time were written for our learning,* including all the Seed of Faith with him; but by the way take notice that *Paul* doth not intend his own writings were written for his learning, but the tenor of his speech reflected upon the writings of *Moses* and the Prophets that were before him, as you may read *Rom. 4.23. Now it was not written for his sake alone, that it was imputed to him, but for us also to whom it shall be imputed, if we believe on him,*

&c. Now minde, this trial of *Abraham* was not written for him, but for the Seed of Faith that came after him; for this you must understand, that what a man writes in his life time, is not for his learning to write it: but I write my revelations in me for the instruction or learning of others that come after me, for in that I have been learned by the Seed of Faith in my soul, therefore I write my knowledge that Christ Jesus is the onely God, for the learning of them that shall come after me, even so the transactions and revelations of *Moses* and the Prophets were left upon record for the Seed of Faith afterwards, as *Paul* tells you, *I Cor. 9,10. For our sakes no doubt this is written,* not for the sakes that writ it, but for the sake of *Paul* and the Seed of Faith with him, the Law and the Prophets were written; for you must understand as there are now, so there was in their days, carping cavelling spirits that would have *Paul* prove from *Moses* and the Prophets how Christ should be the Son of God, and why the Circumcision was not in force, as formerly, as also their offerings and sacrifice; *And brethren, I would not that ye should be ignorant that all our fathers were under the cloud, and all passed through the Sea, and all eat and drank of the spiritual Rock Christ Jesus, I Cor. 10.1,2,3*. Now minde that all the transactions and dealings of God with the house of *Israel, Paul* applies it to the Believers in his days, as in verse 11. *Now all these things happened unto them for ensamples, and they are written for our admonition:* now take notice how many several places *Paul* hath quoted, for the confirmation of the Faithful in his days, that the dealings of God with *Moses* and the Prophets, were onely written for the learning of the Apostles and those that believed in their doctrine, and not for any of the seed of reason whatsoever, though never so great or learned Rabbies of the world; the Scriptures aforetime were not written for *Pilate* and *Herod*, the Scribes and Pharisees, or Rulers of *Israel,* but for our learning, saith *Paul;* not for the learning of them that persecute us, but for the learning of us that are persecuted for the same God, and the same faith as they were, for we the righteous and beloved of the Lord who are the true Commissionate Ministers and Messengers of God as they were, for our learning, and for none other, but for our sakes were the Scriptures written; and therefore it is written, *what hast thou to do to take my words in thy mouth, and hatest to be reformed,* thou seed of reason, that art an enemy to the Eternal God and all his Commands, yea, ignorant of thy eternal happiness? how canst thou say the Scripture was written for thy learning, unless to set forth thy eternal destruction? notwithstanding thou makest use of it for thy advantage and glory, and thereby thinkest to have eternal life, yet from the Lord Jesus I say, they do not in the least concern thee, neither hast thou any part or portion therein; for as they were writ by the spirit of all-knowing Faith, so they onely belong to the Seed of Faith, how canst thou then imagine that thou by thy natural learning canst understand the true meaning of the eternal Spirit? for nature understands it naturally, so cannot interpret the language of faith, because it is spiritually writ by the spirit of faith.

So that take notice, as the Scripture belongs to none but the Seed of Faith as aforesaid, so likewise none but the knowing of that Seed can, or are able to interpret the Scripture; and as you have heard that the writings of *Moses* and the Prophets were onely writ for a few, even for the Apostles, as Paul and the rest so the writings of *Paul* with the Apostles, are onely written so the learning of the third Commission, nay I say, and from the spirit of the Lord Jesus I affirm, that the writings of *Moses,* the Prophets and Apostles are onely written for our learning, and for none other, whatever the seed of reason pretend to the contrary, and though they preach it and read it, yet I say they have nothing to do with it, neither was it written for their learning, unless therein they may finde it recorded, how that their fathers murthered and put to death the Prophets and Apostles, yea that Jesus the Lord of Glory, I say if you impute any part or portion therein, you must take all woes, plagues, and judgements therein threatned, as you may finde a Catalogue of them in *Matth. 23* saying, *Wo unto you hypocrites, which indeed appear beautiful outward, but are within full of all uncleanness, ye also appear outwardly righteous, but within are full of hypocrisie and iniquity. Wo unto you ye build the tombs of the Prophets, and garnish the sepulchres of the righteous, and say, if we had been in the days of our fathers, we would not have been partakers with them in the blood of the Prophets wherefore ye be witness unto your selves that ye are the children of them that killed the Prophets:* I say from the Lord Jesus, if anything were written for your learning, it must be these and such like hypocrisie aforesaid, so that you the seed of reason shall not need to learn this or any other wickeness, because your reason being naturally your School-master, teacheth you all manner of hypocrisie, tyranny, and such like filthiness against the Seed of Faith, so that for the time to come when you cast your eye into the Scripture [mind what you read] it is not for you to learn the steps of your fathers, but to read the sentence of the eternal woes to your selves in your fathers, for you are naturally prone with your fathers, to applaud and honor the writings of the Prophets, and the righteous that you did not know, and to imprison and condemn the writings of them that you do know; for while the Prophets and Apostles were alive, their writings were despised for their persons sake, Reason then judging them men of no learning, and small reputation, could not understand how they should write from inspiration, any more then the Priests and Rulers of *Israel,* who were onely endued with the light of reason, and therefore it was the wisdom of reason in those days did look upon them, and so esteem them as false prophets and teachers, and so by their wisdom of flesh did put to death Christ Jesus and his commissionate Ministers for Blasphemers, and now the last Commission or Witness of Christ the Eternal Spirit, of the same seed is despised and slighted in that they know our persons, they condemn our writings for blasphemy, though truly and really they are the blasphemers themselves; so that I say as I said before, there is none of these three Commissions written for the learning of the seed of reason, but onely for the seed of faith that were then living, and so believed their doctrine in their time and places: But,

4. Seeing the writings of *Moses* and the Prophets were onely written for the learning of the Apostles, and the writings of *Moses,* the Prophets, and Apostles were written for our learning in this last high Commission or Witness of the Eternal Spirit, therefore now I shall give you to understand what it is in the aforesaid writings we are to learn, and what not, that so for the time to come ye may not wrest the Scriptures to your own destruction, by attributing that unto them that cannot be learned by them, or by taking that from them that may be learned by them: For want of knowledge in this secret, some do idolize it, and others do slight it, and very few there are that truly understand wherefore the Scripture was written; so that you the Seed of Faith may rightly use it, and not abuse it, observe that what now I write is for the learning of all the Seed of Faith, so long as this Commission or Witness shall hold, which must not end till time be no more in this Reasons kingdom: so that,

First from the Eternal Spirit of the Lord Jesus I affirm, That the Scriptures were written for our learning, to know God, or Christ God clothed with three Titles in one single person glorified to all eternity.

Secondly, against men and angels I affirm, That all Opinions or Dispensations, though never so heaven-like written, that are not included in one of those Commissions, are counterfeits, so not learned by the Spirit of Faith, but the light of reason onely, so none of the three Witnesses.

As unto the first of these Affirmations aforesaid, I shall clear up from the first Epistle of *John* 5.7,8 verses, where you shall finde it thus written, *For there are three that bear record in heaven, the Father, the Word, and the Holy Ghost, and these three are one; and there are three that bear witness in earth, the Spirit, the Water, and the Blood, and these three agree in one;* from hence ye the blessed of the Lord may without doubting believe, that the Lord Jesus had resolved in himself before he had formed any creature to live in his presence, to make known himself to this unbelieving world by three several Commissioners, holding forth his glorious Person in different Titles, which three were to be sent forth by voice of words from the mouth of the Lord Jesus, to bear witness unto his glorious Name, as the onely true Commissioners till time be no more; therefore *Moses* the first Commissioner, so the first Writer of Scripture, doth bear record unto Christ Jesus under the Title of God the Father, and so what was writ by *Moses* and the Prophets in the virtue of that Commission, was written by inspiration or revelation, so is to be believed for Scripture, the Holy Writ of God the Father.

2. The Apostles were the second Commissioners, so the second Writers of Scripture, and do bear record unto Christ Jesus under the Name or Title of God the Son, so what was written by the Apostles, or any other in virtue of their Commission, was writ by inspiration or revelation, so is to be believed for Scripture, the Holy Writ of God the Son.

3. *John Reeve* and *Ledowick Muggleton* are the third and last Commissioners, so the third writers of scriptures, & do bear record unto Christ Jesus under the Name or Title of God the Spirit, so what is written by this last Commission, or any other in the virtue of the same Commission is writ by inspiration or revelation, so by the Seed of Faith will be believed for Scripture, the holy writ of God, the holy Ghost or Eternal Spirit.

Therefore ye the Seed of Gods owne body, ye are without doubting to believe, That the Lord Jesus is all the Gods that ever was, is, or shall be, in one single person glorified, blessed for ever to all eternity; as also that Christ the Father, and Christ the Son, is both comprehended in this last Witness, Christ the Eternal Spirit, and thus I declare as it is written, *they all three agree in one,* bearing all as one entire record and testimony to Christ Jesus the onely alone everlasting Father, Creator of Heaven and earth, and therefore as the two former had power to curse either angel or man that should preach any other doctrine, but what was held forth by them in their Commissions, so whatsoever after the report hereof is sounded in their eares, do preach any other doctrine contrary to this high, glorious, spiritual Commission, they are held accursed, yea blasphemers against the Holy Ghost the Eternal Spirit; and so to the end of the world let this be in memorial, that we write not of other mens labours, but as our faith within us reveals unto us, that the true meaning of the former Scripture are infallibly interpreted by this last Witness, what the Lord Jesus was, is, and ever shall be world without end.

2. If any of the seed of the serpent by their light of reason, do from this second Affirmation assume authority for their preaching, by vertue of the two former Commissions, *viz. Moses* and the Apostles, let them know this from the Lord Jesus, that at best they are but thieves and robbers, yea by those Commissions declared counterfeit Prophets and Ministers, for this you must know that you are not included in either of those Commissions.

First, in that you were not living in the days of *Moses* and the Prophets, so have no authority by voice of words from God as they had, therefore not endued with the same spirit of inspiration or revelation as they were, neither do you know which of you are Jews, and which of you are Gentiles, so do not worship Christ as God the Father, in manner and form of worship as they were commanded, and did observe, therefore take notice you have neither part nor portion in the first Commission, so are not authorized to preach by vertue thereof, neither do you bear record to the first Witness, that Christ is God the Father.

2. In that you were not living in the days of the Apostles, so have no authority by voyce of words from the Lord Jesus as they had, therefore not endued what the spirit of inspiration or revelation as they were, for there is not any of you the seven churches, *viz.* Papist, Episcopal, Presbyter, Independent, Anabaptist, Ranter, Quaker, that can with peace of conscience say, that the refinest head-piece among you was called into the Ministry by voyce of words, or by inposition of hands received the holy Ghost, as *Timothy* and *Titus* to be Bishops, or Elders, or Presbyter, so not by the same power sent out in point of Ordination to preach the same Gospel as they did, but that ignorance and ambition hath blinded your eyes, I might admire you should assume the name of an Apostle or Bishop without the power, what's a Commissioner without a power? it's like a Lamp without Oyl, of no use but to look upon, as darkness and no light, and yet what a noise you make with anothers Commission, when you might know if ye were not stone-blind, that your fathers put all the true Commissioners to death that had power to ordain others, and yet you will have succession without any Ordination of Apostle or Bishop, when that you cannot be ignorant but that your Ordination was from the Roman Emperors, so the messengers of men and not of Christ: O therefore, if not for fear, yet for shame leave off your rebellion and treachery, and do not damn your own souls for riches and honor, in deceiving of others, for by vertue of this Commission, yea the revelation of the Eternal Spirit, I declare you blasphemous counterfeit Ministers, in that you assume authority by the Commission of *Moses* and the Apostles having no Commission from the Lord Jesus your selves, you make merchandize, and have ready sayl and quick return, for that your fathers then living persecuted and put to death Christ Jesus the Son of God.

3. Though you are now living in the days of the third Commission or last Witness revealed by voyce of words, that Christ Jesus is in the form of a man, all power, life, light, and swifter then thought, so glorious that the sun at his presence will be put forth as the snuff of a candle, yet let me tell you, and yet not I but the revelation of faith in me, that none are included in this last Commission, or Witness of the Eternal Spirit, but such whose hearts are enlightened with the knowledge of divine Faith, to believe the doctrinal writings herein revealed, and from thence are acted forth obedient in their life and conversation.

From my seed-spring within me I say this unto you, that there is not any in the world now living, that in the vertue of this Commission is called forth by the spirit of inspiration or revelation, but onely my self to bear record and testimony that *John Reeve* and *Ledowick Muggleton* are the last Commissioners that ever shall appear in this unbelieving world, I say from the Lord Jesus, I having the same spirit of revelation that gave this Commission by voice of words, that I am endued with divine knowledge to write that for the next generation, the body of which shall not be buried, till this world be buried with thick darkness to all eternity; and therefore ye the seed of the serpent, thou proud reason, and god of this world, despise, scoff, persecute, and put to death what thou canst Christ Jesus, clothed with three Titles, confirmed with three Witnesses; so you that have ears to hear give attention to what I shall now write, which is this, That whosoever despiseth this last Commission, despiseth the two former, yea who believeth not this, believeth not the writings of *Moses* and the Apostles, and so believeth not Christ Jesus to be God the Father in the first Commission, nor believeth Christ Jesus to be God the Son in the second Commission, so cannot believe Christ Jesus to be God the Holy Ghost in this last Commission, one person clothed with three Titles glorified to all eternity, so they believe in no God at all, but an infinite power in thy perishing nature onely, and so at the end of this Commission shall perish with thee to all eternity; for know this, that what is a counterfeit, is a lye, but all that pretends a Commission against this, not being commissionated by one of these three, are counterfeits, so lyers; for as there is but three that bear record in heaven and earth, so three there must be, and no more nor no less, therefore whosoever doth preach forth more then these three, are ignorant of all, and whoso holdeth forth but two, robs Christ of his glory.

But now in the next place, that you may understand a Commission from a Revelation, I shall give you to know what is done or spoken by a Commission, and what not.

And first for the first, all the wonders and miracles that were wrought by *Moses,* were prosecuted by vertue of his Commission that was given him by voice of words from the Lord Jesus, in the name and authority as the Lord God of your fathers, *viz. The God of* Abraham, Isaac *and* Jacob *hath sent me unto you:* this was his name, and this was his message. By vertue of this Commission *Moses* was in stead of a God to the people of *Israel,* as *Exodus 20.19.* they said unto *Moses, Speak thou with us and we will hear, but let not God speak with us lest we die;* so that by this Commission was executed all the plagues upon *Pharoah,* by his Commission were the Red-sea divided, yea by his Commission was the Law given to the people of *Israel,* with all the Statues and Ordinances therein to observe, it was by Commission that *Elijah* said, *there shall be no dew nor rain for these years, but according to my words,* it was by Commission that *Elijah* destroyed all the Prophets of *Baal,* and the Captains and their fifties, so that by vertue of his Commission *Elijah* in a God-like manner effected all his wonders.

2. By Commission was all the miracles done by the Apostles, received by voice of words from the Lord Jesus, in the name and power as Christ Jesus the Son of God, and so all the miracles that

was done, they did it by vertue of that power, *Acts 2.2.* under the title and name of Christ Jesus the Son of God, as it is written *Acts 4.10. Be it known unto you all, that by the name of Jesus Christ of Nazareth whom ye crucified, and whom God raised from the dead, even by him doth this man stand here before you whole, neither is their salvation in any other, for there is no other name under heaven given among men whereby we must be saved.*

3. In this last Commission that was given by voice of words unto *John Reeve,* was these, as Christ Jesus spake unto him *verbatim,* word for word, three several mornings, saying, John Reeve, *I have given thee understanding of my minde in the Scriptures above all men in the world, look into thy own body, there thou shalt see the kingdom of heaven, and the kingdom of hell, I have chosen thee my last Messenger for a great work unto this bloody unbelieving world, and I have given thee* Lodowick Muggleton *to be thy mouth, I have put the two-edged sword of my spirit into thy mouth, that whosoever I pronounce blessed through thy mouth, is blessed to eternity, and whosoever I pronounce cursed through thy mouth, is cursed to eternity; if thou dost not obey my voice, and go where ever I send thee to deliver my message, thy body shall be thy hell, and thy spirit shall be the devil, that shall torment thee to all eternity: Go thou unto* Lodowick Muggleton, *and with him go to* Thomas Turner, *and he shall bring you to one* John Tany, *and do thou deliver my message when thou comest there; and if* Lodowick Muggleton *denieth to go with thee, then do thou from me pronounce him cursed to all eternity. Go thou unto* Lodowick Muggleton, *and take such a woman with thee, and then go thou unto one* John Robins *a prisoner in* New Bridewel, *and do thou deliver my message to him when thou comest there.*

Now you that have divine understanding may discern the variety, and seeming contrariety in these three Commissions, as also in their revelations, for you read the Commission of *Moses* and the Prophets was to deliver messages to Kings and Princes, yea to the Rulers and Elders of *Israel,* which message was to declare woes, plagues, and judgements against them externally as touching their bodies, their goods, and their cattel, &c. and their revelation led them to worship Christ in Circumcision, Offerings, and Sacrifices in Temples made with hands, as *Jerusalem* and such like places, and to call upon Christ by name of the Lord God of *Israel,* or God Almighty, and everlasting Father.

2. You read the Commission of the Apostles was to cast out devils, cure the sick, and raise the dead &c. and their revelation led them forth to preach faith and repentance, by dipping them in water, waving all the Ceremonies and Circumstances of the Law aforesaid, and from thence to baptize them with the Holy Ghost and with fire, not tyed to any particular place of worship, but travelling from town to countrey, preaching Jesus Christ that was crucified by the hands of the Jews, was risen, and that he was the onely Son of God, affirming

by their revelation, that whosoever confessed with their mouth, and believed with their heart that Christ Jesus was the Son of God, should be saved.

Now if you can by the eye of faith behold the transactions of Christ Jesus in both these Commissions, as also their revelations, how various and different they are the one from the other, then you would not stumble at the vast difference of our Commission, that it is not acted forth in manner and form as either of the two former, but rather admire what an infinite fountain of endless revelations there is in Christ Jesus glorified: as,

Thirdly, to consider the nature of this last Commission, the witness of the Holy Ghost or eternal Spirit, declared by voice of words, from the glorious throne of Christ Jesus, *that I have chosen thee for my last Messenger for a great work, unto this bloody unbelieving world, by putting the two-edged sword of my spirit into thy mouth, that whoever I pronounce blessed or cursed through thy mouth, is blessed and cursed to eternity.* Now you may take notice that this Commission is all spiritual, in that the sentence thereof is to curse the despisers of this Truth both soul and body to eternity, not reflecting in the least upon their estates as the former curses did, for all this they may thrive in the outward man, as in riches, honour, and knowledge in the light of reason, this being their onely heaven: but this I know, they decline and wither in the inward man as unto assurance of salvation and knowledge that Christ Jesus is the onely god, and everlasting Father.

So that the nature of our revelation leads us forth to no maner or form of worship, but to do righteous things betwixt man and man, and according to our ability love mercy, and yield our souls to be damned, that is, doing the two former, not troubling or toyling our selves with any duty, we having no command for it, but let the Lord do with us what he pleaseth, and once brought to this pass, my soul for thine, thou shalt never perish. Now this having no form of worship, so the Priest can have no benefit by it, nor Magistrates honour in it, will, what in them lieth, slight it and despise it, to the ruine of soul and boyd; but however the revelation of this Commission being the witness of the Eternal Spirit, so all spiritual, the nature hereof must needs be full of heavenly revelation and divine inspiration beyond all from the beginning to this day, and therefore the Seed of Faith against men and angels will affirm and declare it, till the coming of Christ who is all Faith, that this is the third and last Commission, the revelation whereof is to be believed as the other.

And therefore ye little flock who believe that Christ Jesus was God the Father in the first, that Christ Jesus was God the Son in the second, and now Christ Jesus God the Holy Ghost in this Commission, having from the Spirit of this Lord Jesus revealed unto you what Scripture is, and what not, who was the Writers thereof, and for whom it is written, onely for them in their time, to believe and walk obedient thereunto, and for you the same seed of faith, to observe the various revelations that floweth from Christ Jesus the Lord of Glory. Now I shall proceed to interpret the dark hard sentence in Scripture, for your better confirmation.

PHIL. 2.6

Who being in the form of God, thought it no robbery to be equal with God.

In *Eastcheap London* there lives a Quaker, by name of *Richard Whitpane,* who formerly had been an aquaintance of mine, seeing me pass by, called me to him, and asked me if I had not lately printed a Book, so called, *Look about you, for the Devil that you fear is in you?* yea, said I, there is such a Book of mine abroad, which thou mayest have at *William Learners,* and other places, as also at my house, then said he, I have it, and it's like we shall object against something that is in it, to which I answered, that I question not, and it's as like I shall answer thee; so the time he appointed me to answer what he would object, was the second of *July 1659.* so called by him the second day, the first hour of that day, which in this world is called Monday one of the Clock, at which time I came exactly, onely with our friend *Lodowick,* who with this *Whitepane* was seven or eight more, whose names I know not; so they sitting silent, saying nothing, Friends said I, you know wherefore I am come, therefore either do you set forth your God, or shall I reveal unto you what the true God in his form and nature is; whereupon one of them declared that his God was an infinite Spirit, all life, light, power, that filled heaven and earth with his glory, with words to that effect: To which I replied, this was no new thing, for almost the whole world believed that as well as they, neither was this any God at all, for a spirit is nothing without a body, therefore if thou canst, tell me what form that Spirit hath which thou callest thy God: whereupon they were outragious, contrary to my expectation, thinking they had been moderate and civil in expressions, but they are not able to answer us, upbraided us with filthy, diabolical tearms against the Lord Jesus in his form and nature, so that in obedience to the Commission given by voice of words from the Lord Jesus, resident in the highest of heavens, five of them came under the sentence of eternal condemnation, where they and all their cursed brood that so lives and dies, with their pretended light within them, which at that day of Judgement shall finde great darkness, yea darkness that may be felt, and therefore let that saying of Christ, *Matthew 6.23* be as a Warning-piece to all ignorant souls to *take heed lest the light that is in you be darkness, O then how great is that darkness?* so to conclude with this, I shall evade their rayling, persecuting Rabsheka language, and as in order I shall meet with the chief heads there revealed in the interpretation of this Scripture, I shall give you notice of them, and the Quakers answer to them. But now to the words, *Who being in the form of God, thought it no robbery to be equal with God.*

First, against men and angels I affirm, That both angel and men hath forms suitable to their natures, and that it was their natures that gave them their forms, otherwise all other creatures had been in the form of man; for as Reason hath the form of man, so hath Faith the same form, for from the ever-living word of Faith spoken by Christ Jesus, an innumerable company of angels was created of that spiritual dust above the stars, in forms of men, so by the same of Faith *Adam* was created of this natural dust here below, in the form of a man, so that the angels bodies are spiritual, and their spirits natural, *viz.* pure reason; now *Adams* body is natural, and his soul spiritual, *viz.* divine faith, now in that both these Seeds or Natures were to live in one form, that is, the form of man, therefore in the downfal of that angelical angels form by deceiving of *Eve,* both natures possessed *Adams* form, and thereby it came man hath both faith and reason in his own form, and so hath two thoughts, two motions, two voices, yea subject to reasons temptations,

2. I affirm, that the nature of God is all spiritual, heavenly, divine faith, and no part of reason at all, for this I say, that neither God nor man hath pure reason [but the angels onely] and therefore ye read, when God took his journey in the flesh, *he took not upon him the nature of the angels, but the seed of* Abraham, yea that seed of Faith that was first breathed into *Adam,* so that *Adams* was partakers of Gods divine nature, and therefore that seed or nature that is the same with Gods, he could with safety take upon him.

3. I affirm, that after the same manner, fashion, image, likeness, or form that God had himself, in the very same form by his word speaking came forth both angel and man, and therefore it is written, *Let us make man in our image, after our likeness, so God created man in his own image, in the image of God created he him both male and female,* so that man is in the form of God, and God hath the same form that man hath, so not one, but two, distinct one from another; for the form of man is natural, and upon this earth, but the form of God is spiritual, yea clearer then chrystal, brighter then the Sun, and swifter then thought; now in that no light but faith can apprehend this, so believe this, and the Quakers light within them being but reason, cannot understand God in his form and nature, and therefore it is they having not faith, their light cannot believe it, shall never come to the knowledge of him, as he is God in the form of a man; for this know, without knowledge of the Spirit of Faith there can be no confidence, for if thou be not fully perswaded that God is the same that thou knowest him to be, a God that by his own power laid down

his God-head life, and by his own power, or word of Faith, raise it up again, without this thou canst not really believe that he is able to raise thy soul at the last day; neither canst thou with *Paul* say, *I know whom I have believed, and I am perswaded he is able to keep that which I have committed unto him against the last day;* but when thou believest him onely an infinite eternal Spirit, then thy faith is wavering like unto thy God; for a spirit without a body cannot be known, and so no believe on that which is not: for what man that hath the least assurance of salvation, would commit his soul to that which is nothing, nor knows not where to finde his God? Surely none but a mad man would commit into custody all his estate and life into the protection of one that is a spirit without a body, onely the name of a man, yet no man, for when time of restauration is come, there is none to restore it, in that a spirit hath no substance, so no tongue to answer, nor hand to deliver.

O ye blinde, miserable Quakers, ye were not able to believe this, nor in any measure to withstand this, truth of faith being stronger then your lying reason, you were all mad, yea cut to the heart, that your deluding cheat was found out, and your strong man of reason was bound hand and foot, that you had nothing to say, but to rayl on us, and crying out, prove this, and prove that, when you have no understanding in the proof of it, though I told you the Scripture was not written for you the seed of reason, but we the Seed of Faith, in that it was written by the spirit of faith, so onely understood by the Seed of Faith, yet I gave you this Scripture that now I am speaking on, *Who being in the form of God, &c.* in that Christ was in the form of God, and Christ you could not deny but that he was in the form of a man, then God was in the same form that Christ was, so a man. Now that you might know that God was, and is a man, you might read *Mark 10.18. And Jesus said unto him, Why callest thou me good? there is no man good but one, that is God,* with many more, but all to no purpose, unless you could read a Scripture that should say, that I the Creator of heaven and earth am a man in maner and form as you are, may be then you would be silent, though not believe, for I say unto you, as Christ said to your brethren the Jews, *Why do you not understand my speech, even because ye cannot hear my word?* John 8.43.

Ah poor creatures, you think you of all men do hear, yet faith can finde that you are deaf; you think you see, and yet by the light of faith we know that you are stone-blind as unto life eternal, as by your own words you shall be condemned; for you say, when God breathed into *Adam* he was a spirit, and so in the breath went all his Godhead spirit into angels, men, beasts, herbs, trees, roots, and what not? and so you make God no person of his own, that made all persons, but lives in the forms of these creatures aforesaid, and so cannot believe that God can make his abode in so narrow a compass as the person of Christ, which you shall have revealed that it is so, in its place and order, and therefore ye imagine him to be of so vaste a quantity that encloseth or covereth all things and places through his spiritual bulk or bigness, this is the blinde reasons imaginary's god, that is no God, and therefore ye suppose God being a Spirit, as from that fourth of *John*, which in its place I shall answer, I say from the place you think God is a Spirit without form, and so lives in the form of man that he made, and so they suppose when man dies, hanged, beheaded, or any other death, that then God flies out of them, and so leaves them, supposing life cannot die, when to your sorrow you shall know there is nothing but life that can die, and whither that God or Spirit goes, they cannot tell, and thus they believe God and Christ is in you, and so makes God the worst of all creatures that he made; as if you do but observe if this were, as you imagine and have affirmed, then God lives in a sick, weary, hungry creature, that God lives in a sinful, wicked soul, nay, if it were as you say, then I tell you it is God that is born every day, that dies every day, it is God that is sick, and in pain every day, it is God that weeps and laughs every day, it is God that prayeth and curseth every day, it is God that is arrested and imprisoned every day, it is God that condemns and is condemned, it is God that swears, whores, and is drunk every day, it is God that cheats, defrauds, and murthers every day, and thus the Quakers, Ranters, and almost the whole world may behold what a piteous sinful god you have, that lives onely in perishing nature.

 Therefore ye faithful of the Lord are but few, and that very few that are true believers indeed, yet you that are really so, can by faith evidence in your own souls God in his form and nature without you; for if you Quakers and all others could but understand, that reason in the purest nature cannot comprehend God, then you would see it is out of your reach, and so cannot imagine God to be that he is, for nothing but faith can pierce through death into the highest heavens; *and therefore faith is the evidence of things not seen* [not seen by your light of reason, but the light of faith] for as faith hath no imagination, but motions of revelations that are real, so cannot believe on that God which is nothing, *in that faith is the substance of things hoped for,* and from hence it is that those blinde Quakers having not faith their life and light, but Reason their god and guide, are become blinde in the knowledge of the true God, and therfore Quakers Reason looks for all within, God and Christ within, heaven and hell within, damnation and salvation within, yea the onely resurrection within, and all because they suppose God to be a spirit of reason without faith, and no body, and therefore the Quakers cry, *Hearken to the light within thee,* and that they suppose from *2 Cor 13.5.* that all that Christ that is they affirmed was within them, they being without faith cannot understand the revelation of faith from these words, *Know ye not your own selves that Jesus Christ is in you, except ye be reprobates?* so that because I said Christ was not within me, therefore they judged me a reprobate: therefore ye blessed of the Lord observe how by faith I pursued them, till I bound the strong man of Reason within them, that so ye the Seed of Faith may behold the damnable delsiuons revealed by them.

First it is written, Christ is within you, you that believe in our doctrine, ye Believers of *Corinth*, not the unbelieving Quakers of *England*, these words were never spoken to you, but to them then living, those few of *Corinth* that believed Christ Jesus was the Son of God, *if Christ be not in you, ye are reprobates,* that is, if the same seed of faith be not in you to believe God without you, but however I shall treat with you as though they had been spoken to you, and therefore what doth your blinde reason, or as you call it, your light within you, intend from these words *Christ within you?* do you suppose Christ in his person is in you? or do you intend Christ without a form is in you? now if ye believed that Christ with his spiritual body, that could enter the house the doors and windows being shut, hath in the same manner entered you, and thus you judge Christ is in you, then take notice he is but in one of you, unless you can make it appear that Christ hath as many bodies as there is Quakers, and so this kinde of Christ is in you, then you would say something to prove yourselves what you are, the seed of that dragon serpent devil *Cain:* but now if ye intend Christ is in you as he is a Spirit, and so all that Spirit that you call Christ is in you, then I demand of you what is become of Christs body in which his Spirit dwelt all the time Christ was upon earth? now if you say his body neither ascended into heaven, not descended into the earth, then if ye could ye would tell me. *This same Jesus which is taken up from you into heaven, shall so in like manner come as ye have seen him go into heaven,* that very person of Christ that was upon this earth thirty three years, and laid down his life, which body naturally passed through the grave in a moment, and so raised it self spiritual, and then, and at that time ascended to its glory from whence he came, so that now his body is out of your reasons reach, not in you, but without you, and above you, in the highest heavens glorified; therefore if you could understand Christ is in you, then you would know what Christ was both in his form and nature, you would know that his form is in glory, yea the same form that was put to death by your seed of reason in your fathers, and now spiritually trampled under feet by you Quaking Ranters, and such like cursed brood; but in that you know him not in a form, nor the manner of it, it is impssible you should know his nature, and so as unpossible to have Christ in you, much less to have all Christ in you; therefore I shall proceed in the revelation of my generated faith within me, what gross darkness that is which you Quakers calls a light of your God within you, as you shall finde in these ensuing Affirmations infallibly opened unto you.

First, against men and angels I affirm, That the God which you, or any other call an Infinite Eternal Spirit, was in, yea clothed in that flesh or person of Christ Jesus.

2. I affirm, That God or Christ which you will, is not in this world, neither in Prophets nor righteous, but in the highest heavens in his own single person glorified.

3. I affirm, That the seed or nature of God is in all true Believers, by which they know what God is both in his form and nature, as also that the nature of Christ is in all the seeming righteous and professed wicked men more or less, to their eternal condemnation.

4. I affirm, That all the sufferings of the Quakers in *New-England,* or any other Nation, that they suffer justly as evil doers, and yet neither they nor their persecutors shall escape damnation.

First for the first, I affirm, That there never was, is, or shall be but one God, though three Titles, as Father, Son, and Spirit, yet all comprehended in one single person the Lord Jesus, though you will not, because you cannot believe my revelation, yet you shall know that this Seed of Faith, being the onely interpreter of the Scripture, all along I shall produce Scripture to maintain that God, who was called a Father in the first Commission of *Moses* and the Prophets, that very same God became a Son in the second Commission of the Apostles, as you have it thus written, *Genesis 3.15. And I will put enmity between thee and the woman, and between thy seed and her seed, it shall bruise thy head, and thou shalt bruise his heel.* In this last Commission of the Holy Ghost or Eternal Spirit, it is onely revealed that the spiritual sense of these words is this: The Seed of the woman is Faith, and the seed of the serpentine angel is Reason, they being contrary as life and death, light and darkness, must needs be at enmity, and therefore it was Faith should bruise Reasons head, and Reason should bruise the heel of Faith, in that the seed of the serpent, which is Reason, should make war against the seed of the woman, which is Faith; for if you could understand the contrariety of these two seeds, then you would know how *Cain* the father of the wicked, put to death *Abel* the Seed of Faith; it was this serpents seed Reason that put to death the Prophets of the Lord, it was this seed that put to death Jesus and his Apostles, and so it is the same serpents seed, Reason, that doth persecute and put to death, not onely its own seed, but also the Seed of Faith in our days.

But now, observe though Reason hath power to put to death the Seed of Faith, yet this take along with you, it is but a mortal, natural death, a death that shall end, and be crowned with eternal life of glory; but on the contrary, the death that Faith gives Reason, it is an immortal eternal wound, a death that shall never end, yea a death that shall be crowned with an eternal tormenting misery, so that Faith shall die in the heel, and Reason shall die in the head, that is the crown of life, the top of all that, and there shall Reason receive its deadly wound. Now that you may in short know the intent of Faith in these words, is this, Even as the body of the angel did descend into the womb of *Eve,* so I the God of heaven and earth in the same manner will descend into the womb of the Virgin, that being put to death by Reason, I by my own power of Faith will raise my self to life again, and so keep Reason under death eternal, otherwise there would have been no end of this Reasons kingdom, neither had Christ been Lord over the dead, but onely over the living; so this was his promise, that God would become a Son. As for the plain discovery of these seeds, I refer thee to that Book, called, *Look about you, for the devil that you fear is in you,* and to my other Book, entituled, *A Wonder of Wonders:* Now the Father is a Son, and yet all the God or Father that ever was, is, or shall be, was Christ Jesus, as read *Isaiah 9.6. For unto us a Childe is born, unto us a Son is given, and the Government shall be upon his shoulders, and his name shall be called Wonderful, Counsellor, the Mighty God, the Everlasting Father, the Prince of Peace:* Here was a prophesie that God would be born of a woman, and change his Name to Christ Jesus the Son of God, and yet he was the mighty God and Father of heaven and earth; and to this end the same Prophet in *verse 42 saith, I, even I am the Lord, and besides me there is no Saviour,* so that ye Baptists, with other Churches, if ye were not stone-blinde, you might discern that there is but one God, and one person, even the man Jesus, but surely you conceive that in process of time it would be with God as it is with man, that God should die, and so in his room make his Son heir of his glorious Kingdom, but how the Father got his Son you cannot tell, and so ye imagine a Scripture out of the *Bishops Lettany,* three persons, and one God, when Faith that is of the nature of God, can finde but one God in one person; therefore take notice and remember that the true alone Messenger of Christ Jesus told thee so, that in this belief of thine, so living and so dying, shalt never see the face of the true God at all, but thy blind Reason onely: Again it is written *God was in Christ reconciling the world, &c. I am in the Father, and the Father in me,* with many such places, so that if this were as thou sayst, what a monster would ye make of Christ, if God were a person without Christ, for you read God is not distinct from Christ, but in Christ, [and therefore now ye Ranters and Quakers what will you do with your God that is a Spirit without a body] when you have heard that a Spirit cannot live without a body? so that God being a Spirit must either live in your body, or a body of his own, if you believe as to me you have affirmed, and in your *New-England* Books have recorded, that God is in you, I say now, as we said then, that cursed are you and your god to all eternity; for if ye were not reprobates, the seed of Reason your father *Cain,* you would understand and believe *that the fulness of the Godhead dwelleth in Christ bodily,* that Spirit of infiniteness or fulness was in the person or body of the Lord Jesus, God was in Christ, not in you blinde perishing Quakers that will not allow God a form of his own, that made all forms, unless he will live in your form, not in the least understanding that saying of *John 4. God is a spirit, and they that worship him must worship him in spirit and in truth:* now the drift of Christs speech to the woman of *Samaria,* was to inform her, that invisible Spirit in the body of his flesh and bone, was that Godhead power or glory abiding onely in his person, and therefore the worship required by him from his Saints, was an inward fulness by which their souls were made willing to hearken to the voice or motions of of his most holy Spirit, speaking in them variety of heavenly assurance, and satisfaction concerning the glory of eternity, yea that God that Christ said was a Spirit, the meaning of his revelation was, that his invisible soul was that God or Spirit abiding onely in his person, by vertue of which, to fulfil his own will, could with that body descend from his kingdom of glory through the womb of the Virgin, yea pierce thorow the grave in a moment, and ascend with that same body to his place of glory again, and yet all this time his Godhead Spirit was clothed with flesh, and that in no other shape or likeness but the form of a man; and therefore (ye Caldeans, Egyptians, Magicians, and Soothsaying Quakers) ye sons of reason, that serpents seed, that would enforce a confidence in the simple-hearted ones, that there is Spirits without bodies, or that a Spirit can assume a body as it pleaseth, I tell you from that Spiritual Body of all living Faith, that all they boasting is but imaginarily, and not really; for as no body can move without its soul or spirit, so there is no visible light or sight in the persons of God, men, or angels, but what proceeds from their invisible spirits, they are so united and interwoven as one entire living substance, that they cannot be separated; and therefore none but ye the blessed Seed of Gods own body, by the eye of faith do see that the Godhead Spirit ever was, is, and shall be in the form of man, and that not in the form of Quaking Ranters, but the distinct, single, alone form of the Lord Jesus, blessed for ever, yea for ever, for ever without end.

2. In this second Affirmation I shall reveal, as also from Scripture prove, that God in the person of Christ is not in this world, nor any other creature, neither righteous nor wicked, and therefore ye Quakers that despised us when we made this secret known to you: By the power of our Commission, and in the vertue of my revelation, I charge thee read this, though thou wilt never believe this, in that thou art already condemned for blasphemy against it, onely you poor deluded Quakers, that upon the report of this may be brought in obedience to this, minde what you read, yea I say again observe, that the Lord Jesus who is the onely personal God, from revelation I say is not in this world, not in my self, or any other creature, but in his glorious kingdom above the stars, which when he was upon Trial before the god of this world, he said, *My kingdom is not of this world, if my kingdom were, then would my servants fight that I should not be delivered to reasons cruelty,* John 18. but his kingdom was not from hence, therefore he hid himself when the Jews would have made him king: what shall I say unto you? yea you Quakers that will have a proof for what you believe, though you your selves can believe nothing but your light of nature; [for if that Scripture in words were made your

own in deeds] *faith is the evidence of things not seen, and the substance of things hoped for,* then you would believe God a person in glory, and not God a Spirit in disgrace; then you would see how impossibly this world should contain his glorious presence, when at the sight thereof the light of this world would become darkness. You that say God is in this world, where is he? let me see him, for if he cannot be seen, he is no God, but thy lying imagination onely. *O be not doubting, feel me, handle me.* Our God, which is the onely God, may be felt and embraced, is this your love to Christ, to say he is no other but what you apprehend him to be, onely in this wicked unbelieving world, and in thy blinde perishing soul as aforesaid, as two of your sisters in *Kent* laid naked the deceit of your heart to a friend of ours at *Maidstone*, who being asked what their God was, they said, If the world should but know what god they held forth, they should be stoned as they went in the streets: then said their friend, If all the God that is be within you, what do you think will become of you on the other side of death? to which they replied, That matters not what became of them; so that really believing there is no other God Christ but what is within thee, so that from the Lord Jesus I say, that thy god and thee shall perish to all eternity; for the christ that thou sayest is thy light within thee, is no other but the god of this world, *viz.* reason, which hath so blinded thy understanding, that thou canst not discern the true God at all: So that you may know who is the god of this world, you shall finde it written, *John 14.30. The Prince of this world cometh, and hath nothing in me:* who do you think was the prince of this world that hath nothing in Christ Jesus? surely it must not be Faith, but Reason, in that faith is of the nature of Christ, and reason the nature of the devil: Christ then speaking that he must go and depart this kingdom, for the prince or god of this world is a coming, and who was coming? even *Judas* to betray him. So that if ye were not stone-blinde, ye might see it was man-reason, or man-devil, the seed of the serpent of *Cain*, that is the god of this world. *I have said ye are Gods, but ye shall die as men:* was it any other but the Princes, Rulers, and Elders of *Israel,* Reason, Consultation, that was coming in *Judas* with Clubs and Staves to take Christ? As read I Cor. 2.8. *which none of the Princes of this world knew, for had they known, they would not have crucified the Lord of Glory.* O ye Quakers, why do ye not discern? even because he hath blinded your eyes, and hardened your hearts, lest ye should be converted, and God should save you, if ye were shut up in unbelief, you would tremble to say that God is in this world, so the Millenaries and such like might take shame and confusion of face, to have such a thought of Christs reigning in this world at all, much less a thousand years, [minde what I say] it would sadden the heart of a Believer, if he were in glory, much more the heart of our glorified Christ, to make such a sad exchange, as to leave his kingdom of glory, to reign here in this bloody unbelieving kingdom; if ye could by the eye of faith see what I see, you would then say [It is more inferior for Christ to leave his immortal glorious crown and kingdom, then for an earthly king to leave his mortal perishing crown and kingdom, and reign king over the herd of swine] but however, undervalue him what you please, and dream of what you can, as sure as God by his death hath conquered your Reason, the god of this world, and is delivered out of Reasons power into his own kingdom of glory above the stars, therefore appoint times and seasons, year after year, as *Archer, Horn* and others, with his deceived disciples at *Lyn*, have, and daily do; believe me whether you can or no, from the Lord Jesus I tell you, you shall see him no more reign in this world then you do now, for as ye have been deceived many years, so shall ye be deceived still, and as sure as God is clothed in the person of Christ in his own world or kingdom, *so that heaven or kingdom shall contain him till the restauration of all things,* Acts 3.21. that is, till Reasons kingdom here below shall be restored to its first original, *viz.* a Chaos of darkness that may be felt, and that for ever without end; was not his kingdom from hence when he was here, and shall it be his kingdom now? Oh no, no, his next coming shall be his last coming, and that not to stay, but as lightning from heaven to make a final end in one day, *for a thousand years in the account of the Lord are but as one day, and a day as a thousand years;* so that thousand years shall be but one days work to destroy Reasons glory and kingdom, that so his true Believers may enter their own kingdom, yea the kingdom of glory with Christ Jesus the Lord of glory. Oh when I remember what I was, and what I am now, it causeth chrystal tears of joy, to consider what a glory, yea what a top of glory my soul is raised to, in so much that I say, more on this side death cannot be known, though my loss external was great, yea greater then you all, yet my gain eternal, yea eternal is far surpassing my loss external; so that ye Quakers, if ye could understand my speech, then ye would believe God is not in this world, neither the god of this world, nor in any creature, righteous or wicked living in the world, as in the next Affirmation you shall have revealed: Therefore as Reason is the god of this world, let Reason have its proper right, so long as he is prince or god of this world, but your civil pride is become righteous treachery against the Magistrates of this world, otherwise Scripture would be your rule, and Moderation your guide, and not run wandring up and down this world disturbing the peace thereof, do ye not know where you are, and in whose kingdom you live? even in your own kingdom of Reason, why then do ye rebel against your own Government? for in so doing ye rebel against God, as read *Rom. 13.* the Magistrates of this world are the power of God, so resisting of them, ye resist the Ordinance of God, and so bring your selves under the breach of the Law, for they are Ministers of God to execute the Law on them that do evil, for this cause ye ought to be subject for conscience sake; and therefore ye are to render to them all civil duties required by them, *tribute to whom tribute belongeth, yea honor to whom honor belongeth,* otherwise ye condemn Christs direction in justifying your rejection, for he paid unto *Cesar* the things that were *Cesars,* as Christ will be paid the things that are his. O thou proud *Lucifer* Quaker, shall not Christ be thy pattern? wilt not thou follow him as an ensample? which if thou wert really that which thou pretendest to be, then thou wouldst see that Christ not the Apostles did not enter the Synagogue and Temple of the Jews, to rail on the Magistrates and their Ministers, but withdrew himself from them, and walked in the deserts and private villages, neither was the Apostles refractory, but subject unto them, as read *Acts 23.5. And they that stood by, said, Revilest thou Gods high priest? I knew not he was a Ruler, for it is written, Thou shalt not speak evil of the Rulers of my people.* Now judge you, were not those Rulers as bad as yours? and yet your god within you teacheth you to rail on the Rulers of this world, and that with corrupt tearms and diabolical actions, as some of you have done against the Lord Major, his Aldermen, and others, to the just deserving of your sufferings acted upon you, for were that the light of Faith, as it is the light of Reason within you, then you would know what spirit ye are of, yea tremble to do as ye have done, knowing this is not to do as ye would be done to; as suffer me to reminde you of one remarkable passage executed among you as touching the Ministers of this world, what a Disturbance you have made in their Assemblies, the like was never known; But you yourself say, they are *Baals* Priests and false Prophets, yea Ministers of men, and not of God, so *Cesars* Ministers, therefore must be publickly reproved, that so they may be ashamed, and the people be no longer deceived by them.

Answ. What though they be as you say, as none in the world know; them what they are better then we, yet let me tell you, and yet not I, but the Seed of Faith within me, that you have no Commission or Warrant to oppose or disturb them in their publick Worship; for in your Query it is affirmed they are but messengers of men, and you are no more, as to the Rulers of *New-England* you have acknowledged, that your names were no more written in the Scripture, then the Ministers of *England* old or new, nay, when by the Governour you were demanded to prove your Call, and that you were sent of God, then they would receive you, you could no more make it apparent then their Ministers, for I assure you, that you are as false, if not more counseits then they, for they have Authority to show how they were admitted to their Ministry, yea they have *Cesars* seal to prove them, and the Law to defend them; but as for your Call, you have nothing to show neither from God or man, but onely the imaginations of your reason to guide you, which you call your light within you; and if it be that tithes be their onely portion, and this kingdom all the heaven they are like to have, the more you are to be blamed for disquieting this their onely rest: alas poor creatures, their glorious time is but short, therefore abridge them of nothing that is their due, and for the time to come be at peace one with another, and as you agree in spirituals, so I advise you to agree in temporals, you have all one God, one devil, one heaven, and one hell, why then are you afraid one of another, and persecute one another, being as *Simon* and *Levi* brethren in knowledge and doctrine? what though one is a Scholar, and the other not? what though one will have Tithes, and the other the good will of their hearers, what their house will afford, let not this make a difference or rent in your kingdom, but as you are both of one seed, so heirs of your own crown, therefore fall not out by the way, but refresh one another, for you will have misery enough at your journeys end, so that if they be proud, be thou humble to them. But may be you will say, *You ought to have no mens persons in admiration*, as *Rom.2.11. for with God there is no respect of persons:* from hence ye infer, how that ye ought not to respect one person above another, and so being blinde leaders, as ye have done, causeth your hearers to rebel against God. To the end the deceived by you may be better informed, read *Acts 18.34. also James 2.1* also *I Pet. 1.17.* and then if you can, tell me upon what account the Lord is no respecter of persons, as can you from thence find any clause against the 13 of *Rom.* that you should not give due respect to the Rulers of your kingdom, is it not there intended as unto damnation and salvation God is no respecter of person, and therefore *Peter* said, *Now I perceive that the Gentile shall be saved as well as the Jews,* the poor, as the rich; the ignorant, as the wise, nay herein it is manifest as unto his Royal Prerogative Power of Election and Reprobation, God is no respecter of persons, as it is written in the first of *Cor. 1.26, 27, 28, 29. For ye see your calling, brethren, not many wise after the flesh, not many mighty, not many noble are called, but God hath chosen the foolish things to confound the wise, weak things to confound the mighty, and base things which are despised, hath God chosen to bring to nought things that are, that no flesh should glory in his presence:* This, and onely this is the minde of the Holy spirit, and not in the least forbidding to give honor to whom honor belongeth; for if ye were according to birth the Seed of Faith, so heirs appointed for salvation, ye would in things concerning this Government, give the Magistrates due honour, and not habit your selves with your Hat on your heads without Hatbands, and such childish and vain cogitations, pretending thereby it is conscience, when it is nothing but the pride of your heart, and to the undoing of poor Trades-men in the City and Nation; for it is written, *the humility of the body profiteth nothing,* neither doth the kingdom of Christ require or consist of such things, *onely faith in the knowledge of the true God:* it is not the body, but the minde, as *Acts 20.19.* so *Isaiah 57.15.* for it is written *Rom. 14.17. That the kingdom of God is not meat and drink, but righteousness, peace, and joy in the Holy Ghost,* not plain Clothes, course Diet, or the Hat keeping on, or taking off, as occasion requires. O that the Letter of the Scripture were but your Judge, then you would follow after things which make for peace, and things wherewith you might edifie one another, and not ignorantly or willfully run your disciples into sufferings as evil doers, for if ye were not stone-blinde [ye would know it was not the wisdom of faith, but the wisdom of reason that made the Hat] and therefore the Superiors of that wisdom must, and will have honor by it; for faith is simple, honest, and plain-hearted, yea ignorant as unto the things of this world, faith being a seed of another kingdom: now Reason being the seed, or god this world, is wise and expert in the affairs of its government, and therefore it was Reason had the knowledge to divide this world into kingdoms, and these kingdoms into provinces, counties and shires, and these shires into parishes, and gave their several names which now they have; it was the wisdom of flesh or reason that made a chief Magistrate and all others under him, and called him King, Protector, States, Parliaments, Majors, Sheriffs, Justices, and such like; it was Reason the Governour of this world, that invented all Arts in gold, silver, wood and stone; it was Reason that found out the knowledge of all Science, Tongues and Languages whatsoever, so that the wisdom of Reason could divide years into moneths, weeks, and days, and gave them their names in their moneth, weeks, dayes, and houres, and yet you being Reasons disciples, cannot endure your own language; but you must without a Commission imitate others that had a Commission to change times and seasons, as though you cannot with as much peace of conscience say *Sunday, Monday and Tuesday,* as the first, second, and third day? And where is there a breach of the Law, to say one, two, or three of the Clock, as to say the first, second, or third hour? And why is not *you,* as proper as *thou?* Ah poor blinde souls, it is not humility but prodigality, and when I demanded the reason of your thus uncomely behavior, your answer was, Art thou a heathen, how shall we be known from the world if it were not for our language? so that now minde, if you call Sunday the first day, One a Clock the first hour, then you are no heathens, but Christians: And when you assemble, sit silent, with your hands and eyes to the skie, sighing hum, hum, hum, hanging down your heads like a hounds ear, Jewish-like: Do all condemn you for Pharisaical dissembling hypocrites that hath the words of God, and not the true knowledge of God, as before related, supposing your outside Pharisaical righteousness will commend you to God, so that you work for life, and not from life; now in that I know God, I obey and walk upright before God, for how can I love him or obey him that I know not? therefore ye Quakers, observe what I say, faith begets knowledge, knowledge brings assurance, assurance brings peace, peace brings victory, victory brings vertue, vertue brings glory, so that ye begin at the tayl to attain the head, and that keeps you in chains of unbelief and eternal blindness, to your utter ruine of soul and body to all eternity.

3. Now from the third Affirmation I shall reveal, also from Scripture prove the Seed of Nature of God to be in all men, Believer and Unbeliever, more or less, as you that have ears to hear may

understand, that from hence there is revealed such divine Secrets that never was known till this last Commission or Witness of the Holy Ghost, and therefore no marvel why Faith is of so small a reputation among the wise men of this world, but in that Reason is so ripe, fluent, yea so excellent in their hearts, and that is the cause that some in my hearing have said, *There is no such thing as Faith:* and others have said, *That Faith is of no value,* or at least that Reason is of more excellent nature or vertue then Faith; so the Seed of Faith may discern that your life being the life of Faith, is but death in Reasons account; for as Faith is the life of the just, so Reason is the life of the unjust, and therefore their natures are contrary, as fire and water, God and devil, that if these two could be reconciled, then it is possible all may live and not die, and so, none be eternally damned; So that for the future all that are despisers and ignorant of this precious Seed Faith, may take notice, that it is the fountain of all that is eternal; however by the wisest head-piece of Reason it is slighted, yet the seed of the serpent shall here in part know, but with a witness at the resurrection shall feel, that it is this Faith that shall keep Reason under death eternal, for as by Faith the just shall live eternally, so by Faith Reason shall be kept in eternal death.

Now if you would know what Faith is, minde what you read, it is a secret invisible life, that hath formed it self into a body like unto its nature, *viz.* a spiritual glorious body, full of power, life, light, and motion, swifter then thought, that by its word speaking can create and bring forth what the nature of its Royal will and pleasure moveth to do: now if you ask me to prove this, I tell you as by faith I believe this, so must you, *Through faith we understand by the word of God that the worlds were framed,* so through faith I know that God is in the form of a man, and by that spark of faith within me, I believe that the nature of God is all heavenly spiritual body of faith without me in the highest heavens glorified to eternity, so that knowledge of Faith in God is so contrary to the knowledge of Reason, that it is but as a dream, or as a tale that is told, so that you can believe beyond the light of nature, by the eye of faith can see through the grave, yea pierce into the highest heavens to behold the glorious throne of eternity: the revelation of Faith is so swift, bright, and pure in its nature, that the watery element with all its clouds of thick darkness cannot blinde the eye of faith, but as it were by transfiguration opens it self, at which time there is such raptures that the soul knows not whether it be mortal or immortal; the experience of this *Steven* and *Paul* reveales unto you, as I my self can witness the truth of what I write, otherwise I could not ascend from the throne of grace to the throne of glory, were I not endued with revelation above my fellows, how were it possible for me to set forth God in his form and nature with that power, life, and light that attends him, but that I know there was such a power of life and light in that word spoken from the person of the Lord Jesus, who is all divine Faith, that nothing could withstand what his body of all glorious Faith moved him to do, and therefore I know it was by his word of faith he created the heaven and the earth, that was void and without form, to appear in a form of life and light; I know it was by his everlasting word of Faith that he fixed the firmament of water, by the life and light of those glorious bodies of Sun, Moon, and Stars, that hath congealed it into a body, as you may behold smooth, even, yea firm and sure, at his pleasure to divide the waters from the waters, and to give life and light to the earth and sea; I know it was by the word of Faith that the earth brings forth grass, herb yielding seed, and the fruit-tree yielding fruit after his kinde, whose seed is in it self upon the earth; I know by faith in that word spoken there was a power of life and light in the earth, that brought forth all these variety of herbs, fruits, and living creatures, both in sea and land, or that flieth in the air; I know by faith, that since God created them in their kindes, forms complexions, and natures, that they have no more power, life, and light, then was given them in the creating of them; I know it is by that word of Faith that gave power, life, and light in them at the first, that shall continue in them to the last; by faith I know that all the signs and wonders that hath, or ever shall be betwixt the firmament and the earth, *viz.* Eclips in Sun or Moon, Commets, Blazing-stars, Earth-quakes, Thunder-bolts, Storms and Tempests, Frost and Snow, Draught and Showers, Winter and Summer, Night and Day, continue and motion forth in their times and seasons, by and in vertue of that ever-living Word of Faith that first instituted them, and no more addition from God in the least unto them, and therefore I reveal that all the seeing, hearing, taking notice, care, or providence of God in or over them, that ever Christ that eternal, everlasting Body of Faith did make, is onely contained in that first word of Faith spoken, that gave them their first life and being, as it is written, 2 Peter 3.7. *But the heavens and the earth which are now, by the same Word are kept in store, reserved unto fire against the day of Judgement and perdition of ungodly men*; and therefore by faith against the angel or man, that are void of that measure of faith, so as to despise it, or die ignorant of it, against all such I affirm, that where you finde any such sayings, in either the writings of *Moses,* the Prophets, or Apostles, as, *Behold the fowls of the air, for they sow not, neither do they reap, yet your heavenly Father feedeth them, wherefore if God so clothe the grass of the field, which to day is, and to morrow shall be cast into the oven, shall he not much more clothe you, O ye of little faith,* Matth. 6. *Are not two sparrows sold for a farthing? and not one of them shall fall to the ground without your Father: but the very hairs of your head are numbred,* Matth. 10. I say, and that from the Lord Jesus that spake them, [minde what you read] I affirm that they, or any other creature, have their providence and preservation in, and from that first Word of Faith that first created them, and not any new or yearly supply from God without them; for as Christ by his word of Faith created at once of every kinde both male and female, so that same Word of Faith in its power of life and light shall for ever remain, while there is a generation from them, I say observe, and again observe that those words in *Acts 17.28.* saying, *In him we live, move, and have our being,* is from the first Word of Faith that first created them, and ever since have generated by that Word of Faith, power, life and light, all the Creation lives, moves, and have their beings, and not from new faith, power, life, and light, as Reason vainly imagine, that by preaching, praying, and weeping, God will alter the heaven and the earth out of the bounds that he first made them, as you think by prayer to obtain rain and fair weather, and all other wants contrary to the Royal Prerogative Will of God. In answer to this, you that are the Seed of Faith shall have full satisfaction, though the seed of Reason will be the more blinded, so that you Quakers, with almost the whole world, shall not understand this, so as to receive this [no not any] but you that are heirs of eternal glory; for as God created but male and female of all sorts, so he gave faith, reason, and sense but once, and as ever since from that first Creation, all these innumerable company of men, beasts, and all that have life, have generated, and so faith, reason, and sense have in all generated in its kinde, form and nature.

But on the contrary, minde what you read, what ever was, is, or ever shall be, that was not included in the first Creation, ever had, and ever shall have a new supply of a Word of Faith without them, but the wonders of *Moses,* the signs and revelations of the Prophets, and the miracles of the Apostles, not being created nor generated, had a new supply by voice of words from the Creator; as *Moses* had a special Commission to deliver the children of *Israel* out of *Egypt,* and therefore he had a special word of Faith to plague the earth as often as he would. So *Joshua* had a new supply from God, by which he said, *Sun, stand thou still upon Gibeon, and thou Moon, in the valley of Ajalon.* So Elijah had a powerful word of Faith, when he said unto *Ahab, As the God of Israel liveth, before whom I stand, there shall not be dew or rain, but according to my word;* as also when he called for fire from heaven upon the Captain and his fifty, upon the sacrifice, that divided *Jordan:* this was no created nor generated faith, but a Commissionated faith by which *Elisha* raised the Shunamites son, and smote the *Assyrians* with blindness, to prophesie the plenty of *Samaria.* As you may read *Acts 2.2.* it was a Commissionate faith by which the Apostles raised the dead, cast out devils, and cured all diseases, so you that have the eye of faith may discern, where all the gross darkness and great mistake of almost the whole world consists, in not understanding the faith of God by Commission given to man, and that faith from God generated in man, I say for want of knowledge in this, both priest and people assume to preach, and to pray, and so to be heard and receive an answer from God, as *Moses,* the Prophets, and Apostles did, when in either of the two first Commissions you cannot finde that ever God did hear or give an answer to any private Believer, but onely to the Commissioners of the first and second magnitude, certainly if ye were not overflown with the light of reason, so void or very weak in your generated faith, you might then understand all along as you read the Scriptures, that God never heard the prayers, or took notice of the tears or alms-deeds, so as to answer any but the Head-commissioners, as *Moses,* the Prophets, and Apostles, unless it were upon a special design or great change, that his divine will or pleasure move him unto, as the Conversion of the Gentiles; upon such a special transaction as this, he heard the prayers of *Cornelius,* that being the Conduit-pipe to convey revelations of Christ in the heart of the Gentiles.

And therefore ye weak ones of the Seed of Faith, grieve not that God doth not hear you, so as to answer you, for my own part I should be glad it were in this Commission as in the two former, for then I know whatsoever I requested would be answered, in that I know him in his form and nature, and do those things that are commanded by him; but though my sufferings and afflictions be never so great, they are not remedied, and yet I shall be supported from my generated faith within me, so far as is necessary for me; and therefore as by your faith ye know him, and walk obedient to him, you shall have your wants answered in peace here, and glory hereafter, for there is your God in the person of Christ, there is your home, your treasure, and crown of glory in Christ his kingdom without end.

For your further satisfaction and joy in your souls, I shall reveal unto you the difference of a Commissionate faith from a generated faith, and how the one is ceased, the other not; therefore understand what I shall now write, and you may read that you never heard, as you may read *I Cor. 13.2* saying, *Though I have the gift of prophesie, and understand all mysteries, and all knowledge, and though I bestow all my goods to feed the poor, and give my body to the fire, nay, though I have all faith, so that I could remove mountains, and have not charity, it profiteth nothing.* O admiration! who but the knowing of the Seed of Faith can tell what to make of this intricate saying, that neither understanding, nor the works of mercy, nor our body to be burned, nor all faith to remove mountains, will all these avail nothing without a generated faith? for that the just shall live by, be merciful, and yield to the Lords Prerogative power to do with thee what he pleaseth; so that you must understand this is onely spoken as in the Commission, by which they were authorized to do great miracles, and so had from God a powerful word of Faith to believe, that what ever they did speak or do, without the least doubt would come to pass; and as that Commission did cease in their death, and shall not rise with them in their life, no more shall that kinde or degree of faith, for what need of faith from God without them, when the Commission is ceased with them? but their generated faith shall die in him, and rise with him, yea this faith or charity shall cause him to ascend to behold the body of Christ, who is all heavenly Faith: this generated faith by which man became a living soul, I say this Word of Faith did not all die in *Adam,* but left its seed in generation, and so all other creatures hath in them, bearing seed according to their kinde, and no more created or given but what was in the created *Adam* according to his kinde generates, grows from one degree to another, till it behold that personal Faith from whence it first had beginning.

Thus I have revealed, that though God be not in this world, nor man, or any creature, yet his seed or nature is both in righteous and wicked; in the righteous, by which they know God in his form and nature, and strongly believe above hope, yea against all the Sophistical delusions of Reason whatsoever, for we being partakers of his nature, by that knows the nature of God, as in the *Psalms* it is written, *In thy light shall we see thee all light:* now faith being the nature of God, by that spark of faith we have evidence in our souls of that Reason cannot understand, as you may read, *I Cor. 2.15. A natural man receiveth not the things of the Spirit of God, for they are foolishness unto him, neither can he know them, because they are spiritually discerned.* Where shall we finde a man that will say he is natural, and discerns not the things of God? But rather will say he is spiritual, though truly from the spirit of revelation I affirm, not one of twenty thousand that can discern, or that doth know God in his form or nature, the devil in his form and nature, the nature of the angels, the rise of the two seeds, how they became two, with the effects and operation: in their thoughts, voices, motions and actions, I say not any in the whole world but those that are believers in our Commission can tell, and yet what preaching and praying to a God they know not, when experience all along may teach you, *that whosoever is not of faith is sin,* and yet you will preach and pray for faith, when you read, *that without faith it is impossible to please God,* and yet all you do is for faith, without which all ye do is but vain and abominable, yea the best of your righteousness doth not equal the Pharisees, and so shall never enter the kingdom of glory, but be rejected as hypocrites and counterfeits against Christ Jesus the Lord of glory.

Fourthly and lastly I shall reveal, also from Scripture prove, that the sufferings of the Quakers in *New-England,* or any other Nation, is not for righteousness, so that neither they nor the persecutors, so living and so dying, shall escape damnation.

An. That you may be no longer deluded under your sufferings, nor your hearers any longer deluded by you, for their sakes hear me patiently, and from the spirit of revelation I shall infallibly make known unto you:

1. *Who are the righteous sufferers.*
2. *When they are said to suffer for righteousness.*
3. *Who are the persecutors.*
4. *The reward of the persecutor and persecuted.*

First who are the righteous sufferers, that is the Prophets and righteous of the Lord, and none other, let their pretense be what they will as unto excellent gifts and uprightness of life, yet if they be non-commissionate, their righteousness is nothing; for you may observe that counterfeits claim the same priviledge as the other have, let their sufferings be temporal or spiritual: you shall hear very few say but that they suffer unjustly, let it be for Treason or blood-shed, as your days experience, yet they will plead it was for their duty to their Prince, and in obedience to their General, supposing from hence they suffer not for evil, but for well doing: Also the Jesuits, with other Dispensations, will plead innocency, and that they suffer for a good conscience, so you Quakers are perswaded that you suffer for the name of Jesus Christ; so that it is necessary their should be a clear distinction who are righteous sufferers, and who not, be pleased to read *Mat. 10.16, 17. Behold I send you forth as sheep among wolves, be ye therefore wise as serpents, innocent as doves, for they will deliver you up to the Councels, and they will scourge you in the synagogues, and ye shall be brought before Kings and Governors for my Names sake, for a testimony against them and the Gentiles:* from hence ye may observe they were sent to declare before Kings and Rulers of *Israel*, that Christ whom they crucified was the Son of God, and for that end and purpose was commissionated with power and revelation of the spirit to speak boldly in the name of Christ, as read *Acts 4.10. Be it known unto you all, and to all the people of* Israel, *that by the Name of Jesus Christ of Nazareth whom ye crucified, whom God raised from the dead, even by him doth this man stand here before you whole, neither is there salvation in any other, for there is none other name under heaven given among men whereby we must be saved:* so that you hear, whoever suffers in obedience to his Commission, suffers for well doing, and on the contrary he that counterfeits a Commission, not being sent from the Commissioner, is persecuted justly for a Traitor; but you Quakers are not commissionate, so counterfeits, yea guilty of spiritual treason against that glorious personal Majesty of Christ Jesus; for as there ever hath, so there ever will be false prophets and false teachers, as ye your selves are at this day the falsest of all, unless you could with peace of conscience say, and as assuredly believe that the Lord Jesus is not within you, but without you in the highest heavens glorified, with voice of words did speak unto you as he spake to *Moses,* and to *Paul,* and now in this last to *John Reeve,* I say if you cannot prove your Call, and by his authority sent, then from the Lord Jesus, who by voice of words gave forth unto us his last Commission, by vertue whereof I am authorized to reveal you are traitors, thiefs, and robbers, that have reaped where ye never sowed, and counterfeited their Commission into your lying imagination onely pretending it is the call of God, when you are ignorant what God in his form and nature is, so that neither in my hearing, nor before the *New-England* Rulers, you could not prove your

Call so sent of God: for how unpossible is it for you to plead for a Commission or sent, when you know not the Commissioner who sent you? but as unto the true knowledge of the Lord Jesus that Heavenly Commissioner, you are altogether ignorant of, as in our Conference was revealed you knew not God, but as before related, which when we affirmed was no god, but a devil, for which you came under the sentence of eternal condemnation; for as I told you, if by revelation from a Commission ye knew God, then as others have done, so would ye submit to every ordinance of man for the Lords sake, *I Pet. 2.13.*

2. When are these righteous souls said to suffer for righteousness? that is when they are sent forth by the command of God, to declare the minde and message of God, for which revelation they are called before Rulers, and imprisoned, condemned, yea put to death, then, and not till then they suffer for Christs sake; for had they not been sent upon the Errand of God, there had been no cause of suffering: but on the contrary when you counterfeit a Commission in the name of God, when God never sent you, and in the publishing thereof are apprehended and condemned, then you suffer justly, not in the name of Christ, but your own name you suffer for; but those that are sent, as you read *Matth. 23.24, Behold I send unto you prophets, wise men, and Scribes, some of which ye shall kill. O Jerusalem, Jerusalem, thou that killest the Prophets, and stonest them which are sent.* Such as these that are sent by a Commission of their own, and not anothers, those suffers for righteousness; therefore ye Quakers and all others, ye had never no voice of words from the Lord Jesus to do as ye do, but your light of reason onely, and so suffer justly as evil doers; as do but read *Matth. 7.21,22,23.* and there you shall finde that you yourselves, with the rest, are those whom this saying doth concern, for you assume prophesie, and to cast out devils, having no Commission of your own, but takes up the words of another, and so for all the great sufferings and wonderful works ye have done, this shall be your reward, I profess unto you that I never knew you, and so will have nothing to do with you, and therefore depart from me, and see if your formless god can deliver you from those eternal sufferings that are coming upon you, for counterfeiting a Commission without me, in that ye would then know it was the command of God without you, and so cause a submissive obedience within you: But,

3. Who are the persecutors? If you could understand what seed is persecuted, then you would know what seed persecutes, so that the Seed of Faith being the righteous sufferers, then the seed of Reason are the onely persecutors; for the nature of faith is to do as it would be done to, and the nature of reason is to injure, cheat, and persecute his neighbor, as you may read all along this seed was that persecuting *Cain*, who was a liar and murtherer of his brother *Abel*, so *Ishmael* being the same seed, did jeer and scoff at *Isaac;* and *Esau* the seed of Reason did persecute *Jacob;* so *Pharoah* persecuted *Moses*, and *Saul* persecuted *David*, so *Pilate* and *Herod* did persecute Christ, the

Scribes and Pharisees persecuted the Apostles, and so ever since, and at this day, and so to the end of the world, the seed of Reason will not onely persecute one another, but the righteous of the Lord, as you are not ignorant how they persecute the Quakers and others of the same seed, though as you have heard, the Quakers run themselves into sufferings by their rebellious carriage, so suffer justly, as they at the day of account shall know. That you may the better discern this seed of Reason from the Seed of Faith, I shall reveal the nature thereof in two things: First observe, where this seed is lord, it so ripens his Genius, that he comes to the knowledge of all Tongues, Arts, and Sciences, and so by the wisdom of this seed grows famous, by which he becomes rich and honourable in this world, it being Reasons kingdom, loves its own, and makes him a Governour and Ruler over the Affairs of this world: it is a proud ambitious seed like its father *Cain*, it loves honor, and to tyrannize over its fellow-creature, though in others of the same seed it is more moderate, being under a servile fear of the Law, is not so cruel as the other. But secondly, as unto the knowledge of the Lord Jesus, the moderatest head-piece therein is very ignorant, and yet this wisdom can preach, pray excellent heaven-like language, and thereby judge themselves the onely Interpreters of Scripture, and so what the wisdom of Faith apprehends above them, Reason judgeth it foolishness, if not blasphemy, and so persecutes the wisdom of Faith, that is onely able to search the deep things of God, as you may read at large, *I Cor. 1.2.* that none of the Princes in his dayes knew Christ the Lord of glory, and yet in our days who but Ministers, Princes, Lords, and Ladies, and the learned of this world, are judged to know the mysteries of Eternity, when you read in the Apostles time it was a rare thing to finde a rich man, or a wise man that believed in Christ, and yet here in *England,* yea in this world, they suppose none can know god but the wise Priests and Rulers, when you read all along it is but the wisdom of nature, and a natural man cannot discern the things of God; so you that can, may see it is the wisdom of *Oxford* and *Cambridge* that are the persecutors.

    4. The reward of the persecuted and persecutor: As they are quite contrary in seeds, so they shall be in reward, for the righteous sufferers of the Lord are those, and none but those, as before quoted, which are but few in comparison of them that suffer justly, yet I say those few shall have a reward, as *Math. 2.12. Rejoyce and be exceeding glad, for great is your reward in heaven, for so persecuted they the Prophets which were before you:* for when a soul really knows for whom he suffers, he receives it as part of his portion, and is confident as he suffers for the true God, so he shall reign with the true God, as *2 Tim. 1.12. For which cause I also suffer these things, nevertheless I am not ashamed, for I know whom I have believed.* The knowledge of God emboldens a soul *to fight the good fight, to keep the faith, and a good conscience toward God,* for such is laid up a crown of glory: we suffer not to know God, but in that we know him, we suffer

righteously for him. O beloved, it is life eternal to know God, in that no suffering (though death it self) cannot hinder this soul from the enjoyment of God, it being as it were a hastening from his misery to his glory; for this is thank-worthy, if a man for a good conscience toward God endure grief, suffering wrongfully, O happy is that soul that suffers not for evil, but well doing, which none can truly say, but he that is sent by Commission, Inspiration, or Revelation of the true God; not all that say they are sent by learning, by Churches publick or private, or by imagination, visions, dreams, or flashing fancies, that they suppose they hear a motion or call within them; these, or any of these delusions, let their gifts and parts be never so excellent, they are not sent from the true God, in that they know not him they pretend sent them: Ask any of these counterfeits what he is that sent them, they know him no other then the vagabond Jews, Exorcists, these you may read *Acts 19.13. We adjure thee by Jesus whom Paul preacheth,* they knew not the life and power of *Pauls* Commission, and so they commanded the unclean spirit, by saying *Jesus whom Paul preacheth,* they could not say, we adjure you by Jesus whom we know, and therefore the devil spirit said, *Jesus I know, and Paul I know, but who are ye?* I finde a power and vertue in them, but none in you, and therefore I am too strong for you, so that they suffered justly; and therefore from our Commission as aforesaid, I tell you, what ever sufferings you meet withal you deserve it, there is none to help or deliver you, or will pity you. Again, there is a righteous suffering, when a man impoverisheth himself to feed, clothe, and lodge the righteous Messengers of the Lord, this man shall have the reward of that righteous man, he that persecutes you, persecutes me, he that loves you, loves me, and so with him shall have crowns of eternal glory, as *Math. 25.34.*

2. The reward of the persecutor shall be a flaming crown of eternal misery, therefore hearken ye Rulers of this perishing world, as I have shown obedience to your Laws, so I shall from the Lord shew you the bounds of your Government, to that end read *Rom. 13.3. For Rulers are not a terror to good works, but to evil;* so that you being onely Magistrates of the Civil Law, you are to execute wrath upon him that breaks the Law; for as the Law was made for the lawless, *viz.* the seed of Reason, and not for the righteous, the Seed of Faith, therefore the power of your Government doth onely reach the disobedient, wicked, and prophane, to repel uproars and tumults acted by murtherers and traitors, to keep peace and quietness in your kingdom, that so the righteous, that blessed Seed of Faith, as they do not break your Law, may not suffer wrongfully contrary to your Law; for this end was the Law given you, and for this cause were ye chosen Rulers over the lawless, over swearers, forswearers, drunkards, adulterers, thiefs, cheats, murtherers, traitors, &c. I say these and such like to have to deal withal, and not with any other for matter of conscience, be they right, or be they wrong, be they false, be they true, so far as they are

civil, and obedient to you Law, you have nothing to do to meddle, by the instigation of the Priests, in matter of their worship, though the Priests of *England* new or old, were able to discern truth from errour, as they are not, yet I say, if they were, as we the true Commissioners of the Lord can discern the states and conditions of you all, and as sure as I write it, so sure you shall finde it, so that remember I told you: step not into Christs kingdom, lest you be apprehended for traitors and usurpers over the crown and dignity of Christ the onely God, for so far as ye intrench upon the Royal Prerogative Power of God, so far ye will be condemned for fighters against God; take notice while it is called to-day, that you are Rulers in your own kingdom, and not in Christs, the Government of that must be at his own disposing.

Q. *But may be your Teachers tells you, that such and such are dangerous, erroneous, if not blasphemous, and therefore they call upon you to punish them, because they disturb your form of Worship.*

Ans. What though they were as you are informed, what is that to them? let them look within their own souls, and they shall finde themselves guilty of that they invite you to punish the Quaker for; and as sure as those Quakers notwithstanding their sufferings, so living and so doing, shall be damned, so shall those Priests your informers; therefore ye Priests and Rulers of *New-England* shall as surely perish as the Quakers punished by you: As you that have ears to hear, seriously mind what I shall say unto you, are they traitors? are they blasphemers? are they false prophets? as none but our Commission in the revelation can tell what they are, yet this you are to minde, as you intend to finde mercy, to consider against whom they are traitors, against whom they blaspheme, and on whom they prophesie lies; if against God, as you say, then know it is not against you, so not in your jurisdiction, therefore not for you to punish; for against what King the transgression is, in that kingdom he must receive his punishment: But blasphemy, as you call it, is matter of conscience, so in Christs kingdom, and therefore let God alone: *Vengeance is mine, and I will repay* where I have to do, Oh that ye would let God have the same priviledge in his kingdom, as ye would have in yours, as you shall hear at large in the next Chapter; but if ye will not keep in your own kingdom, to do just and righteous things without partiality, bribery, or deceit, but seek your own glory in the ruine of others, then hear what my revelation in the vertue of our Commission saith, I will overturn you, as I have done others before you. Oh then what will ye do in the day of our Gods visitation, and in the desolation that shall come upon you, to whom then will ye cry for mercy? And where then will ye finde your glory, when then your god will be your devil, your heaven your hell, and your glory your shame, and your oppression and persecution, your fuel of eternal burnings to eternity.

Therefore ye Rulers of *England,* so many of you as have ears to hear, will make this an ordinance among you, That as you are Magistrates in Reasons, and not in Faiths kingdom, therefore you are required to keep within your bounds, and therein to discharge your duty of those things required of you in your kingdom, that is, turn not aside the needy from judgement, nor take away the right from the poor, and appear not an hypocrite in a righteous cause, nor make a man an offender for a word, nor lay a snare for him that reproveth you justly, be free from bribes and deceit, but maintain a peaceable quiet Government, that so the people may have free trading, by which they may pay what is taxed upon them; as this is your kingdom, so this is your government, and this is the work ye have to do, and as sure as Christ is the onely God, this will be required of you, when there shall be none to plead for you. O were you but truly sensible of the great charge that lieth upon you, you would not strive who should be the chief Ruler among you, and then in the day of death it is as though it had never been unto you; as do but recollect your thoughts of that Heroick spirit *Oliver* late Protector, where was a wiser head-piece, and a greater Glory for the time of his reign, and how quickly was it blasted, yea put forth as the snuff of a candle? and is now as though it had never been, and therefore behold your faces in his glass, that as it was with him, so it shall be with all glory here below, one dies, and another lives, and which of you can absolutely say what will become of you on the other side of death, unless you know the two seeds? the nature of which is revealed in you, will manifest what God in his form and nature is, the devil in his form and nature is, and so in the knowledge of the true God, you will know what you are here, what you shall be in the grave, as also in the resurrection, even perfect assurance, which is heaven here, and eternal happiness, which is the kingdom of glory hereafter.

Before I conclude with this Scripture, I shall a little paraphrase with you Quakers as touching those sayings in your *New-England* book, written by *Francis Howgil,* who came under the sentence of eternal condemnation for despising Christ Jesus the onely God in form of a man: the words *verbatim* are these, *That the Quakers are the Royal Off-spring of the family of him who is the first-born of every creature, and the shout of a king is among them, and that the arm of the Lord is the Quakers strength.* To which I answer.

Notwithstanding you have it infallibly proved in the revelation of this Commission, that the Scripture was not writ for any but the seed of Faith, and yet the seed of Reason that are altogether a stranger to Faith, yet they will all say they have Faith and believe in Christ Jesus, so that enquire of all the inhabitants of *London* or else where, and there is not any but they will affirm they believe, and hope to be saved, and yet what preaching and praying there is to make men believe, and yet all the members of the seven Churches will say they believe, and yet in what company soever you come, you shall scarce finde seven of one minde, but divided in their judgements, because they know no true foundation at all, and yet every one hath kindled a fire in which they burn their clay and brick, and in the light of that fire they have kindled, they wander from duty to duty, seeking straw to make their full tale, and thus the blinde Quakers are laboring through the fire of their own righteousness, intending to finde rest, but cannot, in that their foundation is sand and not a rock, and so cannot build a house without secret doubts and fears of eternal condemnation, and yet you read there is a rest remaining to the people of God, which rest is perfect assurance of a mans salvation, which cannot be attained til thou comes to the knowledge of the true God Christ Jesus, who is the saving rock, and everlasting habitation eternally in the heavens, as read *Heb. 12.22,23.* and you shall finde who they were, and how they were come to this heavenly rest: first you finde they were Commissioners as aforesaid, and those that believed in their doctrine that were come to *the Church of the first-born which are written in heaven,* which heaven is not in reason, but in faith, as *Rom. 5.1,2. Therefore being justified by faith, they had peace in God,* and by faith they had access to the kingdom of grace, wherein they then believed: now these that was commissionate by voice of words, that family of those few Believers that had faith in that Commission, was, as *Acts 17.29. The royal off-spring of the first-born, even Christ Jesus the onely God,* and so were just men made perfect in their sprits, by believing that the Spirit or God-head was in Christ Jesus body that was crucified, and no other form or likeness as gold, silver, wood, or stone, as was supposed, *Isaiah 40.18.* and is now supposed by you Quakers, that God is not in his own form, but ye compare and liken him to be in your form as aforesaid, and therefore take notice that so many of you as lives and dies, in that pretended light within you, are the off-spring of that lying imagination of Reason the devil within you, and not the off-spring of Christ the body of living faith without you.

And then thou sayest, the shout of a King is among you, now whether you do intend Christ Jesus the King of glory, or a mortal king of this perishing world, or *James Naylor,* by some of you reported the King of *Israel,* I know not, however if ye pretend Christ Jesus, I say, as again and again I have told you, he is not in you, nor among you, but above you in his own kingdom of glory; but this I acknowledge with you, if you intend *James Naylor,* so reported, and by some of you believed the King of *Israel,* as upon his Examination was confessed, the shout of such a King is among you, I do not deny and therefore remember the revelation of this last Commission told you so, there never was, is, or shall be the shout of any other king, but that kingly imagination of Reason the devil among you.

As do but observe your last diabolical boasting, that the arm of the Lord is the Quakers strength, from your own words you discover your downfal, in that you know not the Lord nor his strength, as before was manifest, for you believe in no other Lord or Christ but what is within you, and what then is the Lords arm but your own, so that your strength lieth in your selves, which you call the arm of the Lord, for

Reasons strength is your protection, in moral civility and Pharasaical righteous-like suffering, by which if it were possible you are those that would deceive the very elect, as *Mark 13.21,22.* as since the second Commission, what preaching, praying, and reading hath there been to finde out the true Christ, one cavelling and disputing with another, saying, Christ is in our assembly, in our worship, and our way, when from the Lord Jesus who is the onely God, I say ye are all false Christs and false prophets, with your counterfeit seducing signs and wonders; And as we are the last and spiritual commission of the Holy Ghost or Eternal Spirit as aforesaid [minde what you read] for by revelation of that nature or seed that is in Christs own body, I declare, and shall seal it with the death of my soul, for a witness against all you that persecute me for my revelation, that we have power, as the Apostles had in theirs, to curse either angel or any of you, that shall gain-say us, despise us, or call our Commission a lie, I say in the vertue of our Commission we have power to curse both you and your god with an eternal curse, that is irrevocable, therefore jest not with edge tools, nor dally with the Law, but observe what faith, which is truth in me, faith, that all the Gods that ever was, is, or ever shall be, was , and every will be in the person of Christ Jesus, though three Titles, yet but one person glorified, to your sorrow, and therefore remember I told you , that whoever after the reading of this, be left to despise it, or die in the ignorance of it, shall both soul and body perish to all eternity, I speak the truth from Christ Jesus, perfect assurance bears me witness that there was to be three Commissions, of which number two is past, and we are the last Commission that ever shall appear in this bloody unbelieving world, and take notice that I am as a brand plucked out of the fire, from the lust of sin, the riches and honour of this world, to bear testimony unto these two Witnesses spoken of in the eleventh of the *Revelation,* which ere long will be interpreted to publick view; and therefore ye Quakers, or any other, believe me whether ye can or no, know this we are but few, and not so many as you Papistical, Episcopal, Presbyter, Independent, Baptist, Ranter, and Quaker are, for very few there are that shall be saved; and as we are commissionate by voice of words from the glorious mouth of the Lord Jesus, so our seed is from heaven heavenly, insomuch that none can give us a name, or comprehend what we are, though all ye are comprehended by us, what ye are, where ye live, and what your god and devil is; so that now ye Quakers observe, that the arm of the Lord is faith, which faith is in us, and among us, by which we have daily strength to declare, that all preaching, praying or suffering, not being sent by voice of words as aforesaid, are but counterfeits, so blasphemous liars, of which sort none shall have perfect assurance of heaven here, or ever enter the kingdom of Glory hereafter, so that despise, scoff, jear, persecute, yea put to death what you please, as sure as Christs person that upon this earth was crucified, is now in heaven glorified, so sure shall none of you see the person of Christ,

Saints or Angels in the highest heavens glorified to eternity, but be raised devils upon this earth, damned for ever, for ever, yea for ever without end.

Rom. 9.11. Hath not the Potter power over the clay, of the same lump to make one vessel unto honor, and another unto dishonor?

Notwithstanding this Scripture is clear for the Royal Prerogative Power of God as it lieth in the conexion of it, as also the Chapter is full of the same matter, confirming that God must needs do with his creature what he pleaseth, otherwise to what end should he have created any living being in his presence, if the creature had power in it self to be saved or damned at his own will and pleasure, surely then were it a madness in any creature to fear damnation, or be troubled at any thing it doth, and that because it lieth not in the power of God that formed thee, but in thy self. O herein lay my sorrow, to consider that most part of the world are plunged into this Chaos of eternal darkness, to believe without any true testimony of any of the three Commissions, that God should not have the power of a mortal King, when you see it daily that Reason, the god of this world, will put to death, and preserve alive whom he pleaseth, and yet Christ Jesus the Creator of heaven and earth, must by his creature be put to death, yea judged a Tyrant by the seed of the serpent, for saying *I will have mercy on whom I will, and whom I will I harden,* which is no less then if he had said, Whom I will damn, I will, and whom I will save, I will, what is that to any man? shalt thou that was formed by me, say unto me, Why dost thou deal so hardly with me? I say man must have power to put Christ to death, not onely in his own person, but in his word and people, and none shall say against it, when as if God doth but write a word, that he hath all power in heaven and earth, man grumbles that he should assume a power to damn, when you see that one creature is lord over another, to devour its inferiour, as a great dog worries a little dog, and great fishes swallows up the little ones, and so great men murther poor men, and yet God must have no power over his creature, but only a name of a God, but no power as a God, unless it be to pardon and forgive all the bloodshed that hath been acted by the seed of Reason against the Seed of Faith, I say this cursed brood will allow God this Prerogative, to feed them with riches and pleasure of this world, to oppress and tyrannize over the poor Seed of Faith, and when death comes, they would have God ask them whether it be their will to be damned, or no, that priviledge Christ could not have of his creature, to know of the Jews whether the sentence of his death might lie at his own disposing or no; this priviledge that God could not have of man, man would have of God, but know this, O wretched rebellious creature, that thou shalt finde in thy soul, with that blasphemous devil largely, who ever thou art that lives and dies in this belief of thine, that thou shalt be eternally damned, and yet not know who it was, though thou canst not believe what now I write, yet thou shalt finde with a witness the truth of thy eternal misery, in that I know thou wert fitted for destruction.

Now the main ground of all this floweth from thy ignorance, not knowing what God and his nature is, and what the devil and his nature is, for if thou didst but rightly understand the one, thou wouldest know the other, whether they are both one, or contrary the one to the other; for if thou knewest that God and his nature were in antipathy to the devil and his nature, then I would know of thee who made them so, and wherefore they were made so, and which of the two hath the preheminence, thy knowledge in these things would yield a submission to the Royal Prerogative Power of God, and not stand cavelling whether God had a power to damn as well as to save; for this I know [if there be none to be damned, then there is none to be saved] so not two, but one, and that one being God and his nature, shall not need to be saved, it being a Savior it self; but if thou understand there is two seeds, so two natures, so a God and a devil, then thou mightiest also know whether God or the devil made it so; if the devil, then his seed hath the preheminence above God; but if God made it so, as he did, then know this, that God hath power over the devil, and so the devil and his seed must be subject to him, or else he must be damned by him, but the devil cannot, nor will not submit, therefore must be damned; and if this seed Reason, the devil, was appointed for damnation, as none but his seed will gain-say it, who must damn him, if not God, for this be sure the devil loves himself too well, to damn himself, or yield himself to be damned; so it being affirmed that there is not one, but two, and these two as fire and water, light and darkness, I marvel much thou shouldest have a thought of their ever being reconciled, of necessity one must perish, and that not willingly from its own will, but the pleasure and will of the other, even God.

Therefore withstand it what thou pleasest, this know that God could die, and by his own power raise himself again, that so he might by his power raise up the seed of his own body from death to life; and as by this power he can raise up his own seed, so by the same power he can keep down the seed of the devil; for this is truth, that if God can damn none, then he can save none: but be not doubting, but believe, that if he have power to save, he hath power to damn, otherwise all power was not given Christ in earth, as well as in heaven, but in that he had power on earth, he can as well raise his own above it, as keep the devil in and upon it, and that eternal without end, if not, there had been no end of this the devils, or Reasons kingdom, had it been so, as it is not, then the devils might truly have said, as now they do falsly, that God had power to damn none, and so his power had onely been in heaven, and not on earth; but if you will believe Scripture, or me, and both as one, you shall finde that God doth damn as well as save, and that not for any evil thing thou has done, but being damned, thou dost little that is good, nor never shalt truly know him as he is God, yea God a power, for if he had no power, he was no God; for it is a power ye pretend to know, and this power to be in you, and not above you, and so ye acknowledge no other God but what is within you, and from hence it comes you perswade your selves to hearken to the light within you, supposing that is all the light that will guide and protect you, and thus ye conceive this God was an infinite nothing, and so made all things of nothing, and of nothing comes all things that are; but however your blindness be great, yea and that light that is in you thick darkness, yet let me tell you [of nothing comes nothing] but an infinite Spirit without a body is nothing, so what power can be in that which hath no person? But you say, God hath no form, then know he hath no power, for without a form there is no life, so God being all life without form, could not give life to man till he had a form, and that life ye conceive that made all forms, breathed it self into these forms so made by it, and so that God that made you, is in you, and what power he hath is at your disposing, if this be true, as I know it is not, then it is no wonder you should say, God made no creature to damn it, in that he made man to live in him, and so if God damn man, he must damn himself with man. *Hath not the potter power over the clay?* what say you? hath not a living man power over a dead lump of clay, can you deny it? no surely, it is consented to by all, that man hath this power, but it is much questioned whether God hath this power as the potter hath, and that because one they see, and the other they cannot, the one is evil, the other is not: for what is the thoughts of Reason, think you? it is a tyrannical act in God to make a vessel for damnation. Now thou proud Reason, devil, what wouldest thou have God to do? thou wouldest have all been made vessels of salvation, and what then, shall not all be saved? for surely as the vessel is made, so it shall continue, for though a glorious vessel in the using of it may gather dust & filth, according as it is used, and so become a vessel dishonorable, in respect of that corruption it is clothed withal, but when that vessel is washed, then it looks as glorious as before; but that vessel that was made deformed, notwithstanding all washing, it will look deformed still; and therefore if all souls had been made vessels of salvation, notwithstanding in their life time they may gather corruption by sins and iniquities, yet all this while they are vessels of honour, as in relation to their creation, or that seed of Faith in them; for all the time that *Paul* was clothed with a corrupted persecuting spirit, he was a vessel of honor as in the account of God, though in himself he was deformed; but when the deformed spirit of reason was kept under that honorable spirit of Faith, then his soul was honorable in his own apprehension, and so did manifest it self a vessel of glory to the view and experience of others. Now you that are not appointed for destruction, may undoubtedly believe that there is a secret knowledge in the breast of the Lord Jesus, who are the vessels of Faith, and who are the vessels of Reason, and this infinite Wisdom hath appointed the means when, and which way this vessel of Faith shall come to the knowledge of his glorious person, as my soul can witness, which on the contrary the seed of Reason shall never come to the understanding of this Royal Prerogative Power of God, but shall weary out themselves with fasting, weeping, and prayer, and yet come short of the knowledge of the true God, as *Matth. 13.15. For this peoples heart is waxed gross, and their ears are dull of hearing, and their eyes they have closed, lest at any time they should see with their eyes, and hear with their ears, and should understand with their hearts, and should be converted, and I should heal them.* You the seed of Reason, that say it is in your power, why do ye not hear? why do ye not see? why do ye not understand? Christ the eternal God is preached to all, you have as much priviledge to hear as another, and yet you understand not what you hear, you think you are righteous, you judge your selves wise, yea so wise, that none understands more, nor so much as you, and why do you not understand that Christ is the onely God, as well as the simple-hearted ignorant fools so esteemed by you? can you tell me what is the ground why you do not hear? are you wiser then your fathers the Jews, the seed of *Abraham*? if you were wiser, as you are not, as they could not, no more can you, as in them you may read your destiny, *John 8.43. Why do you not understand my speech, even because ye cannot hear my word:* you talk of God being your Father, if he were your Father, ye would love me, because I came from God, as I am truth, and cannot lie, I tell you the truth, and why do ye not believe me? ye are witnesses to your selves what seed ye are, the seed of *Abraham* according to reason, but not according to faith, for *Abraham* saw me not, but believed, and you see me, yea I am he that speak unto you, and yet ye believe not, and that because ye are of your father the devil, that wise, proud, despising seed Reason, the serpent, the god of this world hath blinded your eyes, lest you should see the rise of your misery, or the way to eternal happiness; for you must understand if both these seeds were of the nature of God, then all the world would come to the knowledge of the truth, as in *John 8.47. He that is of God, heareth Gods words, ye therefore hear them not, because ye are not of God.* What say you, Millenaries? what say you, Quakers? and what sayest thou, *Richard Coppin*? with all other of this cursed opinion? do ye not believe the words of Christ the eternal God? do ye not read that all is not of God, therefore of the devil?, so will not come to Christ that they might have life? and why will they not come? because they do not believe that Christ was the Son of God, and why do you not believe? because your light of reason hath blinded your light of faith: and why is your faith blinded? because ye are of the devil: and why are most of the devil? because they should be damned from the knowledge of coming to God who is all Faith, and [no reason.] Now herein appears your madness, that God hath this Prerogative Power.

Therefore hear the words of Christ by his Prophets, crying, *Wo unto him that striveth with his maker, let the potsheard strive with the potsheards of the earth, shall the clay say to him that fashioned it, what makest thou? or thy work he hath no hands? Wo unto him that saith unto his father, What begettest thou? or to the woman, what hast thou brought forth?* O wo unto thee *Richard Coppin,* and the rest of the same faith with thee, that thinketh there is unrighteousness in God, because he hath ordained some to condemnation, and therefore that they may have no hard thoughts of God, they will not believe that ever God did purposely create a man to damn him, for what saith this thiefish brood, it cannot stand with his justice, because an unjust heart saith so, when it is written in *Jude, There are creatures of old ordained to condemnation, and others that are appointed to wrath,* as *I Thes. 5.9. For God hath not appointed us to wrath, but to salvation; from the Lord Jesus,* against all the seed of Reason I affirm, if Christ the onely Father of heaven and earth, by his own divine power had not created a seed to be damned, as well as a seed to be saved: then,

First I demand of thee, why doth the Scripture all along speak of two seeds, as *Cain* and *Abel, Isaac* and *Ishmael, Jacob* and *Esau, Peter* and *Judas,* Salvation and Damnation, Faith and Reason, the one for heaven, and the other for hell, if God and devil were both one seed?

Secondly, If these seeds were but one seed, why art thou troubled with thy secret feares of eternal condemnation, in that then all must be saved, or all must be damned.

Thirdly, If not two, wherein consists the comfort of the righteous, or the misery of the wicked? or how or which way would there be any distinction or difference of the sufferer or oppressor?

Fourthly, If there be two, as there is, what think you, are not you arraigned for thiefs and traitors at the Royal Prerogative Bar of Gods justice, so justly damned?

By that time I have opened these in their order, I know there is none but you that are fighters against Gods eternal power, that dare lift up your hand or tongue against this divine revelation of the onely alone messenger of the Lord Jesus, in whose spiritual breast is all power in heaven and in earth, blessed for ever.

First for the first, if there be but one Seed, why doth the Scripture hold forth two Seeds? and if ye believe not Scripture, you may read it as clear as the Sun at noon, but if ye believe not Scripture, then in vain is it for me to waste pen, ink, & paper, but whether you believe it or no, I matter not, I know what it is, and that to this last Commission onely belongs the interpretation thereof, so you that have eares to hear, forget not, but remember what I say, that as touching that, there is two Seeds, and how they became two, and their natures, with the effects and operations of them, it is so clearly opened, how and wherefore these seeds became two in that Book of mine, entituled, *A Wonder of Wonders,* that I shall not need to encumber the Press with the same relation again, onely I shall give you a breviate of these two Seeds upon another account; that so none of the blessed Seed of the Lord may want revelation to increase their Seed of Faith in this world, it is writ, *Abraham* was grieved that there should be any difference betwixt *Ishmael* and *Isaac,* they being both of his own getting, so both of his own flesh, notwithstanding there was a promise to *Isaac* according to the spirit or seed of faith, yet it is written, *Gen. 17.18 That Abraham requested the Lord that Ishmael might live before him as wel as Isaac,* yet the Lords answer was, *As for Ishmael I have heard thee, behold I have blessed him, & will make him fruitful, and will multiply him exceedingly, twelve princes shall he beget, and I will make him a great nation, but Abraham know this, my covenant will I establish with Isaac whom Sarah shall bear unto thee at this set time in the next year.*

Now all you that have ears to hear may understand, that the promise and covenant of eternal life and happiness was invested upon *Isaac* and his seed, although *Ishmael* was his eldest son; but now you may plead the difference of these Seeds did onely consist as one was of his servant, and the other of his wife, so one a Gentile bond-woman, and the other a Jewish free-woman, and so they are two as in relation to the flesh and not the spirit; but then what will you do with *Esau* and *Jacob,* they were one flesh by father and mother, yea both in one womb, and *Esau* was the elder, yet they were two Nations, and two maner of people, *and the elder shall serve the younger?* for it was revealed unto *Rebecca,* that God hated *Esau* and loved *Jacob,* now was not this eternal love, and eternal hatred, from whence *Esau* was eternally damned, and *Jacob* eternally saved, though not revealed to either of them? for if *Esau* had known what I now write, he might have had more ground then any of you, to upbraid God with cruelty, that before he was capable to think, much more to act any evil, should be damned; I say here was matter enough for *Esau* to have hard thoughts of God, and to reply, and say, Why should I not be saved as well as my brother *Jacob?* what evil have I done more than he? I was begot by a faithful man, and born of a faithful woman, nay, and was the first-born from the same womb as my brother *Jacob* was, so that what justice can be in this God to damn me and save him? truly from the Spirit of All-knowing Faith, against, yea against all the seed of Reason that there is in either angel or man I affirm, that if *Esau* had known what I now write, and should have replied against God as aforesaid, that this, or to this effect had been the answer of God, *Esau,* thou sayest I have not done thee justice, thou canst not tell whether I have or no, for thou knowest not that thou wast dead earth and water, neither dost thou understand that of that dead lump I have made thee this living form, and if all the time of thy life thou hadst pleasure, riches, fame, and honor of this world, which if I had not brought thee into this thou art, thou hadst known none of this, and what if after all this thy greatness, pleasure, mirth and joy, thou shalt never die unto a lump of dead dust again, but die from this mortal pleasant life, to live unto a living never dying death, what is that to thee? canst thou deliver thy self? and may not I do with thee as thou hast done with thy fellow-creatures in the day of thy power? may not I by my power keep thee under eternal death to all eternity, therefore in that I made thee life out of death, I will make thee eternal death out of life, *for this purpose have I raised thee, that I might shew my power in thee,* otherwise where had my Royal Prerogative Power been known, if I had not brought forth another seed, and given it a great power to enconnter with me, the God of all power? I say, if God could not by his word speaking have brought forth another seed contrary to his owne, and so another wisdom and power continually to war and oppose him in his word and people, he had not been known to have been a God commanding all power in heaven and earth whatsoever, neither had there been any mention in the Scripture of two, nor no need of any creation at all, so no necessity of such titles as devil, hell, or damnation.

But this as by experience I know there is two, so I know it was resolved in the spiritual breast of the Lord Jesus, that from the beginning there should be two, and that for this very end and purpose, that Reason in the wisdom and power thereof, might oppose and destroy the wisdom and power of Faith, that so God the power of all Faith might suffer death by Reasons power, that so Reason might know Faith had power to pass through their death to its power of life again, as in the 2d Chapter is proved, and for their so doing, that Reasons power might both know and acknowledge, that God who is the ever-living Power of all Faith, is able to keep Reasons power under eternal death, as it is written, *John 18.37. To this end was I born, and for this cause came I into the world,* to raise my own seed, to live in eternal glory with me, and to keep the contrary seed under a living death to eternal misery.

2. If not two, but one, why then art thou troubled with any secret fears of eternal condemnation? for why, if there be but one, and that one the seed or nature of Gods own body, then all that seed must be saved; but on the contrary if there be but one, and that one the seed or nature of the devil, then all must be damned.

Ans. What ever man doth dream, or by their light of reason imagine that there is but one, and that it lieth in the power of man to make two, however it hath by the Spirit of Faith and letter of Scripture been proved to the contrary, what is the matter then that thou that believest this, art now and then troubled with any secret fears of eternal damnation? for this thou must be sure, if God brought forth but one seed, and that seed the nature of himself, that as God is eternally happy, so must the seed of his own body be likewise happy, and therefore why shouldest thou fear damnation? for it is as unpossible for thee to be damned, as God himself: but on the contrary, if thou believe or imagine that this one seed is of the nature of the devil, then it is in vain to have any hopes of salvation, unless thou conceivest the devil shall be saved, but that thou canst not believe, therefore must absolutely conclude thou must be damned: But now comes in a helpless remedy for a deadly wound, that though God made but one, yet man hath made two out of that one, and so comes in his secret feares of damnation. Do but observe what a Castle thou has built in the Air, that God made but one, that is, all that is good, and thou being man, hast made all that is evil, suppose this were as thou sayest, why shouldst thou trouble thy self with damnation? for if it be as thou sayest, it lieth in thy power to do evil, or leave it, for thou having done more then God, mayst thou please undo it again; and thou knowing it is for sinne that thou must be damned, and sin lieth in thy power to act or no, why then shouldest thou have any secret fears of damnation? surely if salvation were at my disposing, I should not have either secret or publick fears of being eternally damned, for if so, I would take my pleasure to satisfie my lust, and please my minde in all that my heart delights in, so long as I have health I would not cease to do any unjust thing, that thereby I might grow rich, famous, and honorable in this world, for what matter though these be the fruits of damnation, yet it lieth in my power whether I will be damned or no, and therefore when I think that death is at hand, then I will leave off all that is evil. Ah pitiful soul, what filthy cogitations lodgeth in thy heart, that thou hast power, and it lieth in thy power whether thou wilt be damned or no, when thou canst not make a louse, much less save or damn thy own soul: no no, thou shalt to thy cost know, *that it is not in man that runneth, nor in him that willeth, but in God that sheweth mercy; for,* as it is written, *I will have mercy on whom I will have mercy, and whom I will I will harden,* with many such places, and yet what a noise mortality makes that damnation is not from God, but by man; for what say these sad creatures? if God made man purposely to damn him, then it is no matter what man doth, for let man do what good he can, if ordained for damnation, he must be damned, and if we do never so much evil, we can but be damned; therefore saith these men, this doctrine will lead men to all manner of filthiness. To which I answer, Though in some measure it is true what thou hast said, yet it doth not follow that thereby man will take liberty to sin, and that because none of you knoweth who are appointed for damnation, and who for salvation, so your ignorance in this Prerogative Power of God, will rather keep you under obedience, and make all men strive to do righteous things before God and man, and thereby you may prevent the damnation of thy soul; but if it were in thy power as aforesaid, then it were an encouragement to take liberty to sin: but as this secret lodgeth in the breast of the Lord Jesus, therefore man no knowing how he becomes damned, his ignorance in this is that which causeth many secret fears, lest he should not walk worthy of the favour of God in point of salvation: But,

3. If not two, wherein then would consist the comfort of the righteous, or misery of the wicked? or what difference would there be of the persecuted and persecutor?

An. For my part I cannot tell what difference there would be between a murtherer, adulterer, a thief, a drunkard, a swearer, or a liar, and an upright, just, harmless, innocent soul, if not two: what difference then between God and devil, heaven and hell, salvation and damnation, yea what matter is it for faith or Reason if all be one Seed, and what comfort is it for me to leave my trade of preaching, by which I might have lived very honorably and comfortably in this perishing world, when as now the short time I have to stay in Reasons kingdom, I shall be in wants, and undergo bad reports, yea imprisoned, if not put to death, I say what comfort can a soul here enjoy, if there were but one Seed? Of these sort *Paul* met withall in his dayes, that would have no resurrection, so no devil, but all God, for if none shall be raysed, then none shall be saved, nor none shall be damned, so that well might *Paul* with me say, *If in this life onely we have hope in Christ, we are of all men most miserable,* to lose our maintenance, our good name, to be reproached, to be in want, yea to forsake all the riches, honor, and pleasure of this world, that we might with reason have enjoyed; if but one seed, then miserable are our days, and happy are the days of the wicked, that is clad in silk and scarlet, and hath his coaches and servants to attend him, that hath no want, but fullness what heart can desire to enjoy, I say if not two, there would be no difference between the opressor and sufferer, and then might we, as Reason hath and dayly doth in this his kingdom, watch all opportunities to pull down others, and so set up our selves, for why the time present would be the onely power, the onely happiness, or the onely misery, and so the wisest head-peece of reason, would be the onely god, the onely heaven, and the onely glory, that would be for ever after: But,

Fourthly and lastly, if there be two, as two to your eternal sorrow you shall one day know, what think you then, are you not arraigned for thiefs and traitors at the Royal Prerogative Bar of Gods justice, so justly damned?

An. What ever you the seed of Reason believe, or from the imagination of your heart suppose, yet this I assuredly know, whether you believe Scripture or no, or whether you own what I write now or no, I matter not, yet from Christ Jesus the Resurrection of all souls, I declare unto you, that whosoever cannot believe, that the salvation and damnation of all soules floweth from the Royal Prerogative Power of God, without any relation to either good or evil done by thee, let me tell thee, and yet not I, but the seed of Gods own body in me, that thou art a thief, yea a spiritual thief, for thou hast in thy thoughts robbed Christ of his glory, which he hath so often said he will not give to another, no not to man or angel, and yet thou pitiful poor mortal soul, thou dost reply against God, in that thou wouldest not have such a thought of God, that he should create a soul to damn it, and so becomes a rebellious traitor, in that thou wilt assume damnation into thy own power, as aforesaid, and upon this account stands guilty before the Divine Justice of God, shut up in darkness of unbelief till the day of resurrection; at which day thou shalt be raised all reason, and no faith, where then on this earth thy soul shall be thy devil, and thy body thy hell, shut up close prisoners to all eternity, and these thy thoughts, words, and actions, shall be the dreadful accusing fiery Law that shall never quench, no never, never end.

For this ye faithful of the Lord may be confident, as by the eye of faith I see perfected in my soul, that so long as a subject stands questioning with a king then in being, of his Prerogative Power, that man at last will query his head from his shoulders, then how much more mayest thou expect, that dares attempt to call God to an account as touching his Royal, Eternal, Prerogative Power, that hath all power in heaven and earth, to do with his creature what he will? who shall question him, or by a Law try him for injustice, when he made heaven and earth, with all creatures in them, and gave a Law for man to be obedient to him? I wonder man should not tremble at any such thought of God, therefore this know, that soul that cannot believe this, and so yield to the Royal Prerogative Power of God in this, shall be eternally damned by this; for all Scriptures that are seemingly against this, you do not understand concerning this, as now by the spirit of Faith shall be infallibly interpreted, for the confirmation of this point in hand, as you have it written, *who will have all men to be saved, and come to the knowledge of the truth, for as I live, saith the Lord God, I have no pleasure in the death of the wicked;* and so he confirms it again, that they should rather turn and live, and there it is written, *Turn ye, turn ye from your evil ways, for why will ye die, O house of Israel?*

Now here seemes to be a flat contradiction to all that I have written in the precedent matter, therefore I shall reveal what death this is the Lord hath no pleasure in, and what not, that so you may not, as your fore-fathers have done, count the ways of the Lord unequal, for want of understanding herein, the Freewillers have to their own destruction made the Royal Prerogative Power of God of no effect.

Concerning this it is written, *Deut.30.19. I call heaven and earth to record this day, that I have set before you life and death, blessing and cursing, therefore choose life that both thou and thy seed may live.* Now ye rebels, what say you, have you not your desire? that before you have so much cavelled about you have a law, which if you keep you shall live by it, but if ye break it, ye shall be destroyed; as observe, *if ye be willing and obedient ye shall live,* that is, ye shall eat the good of the land, but if *ye refuse and rebel, ye shall die,* that is, ye shall be destroyed by the sword; as touching this death the Lord hath no pleasure, but that all the house of *Israel* should keep his Law and be saved, and if they were destroyed they might blame themselves, for they had a Law according to their own desire, which they did promise to keep, as *Deut. 5.27. Speak thou unto us all that the Lord our God shall speak unto thee, and we will hear it, and obey it,* but they were as *Isaiah 30.9.* which if they had performed they had not died; and if possible they might live and not die, he caused the Law to be daily read unto them, and to exhort them again and again, that they might not forget, but walk obedient thereunto: now where-as it is written, *As I live saith the Lord God, I have no pleasure in the death of the wicked,* was as I told you, *that the fig-tree should not blossom, neither shall fruits be in the vines, the labor of the olive shall fail, and the fields shall yield no meat, the flock shall be cut off from the fold, and there shall be no herd in the stall, but their goods shall become a booty, and their houses a desolation:* this is the death and destruction that Christ Jesus hath no pleasure in, as it is written, *Luke 19. And when he was come near, he behold the City and wept over it, saying, if thou hadst known, even thou, at least in this thy day the things which belong unto thy peace, but now they are hid from thine eyes:* these, with many such like places, do all threaten an external death, as unto the death of their bodies, their goods, and their cattel, the Lord hath no pleasure, but as from this death he would have all men to be preserved; which if they had observed his statutes and ordinances, it had been will with them, but as they did not, I will ruinate them from the face of the earth, and therefore attend and give ear thou cavelling rebellious spirit, unto the words of *Isaiah 5.3. Against the inhabitants of Jerusalem, and ye men of Judah, saying, Judge, I pray you, betwixt me and my vineyard, I fenced it, and gathered out the stones thereof, and planted it with the choicest vine, and built a tower in the midst of it, and also made a wine-press therein, so that what could I have done more to my vineyard that I have not done? and yet for all this when I looked for grapes, behold it brought forth wilde grapes, yea whereas he looked for judgement, but behold oppression; for righteousness, but behold a cry; they called good evil, and evil good, darkness light, and light darkness, they are wise in their own eyes, and prudent in their own sight, and did justifie the wicked for a reward, and took away the righteousness of the righteous from him:* Now what could the Lord do less then to send them to Captivity, and utterly destroy them tall and branch? which if they had kept his Law, he had continued his mercy, *for as I live I had no desire to sell them to the hands of the Heathens.*

 Therefore *Richard Coppin,* and the rest of the free-willers with thee, what advantage can you reap from this? or wherein can you finde that the eternal death of all soules is not reserved in the spiritual breast of the Lord Jesus, though you say it lieth in your power to commit evil or no? yet let me tell you, very few of you can so far keep the Law, so as to perserve your selves from prison, but for all your power of freedom in the flesh, you are now and then curbed by a power of flesh, but however you may now and then escape this, yet minde what I say, you can no ways free or deliver your selves from eternal death, though you shall never know how nor which way it comes, no not any of you that shall be damned, shall but onely understand that your destruction is of your selves, though I know the rise of your damnation is from the Royal Prerogative power of God, as is confirmed by *Isaiah 6.10. Make the heart of this people fat, and make their ears heavy, and shut their eyes, lest they see with their eyes, and hear with their ears, and understand with their hearts, and convert and be healed.* So likewise you read *Rom. 11.7,8. that God hath given them the spirit of slumber, eyes that they should not see, and ears that they should not hear unto this day; what then? Israel hath not attained that which he seeketh for, but election hath obtained it, and the rest were blinded,* and yet, as *Isaiah 10.15. shall the ax boast himself against him that heweth therewith? or shall the sawe magnifie it self against him that shaketh it? Or as if the rod should shake itself against them that take it up? Or as the staff should life up it self as though it were no wood:* So as *Isaiah* said to your fathers, so I say unto you, as if it lay in your power to damn or save your soules, you boast your selves against Christ Jesus the Lord of glory, as thou *Richard Coppin* in thy last Book lately printed, and before a friend of ours at *East-maulden* in *Kent,* thou declaredst, that the cause wherefore thou writest or preachest against the Ministers of *England,* was to preach down their preaching: why, what is the matter? is *Ephraim* against *Manasseh,* and *Manasseh* against *Ephraim?* what, will you by the name of Belzeebub cast down devils? O friend, it is unpossible, for they have a Call to preach, and you have none, they can pray and preach better then you, and are a little nearer the truth then you, so that you cannot preach down their preaching, but thou must preach down thy self, for you have one God, and one devil, one hell, and one heaven: But may be thou wouldest preach downe their Tithes, and what then? must they wander up and down the Countrey with you, and take the benevolence of men and women, as you do? therefore cease their pen against them, and write against thy self, you being all Non-commissionate, so not sent to preach, therefore ought not to judge one another, you being carnal, and not spiritual, reason, and not faith, cannot judge with righteous judgement, for that alone belongs to our Commission, the spiritual revelation thereof judgeth all things, yet cannot be judged of any; and therefore mind what I say unto thee, even the same that I have said of the Quakers, that though thou canst not now believe it, yet when it is too late thou shalt find the truth of what I now write unto thee, as thou canst not love a woman that is onely a spirit without a body, so no more can that god be believed that is a spirit without a body; for if a woman could be no more felt or embraced then a spirit, there would not be so much adultery as there is among the seed of Reason. So to conclude, take notice what I say unto thee, and all of the same faith with thee, that so many of you that lives and dies in that belief of thine, will both soul and body perish to all eternity.

Post-script.

Reader, when this comes to thy view, do not peruse it lightly, but solidly; read it over again and again, for as in the first Chapter thou shalt finde this is the revelation of the last Commission, that was sent forth by voyce of words from the glorious mouth of the Lord Jesus, as Moses and the Apostles were, therefore being spiritual, hath power to judge all Dispensations that shall either act or threaten to persecute the Author, or burn the said revelation, with eternal sentence for ever.

FINIS

A Paradisical Dialogue Betwixt Faith and Reason:

Disputing
The high mysterious Secrets of Eternity,
the live never extant in our Revelation.

As touching God in eternity, how he became time
in flesh, how he dyed in the grave, and
ascended to his glory again.

Also
What the Angels are in form and nature, and how the Angel
became a Devil, and that Devil man; and that this
World was prepared for the Devil, so this the Devils
Kingdom; and what the Soul is, with the place
of its glory and torment.

With a brief Narration what a Commission is, and how many Commissions there are; what the difference of their worships, and how that the Law was given to the Devil; with a brief discourse on the Catechism, the Lords Prayer, and the Creeds; as also, a Divine Prospect to the Elect of the Lord.

Written by *Law. Claxton*, the onely true Bishop and faithful Messenger of Christ Jesus, Creator of Heaven and earth.

London, Printed for the Author, and are to be sold by *William Learner*, at the *Blackmoor* near *Fleet-bridge*, 1660.

INDEX

Chap. I   *Shewing whether God be a Spirit without a body, or that God is a body of flesh and bone glorified.*

Chap. 2   *Shewing whether the Father became not a Son, which Son was Christ, and by death became a Father to all Eternity, now in heaven glorified.*

Chap. 3   *Shewing Christ is the onely God and Father, Creator of Heaven and earth, now it is to be revealed what God and Father that was, and where he was, that Christ so often called upon, when he was upon earth.*

Chap. 4   *Shewing whether the Angels were the first that God created and of what he created them, with their nature and form, and what was the cause of the Angels fall above all the rest.*

Chap. 5   *Shewing whether this world was before the Angels or no and whether this World was made of something, or nothing, and how it came into form and being, and whether it shall for ever thus remain.*

Chap. 6   *Shewing of what matter* Adams *body was created, and what was his nature, soul or spirit, and by what means he came to lose that estate he was created in.*

Chap. 7   *Shewing who it was that tempted* Eve *and* Adam, *whether it was the Angel aforesaid; and if so, why is he called a Serpent, Beast, or Tree, &c. and how and which way they were deceived and what effect it hath ever since produced.*

Chap. 8   *Shewing whether* Cain *was not the first Devil, and who are his seed or children, and what Devils those were, so frequently spoken of in Scripture*

Chap. 9   *Shewing what the soul is, and what it is that dyes, how that it is none but the soul which is the life of the body that can dye.*

Chap. 10 *Shewing what Heaven is, and how many heavens there are, what the nature and form thereof.*

Chap. 11. *Shewing what Hell is, and where it is, what the form and nature of its torment.*

Chap. 12. *Shewing what Authority and Commissioner hath in the vertue of his Commission, what the effects and operations thereof.*

Chap. 13. *Shewing what the Law is at large, and in short, and whether any can keep the Law, and when he is said to keep the Law, and when not.*

Chap. 14. *Shewing whether that prayer doth not belong to all and whether by prayer we may come to the knowledge of God, and whether it is our duty to make use of the Lords prayer?*

Chap. 15. *Shewing whether there be any truth in the faith of the Church of England, expressed in the Creeds or Articles recorded.*

Chap. 16. *Shewing in eighteen Propositions, the invincible mighty great Authority that is intrusted with a Divine Commissioner: Also, an eternal whip or scourge for the Quakers, for belying the Holy Ghost.*

A PARADISTICAL DIALOGUE BETWIXT FAITH AND REASON:

Disputing the high Mysterious Secrets of Eternity, the like never yet extant in our Revelation.

CHAP. 1.

Shewing whether God be a Spirit without a body, or that God is a body of flesh and bone glorified.

Friend, having such a convenient opportunity to have some conference with you, my request is, to know your judgement as touching the true God, and that the more in this distracted age: There are so many opinions concerning him, That some holds him forth an Infinite Spirit, &c. other say, Though God be a Spirit, yet there are three Persons in the Godhead, the Father, the Son, and the Holy Ghost, and these three are one God, the same in Substance, equal in Power and Glory: Now if thou please, let me hear what thy judgement is of God Almighty.

Faith. Notwithstanding this hodg-podg, it matters not me, what thou or all the wise men of the world hold: For from the Spirit of Revelation I infallibly against men and Angels affirm, That God the Creator of Heaven and earth is in the Person and Form of a man.

Reason. How? is it possible that God the Creator of all forms, should admit a form of his own?

Faith. I say, unless that Divine heavenly Faith or Nature, had a Form or Person of his own, he could not have created man after his own form, image, or likeness.

Reason. Yea, I grant *God created man after his own image in righteousness and holiness*, but no otherwise.

Faith.   Ah pitiful, Soul, how thy riches choaks thee, and thy wisdom blinds thee from believing in the true God, that thou shouldst conceive, that righteousness or holiness can be created without a form! or didst thou ever read or hear of any holiness in any other creature but man onely; so that thou canst not say this or that is holiness without a form, and that the form of man above.

Reason.   What necessity, or what ground can be shown, that God who is the Creator of all forms, should admit of a form his own?

Faith.   It was the greatest ground of all; for if God had not a form of his own, it had been in vain to create either Angel or man, in his form, and that because he created them to behold his glorious person.

Reason.   Why, cannot the glory of God be seen, unless he admit of a Person? and what matter of glory can be delighted onely in a single Person; for I conceive him more glorious when he is a Spirit without a body; for then he can fill Heaven and Earth with his glory, and every creature that he hath made then beholds it, in that they enjoy part of it.

Faith.   I say, no glory can be seen without a Personal Substance; nay, it cannot bear the title of glory without a body; for the glorious Spirit that ever was, if it had not a body, were nothing at all, in that a Spirit cannot be seen, so no delight in that which is not; for what delight could man have with his wife, if she had no person? And whereas thou sayest, God having a Person, cannot fill Heaven and earth with his glory, I say, without his Person he could fill nothing at all: As for instance, what glory can there be in a King without a person? whose person being enthroned in his Crown and Dignity, with all things suitable to his Majestie, is that which fills his Court and Kingdom with renowned glory; not that the Kings person is in every place, but onely in his Court, yet the hearts of his subjects over all his Dominions, is filled with the report of his great power and glory: so that the sound thereof, as *Solomons*, doth ring of the glory and greatness of his person; so it is not the person of God, but his powerful nature, flowing in the hearts of his people, that supports all things created by him; neither is his person in any other place but his Kingdom of glory onely.

Reason.   If God admit of a form, that God is not infinite, but finite, and so is not in every creature he hath made: And if so, how will this stand with those sayings, *In him we live, move, and have our being:** Now from hence I conceive, God is in every creature by his

---

* Acts 17. 28.

Spirit; and hath no form of his own, but lives in all forms that he hath made.

Faith. Did I not know thee, I should admire at the ignorance; but however, I shall exactly answer thy Question, that God was in the form of man, before he became flesh in the same image and likeness as now he is, though then he was not flesh and bone, as now he is; yet as he is now, so he was then a flame of bright burning glory, that no Chrystal or Sun can stand before him; yea, his body is softer then down, and swifter then thought; and with that body so glorious, can ascend or descend in his Kingdom of glory; that he can be infinite as he pleaseth, and yes when he will, can confine his Godhead glorious, Majestical Person, to as narrow a compass as any man; which if, as thou saith, God had no body but a Spirit, and that Spirit in every creature, then God were finited and limited indeed, that the Creator of Heaven and earth should be imprisoned in thy mortal, corrupt, sinful body; nay, not only so, but God was in Horses, Hoggs, Dogs, Toads, Snakes, Spiders, and all other creatures, which if it were as thou saith, God were the worst of all creatures that he made: Nay, if it were so, then from my Seed Spring I say, God is no Creator, but a deformrd, sick, weary, sinful creature like thy self: And as for those sayings, *In him we live, move and have our being,** is thus to be understood, that a true believer, as *Paul* was that spake it, doth by faith live, move and have their being from the first word of faith that created *Adam*, and not from any in-dwelling of God in him; as it is written, *Christ in you the hope of glory*; and, *Know ye not, that Christ is in you, except ye be Reprobates,* is not thereby intended, that God or Christ, as he is a person, is in you; but as Paul saith, *Christ dwells in our hearts by faith:* It is faith which is the nature of God of which I am partaker of, and by which it evidenceth in my soul, where God is, and what God is, both in form and nature.

Reason. Thou faith, God hath both form and nature; if so, his form and nature must be one, and if one, cannot be divided; so he that hath one, must have both, therefore it will follow, where the nature of God is, there God must be himself; for I conceive they cannot be separated, in that it is written, *That they all may be one, as thou Father art in me, and I in thee, that they also may be one in us*[†], &c. and again it is written, Jacob said, *Surely the Lord is in this place, and I knew it not*[‡]; so that I conclude, God is in all creatures.

---

[*] This is no Scripture of faith. Acts 17. 28. But a Poets judgement in reason. 2 Cor 13. 5.
[†] John 17. 21.
[‡] Gen 28. 16.

Faith. Though the nature be in the form, yet it is not the form; and therefore it is written, *That by these you might be partakers of the Divine Nature**; though not the form: As instance, the Sun shines upon the just and unjust, yet the body is in the firmament; we feel the vertue or nature of the body of the Sun, by its heat and light, yet we have not the Sun; so in my Soul I have the nature of God, but not the form or body of God; and therefore it is written, *I am the vine, and ye are the branches†*, that is, I am the vine and body of faith, and ye have the branch or nature of faith; so by my nature ye abide stedfast in me, and I in you: *As the branch cannot bear fruit of itself except it abide in the Vine, no more can ye except ye abide in me,* by that nature flowing from me; and therefore it is written, *Christ dwelleth in my heart by faith, by which Christ is in me the hope of glory‡*: and if I know not that Christ is thus in me, *I were a reprobate;* not in me by his body, but by his faith God or Christ is in me.

Reason. What then is God in his person in heaven above the stars, and his nature in thee here below? then to me it is clear God and his nature is parted, and so God looseth part of himself, which to me is contrary to reason, so not to be believed.

Faith. However, it is so to thee, yet I know that God is in his glory and nature here below in mortals, (so really parted) and yet no damage to God at all, no more then a Fountain to cast out a Floodgate of streams, and yet retain its fullness in its self; so the eternal Godhead, fountain of all endless glory can stream, yea, hath streamed into all the seed of his own body, such a Well-spring of eternal Assurance, that all that are partakers thereof, have perfect peace and belief in God the fountain of endless Glory, and yet God all fullness in himself, as *David* saith, *With thee is the Fountain of Life§*: and Christ said to the woman of Samaria, *Whosoever drinketh of the water that I shall give him, shall never thirst; but the water that I shall give him shall be a Well of water springing up to everlasting life; For in him dwelleth all the fullness of the Godhead bodily, yea Christ is all in all***. So that I affirm it is no more loss to God to distribute his eternal Light into his creature, then for the Sun to give light to the face of the earth, and yet retain its essential light in its own body; for as *Jacob* in his Vision saw a Ladder upon the earth, and the top of it reached to heaven, and behold the Angels of God ascending and descending, and behold the Lord stood above it, and said, I am the Lord, it is no more but what *Stephen* and *Paul* saw by revelation of their Faith; as several

---

* 2 Pet. 1. 4.
† John 15.
‡ Verse 4
§ Col. 2. 9.
** John 4.

times I have seen in my own Soul, as the Tide doth ebb and flow into the Ocean, so doth the Revelation of Faith ascend and descend, beholding the glorious throne of Eternity with unspeakable rapture, not utterable by pen or tongue.

Reason. I cannot understand how God being a person, and yet a Fountain of endless Glory, should fill heaven and earth, in that a person is finite in one place, and heaven and earth is large, so that if Gods glory be in every place then there his person must be also.

Faith. Dost thou not see in nature that one fountain doth supply many families; how much more then can the Eternal Fountain supply many Souls with that heavenly divine water, and yet from his single person in heaven glorified; and as that fountain from *Ware* is directed to supply the necessity of *London,* and yet the head spring keeps its place, so doth the fountain of Eternal glory retain itself in its being, and yet fills heaven and earth with its streams of glory.

Reason. Thou sayest, God is onely in heaven, and yet it is written, *the heaven of heavens cannot contain God,* he is of such a large infinite vastness, and spiritual bulk or bigness, that not onely heaven, but earth also must be his habitation, and therefore it is written *that with a humble and contrite Spirit God will dwell:* And again it is written, *Heaven is his throne, and the earth his footstool: And the earth is the Lords, and the fullness thereof.* So that I believe God is not onely in heaven, but earth also; so that from these and many other places, I judge thou limitest the unlimited God, and so makest him that is infinite in heaven and earth to be finite onely in heaven, and that in one single person of his own.

Faith. Thou takest upon thee to prove thy reason by Scripture, when Scripture were never written for thee, neither doth it belong to thee, as in its place thou shalt hear, and therefore have patience and I shall interpret the meaning of those Scriptures. First thou sayest, *the heaven of heavens cannot contain God*,* and yet it is written, *whom the heavens must receive till the restitution of all things*[†]. Now when Faith compares these two together, it knows the truth of one from the other; for when I consider *Solomon* endued with thy wisdom & that he spake those words not experimentally but dubiously, as minde the 27 verse, and then peruse that chapter, and thou shalt finde it in three several places recorded thus: *And hear thou in heaven thy dwelling place:* how should heaven be Gods dwelling place, if heaven of heavens cannot contain him? So that in truth those words of the Apostles who were endued with the spirit of

---

* I Kings 8. 27.
† Acts 3. 21.

revelation is to be believed when *Solomons* cannot, in that he spake not by revelation, but from the intricate promise of God to his father *David*. And in the same chapter he acknowledgeth Gods dwelling-place to be in heaven, and not in the temples and where it is written, *with an humble and contrite heart God will dwell,* is not there intended God will dwell in my heart by his person, but by faith, as it is written, *that Christ may dwell in your hearts by faith** &c. as minde the words of the Prophet, *Thus saith the high and lofty One that inhabiteth Eternity, whose name is Holy, I dwell in the high and holy place,* by my person there I dwell, and by my faith in an humble heart; and where it is written, *Heaven is my throne, and the earth is my footstool†,* do still confirm that God hath a body, otherwise what should he do with a throne or a footstool? But now to convince thee, that it is not to be understood this earth, but that glorious earth above the stars, where God, when he pleaseth, doth stand as firm & in as narrow a compass, as I do upon this earth: *And that the earth is the Lords, and the fullness thereof,* is not by me denied, but that it is the Lords by creation; For God by his person is not in this world, but by his Law or powerful word of creation, therefore faith *David, Whom have I in heaven but thee?* So that it is no limitation, but his infiniteness to be in heaven, and not in this earth at all.

Reason. Notwithstanding all this, I cannot understand how God should be in the person or form of a man, but there must be some other above him that must create God in that form.

Faith. Though thou canst not understand, yet to me it is revealed, that God without beginning had a form, and none but Divine Nature did create himself Creator, and yet he knew not how he came to have his being.

Reason. O admiration! what shall I say of thee? that God should not know how he came to be God: by this thou makest God finite, yea ignorant of things past, present, and to come.

Faith. Say what thou pleasest, yet this I will tell thee, that it is the nature of infiniteness not to know itself, for that which knows things past, present, and to come, is not infinite, but finite, in that there is an end of any further knowledge; but the infiniteness is to know no beginning, nor no ending: for if he had known how he came in being, then he would know his ending, and so in process of time cease to be God Eternal.

---

* Eph 3. 17.
† Psal 14. 1.

Reason. I have read in *Revelation 1**that it is written, *I am Alpha and Omega, the beginning and the ending, which is, which was, and which is to come the Almighty,* so that from thence I understand that God had a beginning, and knew how he came to have his being.

Faith. Thou hast read, but dost not understand what thou readest, as observe it is not there intended, I am the beginning and ending of my self, but this is the meaning: I am the beginning and end of the Creation, so that without me the world with all creatures therein, had no beginning, nor no ending without me; as unto this I am Alpha and Omega, and neither the beginning or ending of this world is hid from me, for by my knowledge it came in being, and so must have its ending; but as unto infiniteness or eternity, *It is without beginning or ending of dayes;* and the not knowing either it beginning or ending, is that which makes it eternal, and yet there is nothing done but what flowes in the glorious body of God.

Reason. Notwithstanding this, I am not satisfied that God admits of a Form, but a Spirit onely, for it is written, *God is a Spirit, and they that worship him, must worship him in Spirit and Truth*[†]; and then it is written, *Feel me, a Spirit hath not flesh and bone as ye see me have;* So that it is clear God is a Spirit without flesh and bone, so an infinite Spirit onely.

Faith. As God is a Spirit, so man is a Spirit also, and yet the Nature, Soul, or Spirit of either God, Angel or Man, cannot be worshipped without a body, for there is no Spirit whether immortal or mortal, celestial or terrestial, but it hath its own body, and that sutable to its own nature: as if its Spirit be an immortal glorious Spirit, so is his body immortal glorious also, and if its Spirit be mortal earthly, so is his body mortal earthly also; and this I say, all bodies whether of God, Man or Beast, are invisible, and seeth that which is without, yet it self cannot be seen by any outward sight; For who seeth the Spirit of a man, save he that hath it? So that I say, if God were a Spirit without body, he could not be seen; so not worshipped, no more than a Kings Spirit without a body could be honored; and therefore God being a spiritual body, must be worshipped in Spirit: And where thou sayest, *Feel me for a Spirit hath no flesh and bone, as ye see me have;* I say, from those words of the Lord Jesus, it doth not in the least conclude that a Spirit is not cloathed with flesh and bone; for I affirm the Apostles, as well as other, were dark in many things till Christ was glorified, they supposing that Spirits might be seen without bodies, and that by the eye of nature; therefore Christ walking upon the Sea, and appearing among them, the Doors and Windows

---

* Rev 1. 8.
† John 4.

being shut, was the main cause of their sudden fear, supposing they had seen a Spirit; so that for the future and clearer satisfaction, Christ tells them a Spirit hath not flesh and bone as ye see me have, though I be all Spirit, yet feel me, and behold my wounds and the print of my nails; so that understand a Spirit without flesh and bone cannot be seen or felt, unless a spiritual body; so that against Angels and all thy seed I affirm, that God, that Christ which said to the woman of *Samaria,* God was a Spirit, I say that self same Spirit was not in Heaven, but in Christs body alone.

CHAP. 2.

Shewing whether the Father became not a Son, which Son was Christ, and by death became a Father to all Eternity, now in Heaven glorified.

Thou hast told me all along that God hath a body in the form of man; and now thou sayest, that the Spirit of God was in Christs body, and not in the body of God the Father, Where then was the body of God when his Spirit was in Christ?

Faith. I shall affirm that as the Spirit of God was in Christ, so the body of Christ was the body of God, Creator of Heaven and Earth, not two but one, yea the very self-same body.

Reason. Oh Friends! this is a strange saying indeed, that the body of God the Father should be in the person of Christ, If so, how or which way came he down from Heaven to Earth? it is so mysterious that it is beyond my reach or understanding.

Faith. What is strange to thee is familiar with me, for thou reads and understands not, though it is frequently written in Scripture, *That Eternity was to become time;* yea, immortality was to become mortal, which is no less, that the Father was to become a Son, as it is written, *The seed of the Woman shall bruise the head of the Serpent**; and to *Esaiah*† it was revealed these sayings, *For unto us a Child is born, and unto us a Son is given, and his Name shall be called wonderful Counsellour, the Mighty God, the Everlasting Father, the Prince of Peace;* and again it is written, *In the beginning was the Word, and the Word was with God, and the word was God, which word was made flesh, and dwelt amongst men*‡; So that I affirm the coming

---

* Gen 3.
† Esay 9. 6.
‡ Joh. 1. 1,2

down of the immortal personal God was clouded in those sayings, *The holy Ghost shall come upon thee, and the Power of the Highest shall overshadow thee; therefore also the holy thing that shall be born of thee, shall be called the Son of God*[*].

Reason.   I do not deny the truth of those sayings, but do believe that Christ was the Son of God, conceived by the holy Ghost, but how or which way God was this Son, I cannot tell, neither do I believe that God did any more unto her then he did unto *Adam*, when he made him a living Soul, the Scripture saith, *He breathed unto him, and he became a living Soul;* so in the same manner I conceive God breathed into *Mary*, and by that breath she conceived the Seed of God in her womb, and so she not knowing of man, called him the Son of God, and not God, for God was in Heaven when he was upon the Earth.

Faith.   From my Seed-spring I say, that the Childe that was conceived in the womb of *Mary* so called a Son, *was the Mighty God, the Everlasting Father, and Prince of Peace;* yes, that Babe in her womb, was the very God; *For the Word was God and became flesh,* and who was the Power of the Highest that overshadowed *Mary*, but God Creator of Heaven and Earth: take notice that the knowledge of these sayings was not to be revealed to thy Seed, for saith the Prophet, *Unto us, yea unto us Prophets and the Messengers of the Lord, a Son is given, and a Child is born;* and therefore thou canst not tell, how God the Creator should become a Son and Saviour, but imagines God as he was a Spirit breathed into her womb as he breathed into *Adam*, and so by that breath she conceived a man-child; as touching this, I tell thee, there is great difference of a living and a dying Seed, for by that breath *Adam* became life, and by her overshadowing she was not made alive, but had a conception in her living womb; now there can be no conception without a Seed, and that Seed must first dye before it quicken to life again, as it is written, *Before the Wheat grain dye it abideth alone:* So that against Angels above, and all their Seed below, I affirm, as from the Scriptures before is proved, that God the Creator in the form of a man, who is the onely Power of the Highest, did descend from his Throne and Kingdom as swift as thought, and his whole body pierced through her secrets in a Trance, and in a moment dissolved into Seed, and there died from an immortal Father, and quickned there to a mortal Son, of flesh, blood and bone, so called Christ Jesus the Saviour of the world.

Reason.   Oh admiration! this is a report of astonishment, that for my part I never never read or by the hearing of the ear ever heard till now, that God in the form of a man should as thou sayest, with that form descend from Heaven, and for ought I know, of a large

---

[*] Luke 1. 35.

proportion and bigness as thy self, enter the womb of *Mary;* and the greatest wonder of all is, that God with a body as big as thine should descend like lightning from Heaven, and pierce through her secrets as thou sayest in a moment, and yet not be seen by any, nor she stand amazed, yea trembling in fear at so sudden appearance and dissolution of this swift motional substance into her body, for my part I cannot understand it, neither will Scripture prove it, so cannot believe it.

Faith. Well may his dissolution into the womb cause admiration, when at his birth, which was no strange thing, there should be such a multitude of Heavenly Host rejoicing with such Heavenly Harmonies; that the Shepherds were amazed with fear, yes a wonder it was to them that heard of it far and near, which if there had not been a conception more than ordinary, the birth of that conception had not caused such astonishment round about; but now God was become a Child, yea Eternity become time, and for a season to dwell among his Creation; and therefore if thou knew that the body of God was of a bright, glorious, Chrystal, soft, thin, transparent substance, swifter than thought, who at his Divine pleasure can transmute himself as high or as low, and into as a straight a passage as can be thought on, then thou wouldst cease reasoning, and believe what I speak to thee, that the body of God consisting of such Divine, Spiritual and Heavenly matter as aforesaid, could without the sight of any descend from Heaven to *Mary*; And why or wherefore should she be amazed, when she had tidings of what should be before? Neither was his dissolution any prejudice at all to her, but raptures of joy springing up in her Soul to her Eternal comfort.

Reason. What then was all the God that created Heaven and Earth in the womb of *Mary*? and was that the very God that was born in a Manger, that was swadled, suckled and dandled upon the knees, and carried up and down the Countrey in the Armes of his Mother? was this God the Father, that created all things, that now hath life in them, that once could not go nor feed himself, but be led and fed by its creature? As unto this, answer me plainly and really what is the thought on this great mysterious Mystery.

Faith. From the Spirit of Revelation I tell thee, that was the very God that the Wise Men went to worship, and that *Herod* did seek to kill, was the very Godhead, Spirit or Life of that Christ Jesus; so that *Pauls* Revelation told him, *The fullness of the Godhead dwelt in Christs body, and God was in Christ reconciling the world*[*], with many such places; and therefore the words that Christ spake[†] *was Spirit*

---

[*] Col 2. 9.
[†] Joh 8. 24.

and Life; and again saith Christ, *Except ye believe that I am he, ye shall dye in your sins;* So that if the Eternal God-head had not sprung up this Revelation, he could not have uttered those sayings as his own.

Reason.   However thou hast quoted some certain places that confirm what thou sayest, yet I cannot find but all along as I read, God and Christ is two, and not one; so that there was a God in Heaven when Christ was upon earth; and me thinks it is contrary to reason, that God which created all Creatures, should walk, talk, eat and drink with them, and be affronted by them, and as it were have his livelihood by them that he created.

Faith.   Well Friend, think of it what thou pleasest, yet this I'le assure thee, that God and Christ is not two, but one; For what necessity was there for God to have a Son? Surely, if it were as thou sayest, either God was in process of time to dye, and so make his Son Heir, or else he wanted a Companion to keep him Company; if not so, then the world was too great, and so got a Son to assist him; yet however, I tell thee there never was but one God: And surely then he that died for us, must save us; and if Christ be our Saviour, then he must be our Creator; and yet what striving here is for two Gods, when in the beginning of *Moses* and the Prophets we read but of One, as it is written, *Before me there was no God formed, neither shall there be after, I, even I, am the Lord, and besides me there is no Saviour*[*]; and then confirms it, saying, *Neither is there Salvation in any other, for there is none other Name under Heaven given among men whereby we must saved*[†]; and yet what a flutter thy seed makes about God and Christ, so two Gods, as though one God should Create, and the other God should Save; O for shame leave off these things, and be silent in thy ignorance, for thy seed is so various, that some of you will have God a Spirit, and Christ the Son a Person, and others of you will have three persons and one God, and the rest will have no Person at all, but an infinite formless Spirit; so that from my Revelation I tell thee, and all thy seed with thee, as by the Prophet *Isaiah* is proved, there was no God formed before Christ, nor never shall be after him; yet this I know, there is three titles, & but one person, which person ever was, is, and shall be Christ Jesus alone; for Christ had the title of God the Father in the Law, and the title of God the Son in the Gospel, and now God the holy Ghost in this our last commission, to which is onely revealed the Christ Jesus is the onely God.

Reason.   Then tell me what was that which died in Christ when he was crucified, and said, now it is finished, and gave up the Ghost?

---

[*] Isaiah 4. 10,11.
[†] Acts 4. 12.

Faith.   That was, he gave up his Soul to death, which Soul was the Eternal Spirit, or Godhead Father; and therefore it is written, *He poured out his Soul to death, and was offered through the Eternal Spirit**; So died in mortality, and was buried in the grave, which Soul, Spirit or Godhead in the twinkling of an eye, quickned to immortality or spiritual form again.

Reason.   If the Creator of Heaven and Earth was that which died in Christ; so that the God of all life, being then become death, How came he, or by what means could he be quickned or raised to glory again?

Faith.   Yea, it was the Soul Spirit that died and was perfectly dead, that gave life to all, and that life that died in a moment, did quicken it self by its every living Word of Faith spoken before his death, that raised him to life, saying, *I have power to lay down my life, and I have power to take it again*†; there being no let or doubt in Faith, that could hinder is what it had purpose to do.

Reason.   Was all the Power that created Heaven and Earth dead and buried at the very same moment, and no power left without Christ, to quicken that which was dead within the body of Christ Jesus?

Faith.   No more than is in a grain of Wheat, and yet that dies, and in season quickens again; so that there was no God, Spirit, Power or Father without the body of Christ, to quicken that which was within the body of Christ, but lay in its pure Seed onely.

Reason.   And did that pure Seed without the help of any other powerful life without, quicken it self again?

Faith.   Yea, without the assistance of any without at all, for let me tell thee, there was no such powerful life without the body of Christ, as was dead within the body of Christ; therefore impossible that which received life from Christ should quicken the life of Christ, that created it; no, I say, the power of dying and living again lay in its own nature only; so that there was neither any infinite Spirit, God or Father, besides Christ that did quicken the Seed of Christ, from death to life in the grave; but his ever living Word of Faith spoken before his death; I say, that pure Heavenly Faith is death in life, and life in death, and this was that which redeemed his Soul from the power of the grave, as it it written, *O death I will be thy death, O grave I will be*

---

* Heb 9. 14.
† Joh. 10. 18.

thy destruction*; this Power was dead and raised it self from mortality, with a spiritual body without the help of any other, to immortality again.

Reason. Did he raise that same body that he was crucified in, and buried with? If not, What became of that body, and with what body did he rise?

Faith. I say, Christ did rise with the very same body that he was Crucified in, that same body was raised and no other.

Faith. How came it then from a mortal body to an immortal body, seeing it was the same body which was capable to dye? How could that same body be made capable to live again a life Eternal?

Faith. If the immortal body of God the Father had not died in the womb of *Mary,* to a mortal Son of flesh, blood and bone, he had not been capable to live in this world among his creatures, and upon the Cross have died again as a mortal Son, he had not been capable to live in that immortal glory from whence he came; so that Christ as he was God, twice passed through death, *viz* from immortality to mortality, and from mortality to immortality again. Now to Answer, how that body which was made capable to dye, was made capable to live in glory, was thus, That which was mortal, *viz* Water, Earth and Air being dead, I say, that spark of Faith did kindle it self throughout the same form so raised the same body without any of the gross Elements aforesaid; so that now it was a body without blood, onely the same flesh and bone purified, yea refined into a soft thin, bright, spiritual form, swifter then though; so that now having raised it self, to the same it was when it descended from Heaven to the womb of *Mary,* now it was able to appear among his disciples, as it did in the womb of a woman, their windows and doors being shut, yea able to ascend to his kingdom of glory, from whence he came, and so sate on the right hand of his Father, or the right hand of the Majesty on high, where now he will remain to all eternity.

CHAP. 3.

Shewing Christ is the onely God and Father, yea the Creator of heaven and earth: now it is to be revealed what God and Father that was, and where he was, that Christ so often called upon when he was upon earth.

---

* Hos. 13. 14.

Reason. From thy last answer thou hast raised more objections, which I would desire thou wouldest be free to answer, and that is, if thou canst reveal unto me what God or Father that was, and where he was, that forbid *Joseph* in a dream, not to turn away his Wife, saying, *That which was conceived in her womb was by the Holy Ghost;* and when Christ was born, who it was that sent *the Angel with the whole host of heaven, singing and praising God.* And when the wise men went to worship Christ, that fore-warned them to go into their own country another way, and told *Joseph* that he should take the childe with his mother, and flee into *Egypt,* and when *Herod* was dead, commanded him to return back; And another time, *This is my beloved Son in whom I am well pleased;* these with many others I could relate, which I desire thou wouldest answer, seeing thou affirmest Christ was God the Father.

Faith. Though I tell thee, yet thou canst not believe me, so that I may leave thee excuseless, I am made free to speak unto thee, and let thee know where it is written that Christ uttered a parable which was to this effect, viz. *There was a certain man took his journy into a far countrey, and set his house in order, and gave authority to his servants, and bid the Porter watch**; so that I affirm this parable was concerning his hard and sad journy he was then undertaking: now the servants he intrusted with his divine Authority was *Moses* and *Elias,* they were his porters that were to watch over Christ Jesus the Creator of heaven and earth, that there was *Angels which should have charge concerning him*†; which Angels were *Moses* and *Elias* in a fiery chariot‡, which none of the Prophets was so suddenly transmuted into glory as they were§, and therefore it was for some great design more then ordinary otherwise there had been no necessity of raising them more than any other of the Prophets**. And then again thou mayest read, there was none so much represented the Royal Prerogative Power of a God above, as they did here below, as at thy leisure read those Scriptures quoted in the Margent.

Reason. Why could not God make use of some of the Angels then in glory, to be as thou sayest, his Steward or Deputy-father, and to watch over his person the time he was upon earth? they knowing him, and was always obedient to him, might as well officiate the place of trust, and represented that authority as well as *Moses* and *Elias.*

---

* Mark 13. 34.
† Psalm 91. 11.
‡ Exod 20. 19.
§ I Kings 17. 2.
** 2 Kings Cap 1

Faith. Why, or wherefore God was necessitated to take up *Moses* and *Elias* was, in these ensuing particulars will appear: First, because *Elias* was the seed of Gods own nature, and so are none of the Angels; therefore not safe to God to trust a contrary Seed, they being but pure reason, when as the nature of *Moses* and *Elias* was Faith; so that God knew it was impossible they should falsifie their trust committed to them. Secondly, if God had left the Angels to take care over him, then had Christ in his infancy perished by the hands of *Herod,* in that the Angels are not able to subsist one day without the revelation of the person of Christ, therefore he being here below, they would have brought all to confusion above; as also Christ had not been preserved his appointed time; but the revelation of *Moses* and *Elias* being of the nature of God, and a well-spring within their souls, was that which did not onely support themselves, but fed the Angels also, and so kept them with that glorious Kingdom in due government, and perfect obedience, so that they had power as God himself in all things (except creating) and therefore it was they fore-warned *Joseph,* and sent the Angel with a heavenly Host to the shepherds, and commanded *Joseph* to flee, and said, *This is my beloved Son, in whom I am well pleased**: I say they had power as God to do what you finde written.

Reason. With what bodies did they represent the Place, Throne, and Dignity of God?

Faith. With the very same body of flesh and bone, without blood, yet this I say in the transmutation of *Elias,* all the mortal gross elements were struck out of his body, *viz.* water, earth and air, and that spark of fiery life did divert the former elements into a flame of immortal glorious purity, that the body which formerly was of a heavy gross substance, was totally dissolved and refined into a glorious, immortal, spiritual body, like God himself; so that now they were no mortal creatures, but immortal glorious Saints, clearer then Chrystal, brighter then the Sun, and swifter then thought; this was the glorious immortal creature that represented the Authority of the Eternal God.

Reason. Did Christ when he was upon earth know that he had *Moses* and *Elias* to be his Steward, or Deputy-father? and if he did; whether Christ knew that himself was God and Father, Creator of heaven and earth? and if so, why did he so often, and so seriously call upon a Father in heaven, which if as thou sayest, was but his creature, and so God became a Son to his servant?

Faith. I say after the immortal God and Father was become a mortal Son, [take notice] as he lost his title, so he lost his knowledge,

---

* Luke 2. 9,13.

as touching he was Creator of heaven and earth; for it was impossible for that which was become time, to know it self as he did in eternity; or while it was mortal, to know what it was in immortality; if he could have known it, he would not have denied it, neither have been by the seed of reason suffered to breath in this world, so that I say Christ knew no other but that *Elias* was his God and father, onely this as he grew in yeares, so his Godhead revelation grew to the greatest height of knowledge, that ever was to be in mortality, so great that none was able to dispute with him; and therefore it is written, *Never man speak like this man**, and his revelation was so high that he knew none was so near related to the father as Christ, therefore he said, *Philip, hast thou seen me, and not seen the father, knowest thou not that the father is in me, and I in him, and that I and the father am one*†? &c. and yet from my seed-spring I say, Christ knew not that he was the eternal father, for if he had as aforesaid, one time or another he would have told it his disciples, saying, *All things the father hath made known to me, I have made known to you*‡, therefore who do men say that I am? The answer was, Some sayest thou art *John the Baptist, Elias, Jeremias,* or one of the prophets; but whom do ye say that I am? *Peter* replies, *Thou art Christ the Son of the living God*§. Now Christ owns this and no more, saying, *Peter, flesh and blood hath not revealed this to thee, and upon this rock I will build my Church,* &c. so after Christ was risen with a spiritual body, yet he knew not that he was the father: as mind his words to *Mary, Go tell my brethren and thy brethren, that I ascend to your father and my father, to your God and my God***, so that till he was glorified he knew no other but that he had a father, so that though Christ was the very God, yet he bore the title of a Son, and though *Elias* was but a glorified saint, yet for that time was he honored with the title of God and Father.

Reason.   If thou canst tell me, and therein deal planly with me, what necessity was there for God thus to lose himself both in honor and knowledge; and for what, or wherefore was the cause that he laid down his life, or poured out his soul or Godhead-spirit to death, and whether it be matter of salvation, to search into these deep secrets and other things depending thereon?

Faith.   If that eternal, divine, ever-living Body of Faith could in his royal will and pleasure, been moved to any other way, there had been no necessity to leave his glorious kingdom, by which he lost his glory and honor, both in title and knowledge, but there was no other

---

* John 7. 46.
† John 14. 9, 10.
‡ John 15. 15.
§ Math 16. 17.
** John 20. 17.

way, so of absolute necessity, and therefore he declares it as his promise, *that the seed of the woman should bruise the head of the Serpent,* that as he had permitted the angels seed to deceive his own, so he would by the same way undeceive it again, to its former state before its fall: and where it is written, *John* withstood him at his baptism, *Christ said, Suffer me this once to fulfil all righteousness**, or fulfil all that the prophets have written of me; as also it is written by *Moses,* and most of the prophets, of what befell him, how he should be born of a woman, and where he should be born, and when led to death, *he was as a lamb dumb that opened not his mouth,* and that he should be as one despised, forsaken and lost, as unto title and knowledge, and suffer the shameful death of the cross by the seed, that so he might keep thy seed under eternal death, without which he could not have raised his own seed to eternal life, & the seed of the serpent to eternal misery; and I say till he had thus suffered, *all power in earth was not his own, as it was in heaven,* neither had he been Judge of the dead, but living only; so that from my seedspring I say it is the greatest concernment of a Souls salvation, to know whether Jesus Christ, be the onely God or no, what he is both in form and nature, by which the Devil is known in his form and nature; without the knowledge of these things in one measure or another, no soul in mortal flesh can be saved.

CHAP. 4.

Shewing whether the Angels were the first that God created, and of what he created them, with their nature and form, and what was the cause of the Angels fall above all the rest.

Reason.   What was the first creature God made? And of what created he them? and what was their nature and form?

Faith.   I affirm that the Angels were the first sensible living Beings, formed by the Creator, and that he created them of that dust, without or above this visible heaven, yea I say by his word speaking, unto that spiritual dust aforesaid, there came forth an innumerable Angelical Host in persons or forms like men, and not bodiless spirits, as thy seed vainly affirm; and the nature of their Angelical Spirits are pure reason onely.

Reason.   And was the fallen Angel created of the same matter as the other were? And had that Angel the same form and nature as the

---

* Mat 3. 15.

rest of the Angels had; if so, why did not he stand with the rest, or the whole host of the Angels fall with him?

Faith. I affirm that Serpent-Angel was created of the same matter and had the same form and nature, yet was more wise or God-like in his creation than all the elect Angels of glory: I say, why he could not stand with the rest, was the Creator fore-knowing that his Prerogative Royal would compel or move him to create this Angelical Reprobate in reference to his divine justice; so that the manifestation of his most glorious power unto elect men and angels, his wisdom say it most fit to endue this angel with more piercing, rational wisdom, and brightness of person, than all his Angelical companions, and that because he was decreed to the greatest shame and pain; and not onely so, but because the elect Angels should admire their Creators wisdom and power, when they should see the out-cast condition of the highest created glory, and themselves be filled with new declarations of honor, praise and glory unto the Divine Majesty for his free electing love towards them, through which they were ensured eternally to reign in their created purity. This, and no other was the cause why this Angel should fall from the rest.

Reason. I have read, as it is thus written, *That God spared not the Angels, but cast them down into hell, and delivered them in chains of darkness, to be reserved unto judgment**; so that I believe there was more then one, in that the Scripture speaks in the plural; and not the singular, *viz.* Angels, and not Angel.

Faith. I infallibly affirm, there was but onely one Reprobate Angel created at first; for know this, as there was but one man *Adam* cast out of his heavenly Paradise of created purity in soul and body; as also all this seed or generation were cast out of their spiritual peace with him; so likewise there was but one angelical Serpent cast from his rational created purity, and that was the Serpent-devil which deceived *Eve:* Now the Angels which were cast out with him, were of his seed or generation through his union with the intrals of *Eve,* where he had this world prepared for him and his generation.

Reason. And was there no other way to manifest the greatness of his glory, but by creating a seed or generation against himself and his seed, that so he might damn one, and save the other? or what prejudice had it been for his Divine Majesty, to have formed all in nature like himself, as well as in form, so that all might have enjoyed eternal happiness?

---

* 2 Pet 2. 4.

Faith. I say, there was no other way to manifest his divine excellencies unto angel or man, but what he hath done; if there had, I am confident he would never have created anything on purpose for eternal sufferings, and that the more thou mayest think the wise Creator would never have suffered any creature to become rebellious against himself, for the occasioning of such strange transactions in this world, and suffering both of himself, angel and man; I say, if he could have possessed his infinite glory in creating of every thing unto eternal pleasure.

Reason. Why, who was besides himself, that should let or hinder what he had a mind to do, but he might form all of the nature of himself, as aforesaid?

Faith. It is true, though there was none besides himself, yet I say, that the Creators Royal Will and Pleasure was that glorious wheel that moved him to create or form any creature at all, and sure I am it was unpossible for God to create the spirits of angels and men to be both of the nature of his own spirit, or either of them to be of his divine nature, then would the variety of wisdom, power and glory been all lost for want of distinction: Moreover, if angels and men had been both of Gods divine nature in their creation, then instead of their being capable to be transmuted into a higher or lower condition, at the divine pleasure of the Creator, would they not rather have been unchangable Creators, then changable creatures, therefore that God might impede all that might prevent his divine purpose, he created the bodies of the angels spiritual, and their spirits rational, and he made the body of the man *Adam* natural, and his soul spiritual, and the cause was this, that if their spirits and bodies had both been of the divine nature, then it had been unpossible for them to change or commit any evil, no more then the Creator himself, where then had been all the wonderful transactions of his glorious Majesty, or what had been formed in stead of creatures, but Creators onely?

Reason. How, or which way came the angels for living creatures, if that life that brought forth their forms had not been in God, so came forth from God infused into them, as it was into *Adam?*

Faith. Though the angels came forth living bodies in the forms of men, yet that life was not in God, nor of the nature of God, but onely a created light of sensible life of divine joys, proceeding from the eternal spirit, by vertue of a word speaking through his heavenly mouth unto those elements aforesaid, for I say, that the uncreated essence or Godhead-spirit of an infinite Majesty was utterly uncapable to be conveyed unto finite created being, for infiniteness is onely capable of its own glorious center, and after the angels were formed into living bodies, the divine Majesty and those created beings, were become distinct in their essences for everlasting; also the angels by apparent sight of their Creators face, might know themselves to be but creatures, yea subject to the divine pleasure of God that made them.

Reason. I all along judge Gods nature to be pure reason, and the angels nature the same, and if not of the nature of God, how, or by what means came they obedient to the commands of God?

Faith. Whatever thou hast judged of Gods nature, thou art altogether mistaken, for the nature of God is all-divine, heavenly Faith, and therefore the nature of the angels was, and are of a contrary seed, subject to mutability; for the angels spirits are pure reason onely. And what is the purest reason, is it any thing else but all pure desires? and what is the original of the most purest and perfects desire, is it not a want of something that is desired, or a kinde of unsatisfaction until its desire be satisfied, from something that is not inherent in it self? and therefore from the Lord of everlasting faith, I say, it is thy ignorance that undervalues him, nay it is umpossible that there should be the least motion of the purest desire in that nature, which is all fulness of divine satisfaction in it self, or how it is possible that spirit which hath desire in its nature, shoud enjoy fullness of content in its self; therefore though God created that Angelical Reason of all pure desires, I say, no spiritual man will call it the Divine Nature of God, because there can be no kinde of desire in that Nature of the immortal God, that is variety of all glorious satisfaction in it self, but this I know from the eternal Light of life, that the Creator by his infinite wisdom and power from a word speaking unto that dust aforesaid, could create, yea did make divers living creatures, and yet not one motion of those created beings was inherent in his Heavenly Spirit; so that I say, the Spirits of the Elect Angels are not in the least of any part of the glorious Nature of his Spirit, but onely a created rational Spirit of all pure desires; so that I affirm the uncreated Godhead it self, is unto the created being of Angels or men, either a Law of perfect Faith, and pure burning love in them towards God unto life Eternal, or else a fiery Law of unbelieving burning envy in them, against Gods Elect men and Angels unto Eternal death; and therefore from the Lord of all Light and Life I affirm all the Angels were equally created under one Law, the which mortal Law was written in their Angelical Natures, motioning in them that all obedience was properly due unto their Creator, which had made them such marvellous creatures.

Reason. But then, how or which way came this about, that this Angels nature was pure Reason, and that as thou sayest in a more greater measure than the Elect Angels? Now if their standing or falling lay in none of them, How came it then this Angel could not keep his standing, as well as the rest?

Faith. I know that though their spirits were created perfectly pure in their kind and measure, yet if they were not continually supplied with inspiration from that Divine glory which gave them their beings, instead of continuing in their Angelical brightness, their spirits would become nothing else but a bottomless pit of imaginary confused darkness of aspiring wisdom above the Creator; for the Elect Angels spirits being pure Reason, the very nature of them, is to desire after the knowledge of the incomprehensible glory which gave them their being; and I say, it is the variety of his Divine Excellencies flowing to their desiring natures, is that heavenly food that is prepared for their eternal preservation; therefore I say, the continuance of the reprobate Angels being expired, the Creator onely withheld the inspirations of Divine glory from him, and immediately for want of that spiritual meat to satisfie that desiring nature, his God-like purity became nothing else but imaginary impurities of secret aspiring desires above the Creator; so that his former pure Reason, was become nothing but a loathsome sink of unclean reasoning, concerning the true knowledge of the Creator, whether he were the Creator or no; and instead of honoring the Creator for his unsearchable wisdom, of forming out of a little dead dust such an innumerable Host of Elect Angels, for his personal Society; I say, this Angel at the blind barr of his lying imaginations, he secretly arrains the wisdom of the infinite God in creation, and condemned it as weakness it self, in comparison of his imaginary wisdom: this Angel being lifted up with the wisdom of the spirit and glory of his person, he beheld the Wisdom and Persons of all the Elect Angels, as simple uncomely creatures, in comparison of him and his wisdom, and then beholding himself with the Creator, he imagines his personal wisdom more capable of a Divine Throne, than he that sate thereon; also he began to imagine a new creation of his own supposing, as if he had been the Creator he could have formed more glorious creatures than the Angels without dust or any other matter, or if he must have matter to form things withall, he imagined by his word speaking, or thinking, he could have created as many spirits without bodies as he saw fit; or if he saw good, he could have transformed their spiritual bodies into any other nature or form after he had corrected them, and not to continue in one nature and form alwayes, for he thought it want of wisdom and power in the Creator, that the bodies of the Angels might not be transmuted into any condition at the pleasure of him that formed them; therefore in the midst of these and such like his irrational wisdom of imaginary impossibilites so elevated his outcast spirit, that secretly he utterly abhorred that the Creator or any other creatures should remain in being, unless he onely might bear rule over them all.

So that when the secret pride and envy of the Angelical reprobate was at height of unthroning the Creator, or else a dissolution of all, then the glorious Creator revealed his spiritual cruelties unto his holy Angels, and answerable to that he would have done for a Creators glory in the visible sight of his Angels, God condemned him to be cast out of his personal presence, and Heavenly Throne or Kingdom for everlasting, and immediately like unto lightning he was thrown down into this perishing world, where his desired Kingdom of God-like Government was prepared for him and his lineal Angels, where they are reserved in everlasting chains of darkness and unbelief, until the Judgement of the great day.

Reason. What advantage did the downfal of this reprobate Angel produce, to the rest of the Angels? and wherein did any glory redound unto God? and whether was that Angel thrown? and what became of him after his fall?

Faith. As unto the Elect Angels there was great advantage, for thereby they were all filled with variety of new Heavenly praises in their mouths, of Honour, Power, Praise, Glory, Majesty, Wisdom, Mercy, Meekness, Justice, Righteousness, or any other Divine Excellencies that could be name to their glorious Creator, for his electing free love unto them eternally, to abide in the created purity to behold his glorious face, and for his wonderful wisdom in creating such Angelical perfection in them, from an everlasting rejection of desperate burning envy in utter shame, and from this it was great glory did attend the personal Majesty of God, and the place he was thrown unto was this earth prepared for his kingdom, where here he was in his spiritual form, onely the nature of his spirit was changed, as aforesaid.

CHAP. 5.

Shewing whether this world was before the Angels or no, and whether the world was made of something or nothing, and how it came into this form and being, and whether it shall for ever thus remain.

Reason. Seeing thou hast thus far revealed thy knowledge of these secrets, let me hear thy thoughts whether this world was in being before the Angels, because thou sayest the Angel was thrown into this world.

Faith. Thou hast raised that, which neither thou nor any of thy Seed can answer, in that this and other that shall be revealed is onely to the Seed of Faith; therefore for thy conviction, and the satisfaction of the Seed of the Woman, I against Angel and man declare, and infallibly affirm, that the substances of earth and water in this world, and that glorious World above, were from all Eternity in the Creators presence, uncreated, senseless, dark, dead matter, like unto water and dust, that had no kinde of life, light or vertue in them in the least; so that I say, this world upon the account aforesaid was before the Angels creation.

Reason. By the learning of this world we have understood, that those substances of earth and water was not Eternal, onely the Creator speaking the word, so they came in being; also it is written, *In the beginning God created the Heaven and the Earth**; so that I understand there was no earth nor water, till it was created.

Faith. As I have said before, so I say again, this doth not belong to thy seed to know it; for it is written, *Through Faith we understand the worlds were framed by the Word of God*†; So that by Faith I say, that earth and water was Eternal; and the word frame or create, is to make formless dead water into sensible living forms, for thou maist read, *That earth was without form and void, and darkness was upon the deep, &c.* So that there was an earth and water, though dead and dark, so without form. Now the word creating or framing, was to give life and light to those substances of death and darkness; and therefore it is written, *The Spirit of God moved upon the waters, and said, let there be light, and there was light*‡; So that against Angel or man I positively affirm, that the earth and the deep water were essentially one Chaos of confused water, distinct from the Creator; and whereas it is said, *In the beginning God created Heaven and Earth;* is thus to be understood, that of the matter of water and earth, that was formless and void, God by a word speaking did create a formable world, as a place of convenient residence for such mortals as thou and I to inhabit in.

Reason. Though it be consented, that the earth and water in the beginning was dead and dark; yet I cannot see but they were created, so not eternal; for it is written, *I create light, and I create darkness*§; so that it will follow, God created them without form and void.

Faith. In answer to this it is written, *That God is light, and in him is no darkness at all;* yet it is written, *Darkness was upon the*

---

* Gen 1.
† Heb 11. 3.
‡ Gen 1. 2.
§ Isaiah 45. 7.

deep*; So that I know from eternity, the Divine Nature of the Creators Spirit was nothing but immortal fiery glory of Life and Light; so without Controversie the dead earth and dark deep water never proceeded all Life and Light out of his glorious mouth; and whereas thou sayest, *God created darkness,* is not intended as thou supposest; but the meaning is, that he created those Souls that were naturally dark, *into a marvellous light,* as these Scriptures will plainly manifest, *The light shineth in darkness, and the darkness comprehendeth it not;* and again, *I will open their eyes, and turn them from darkness to light, and from the power of Satan unto God*†, with many such places, but not one Scripture that God created or gave any being or beginning unto dead, dark, senseless earth and water, aforesaid.

Reason. I cannot yet understand, but that God created that confused Chaos of water and earth; and so of nothing by his word speaking, this world was made.

Faith. Though thou be the Seed of Reason, yet in this thou art unreasonable to think that ever those dark, dead Elements of earth and water, should have their Original from his glorious Spirit; I say, their natures being so contrary, it is impossible they should proceed the one from the other; For alas! What is death or darkness, is it not through the absence of life and light? And is not life, being overcome by death, absolutely become death or darkness, or utter silence for a moment? And if light and darkness, life and death meet together, is there any peace between them, until one hath swallowed up the other? If this be so, as it is so, then without Controversie earth and water were uncreated substances, eternally distinct from the God of Life, Light and Glory; and that the more it is written, *And darkness covered the face of the deep;* therefore I say, it is but a dream and a lye, to say that God created all things of nothing, or that God created that confused Chaos of water and earth; it is all one as if thou shouldst say, there was no Creator at all, but earth and water, and such like dead stuff as they are.

Reason. It is written, *God made a firmament, and divided the waters that were under the Firmament, from the waters which were above the Firmament;* Now was this Firmament Eternal, as the rest?

Faith. I say, the Firmament that is visible, was Eternal, though it was of that dead, dark matter, as the other was: Now the word, making (is the same, creating) which is no other then as aforesaid, to make that which was dead and dark, to be lively light;

---

* 1 John 1. 5.
† John 1. 5.

and therefore God made Sun, Moon and Stars, and set them in the Firmament, to give light upon this earth; so that the Sun is the life of the earth, the Moon the life of the waters.

Reason. What then is the Nature of the Water and the Earth above this visible Firmament, the same with this water and earth in this world?

Faith. No, in nature they are not the same, for that above the Firmament is immortal spiritual, when as this is mortal natural; And therefore the Angels and all the creatures therein, being created of that matter, are spiritual immortal bodies, when as man and all creatures herein, are natural mortal bodies; and therefore it is written, *There are Heavenly Bodies and earthly bodies, celestial and terrestial;* the one above durable, this below perishing; that above sutable for such a glorious personal Majesty as the Creator is.

CHAP. 6.

Shewing of what matter Adams *body was created, and what was his Nature, Soul or Spirit, and by what means* Adam *came to lose his state he was created in.*

Reason. Then tell me of which of the two substances was the body of *Adam* created, of that above, or this below?

Faith. There is no Dispute to the contrary, but that *Adam* was created of this earth below, in that he is numbred among this visible creation, as in *Genesis* related, *And that Adam was to be Lord, and rule over them;* and the Scripture tells thee what substance he was created of in those words, *The Lord God also made the man of the dust of the earth after his own likeness, yea in the Image of God created he him;* so that I say, he made *Adam* of this dust below; and therefore it is the body of man is natural, so of a heavy gross substance, *viz.* flesh, blood and bone.

Reason. How or which way was man framed in the image of God, and so completely made in the similitude of the Creator, seeing mans body is of such gross mortal substance, and Gods body thou sayest is of a bright, fiery, glorious, chrystall, immortal substance, what likeness or image can mans be like unto God, then tell me?

Faith. In the creating of man the Lord God onely spake the word onely unto the dust of the earth, and immediately the vertue thereof brought forth a living man of pure flesh, blood and bone, like unto God himself as near as could be; so that I say, it was not the visibility of their persons that differed in the least, but the glory of them onely, for this by Faith I know, God was an infinite spiritual body in all parts perfectly holy, and *Adam* was a finite natural body of perfect innocency, resembling that Divine form of God that created him.

Reason.   What then was the nature or spirit of *Adam* Angelical? Or was it Divine?

Faith.   I say, though *Adams* body was made of the dust, and appointed for generation so natural; yet this from an unerring spirit I know, that his Soul was not natural; but supernatural or Divine, and that because it was formed according to the invisible glory of the Eternal Spirit.

Reason.   What then was not *Adams* nature Reason, so a reasonable creature, if not, then *Adam* was unreasonable, so not like unto God?

Faith.   From the Lord of Glory I say, that if the nature of *Adam* had been rational in his creation, then it could not have been Divine, but of Angelical desiring nature, of unsatisfaction in its self; but that Divine Soul of *Adam* which was created after the likeness of the Eternal God, did consist of several Heavenly properties in its measure, answerable unto those Divine qualifications in the glorious Creator above all measure; for the Soul of man is not without its several properties, and yet they are all in a Heavenly Harmony, in that the joy of Soul that *Adam* did was possess arose in him from one Divine Heavenly voice, called the Spirit of Faith, which was all satisfaction in himself with his present condition, not having the least thought of further happiness, then what he enjoyed already; thus as the Divine nature of the Eternal Spirit, was variety of infinite satisfaction in it self: So likewise the Soul of *Adam* being composed of the same qualifications, was variety of satisfaction in it self also, according to its measure. Now if the nature of *Adams* Soul had been as thou sayest rational in his creation, the through want of the Divine nature of Faith, *Adam* would always have been desiring after something that he wanted, like unto the Elect Angels; for this I know, the nature of *Adams* Soul could not possible have any reason in it, and that because the very nature of reason is not onely as aforesaid, but it is too serious in its consideration, whether things be good or right that are propounded to its understanding, when on the contrary that nature or breath of Faith which singly was intirely given to *Adam* without the least consideration, perfectly knowing the excellency of a thing as soon as ever it is presented unto it: and therefore *Adams* nature must needs be Divine as Gods is, and supernatural, though cloathed with pure nature onely.

Reason.   If it be as thou sayest, that Gods nature is all Divine Heavenly Faith, without pure reason at all, and *Adam* was onely partaker of that nature, which thou sayest is so immortal pure, that it is all Divine Heavenly satisfaction in its self; How came it then that *Adam* having that nature of Divine satisfaction in his own Soul, did fall from that happy and innocent condition wherein he was created?

Faith.   From the revelation of faith in my soul I declare, that in the nature of God there is not the least motion of the purest reason at all, that being onely the angels nature, as aforesaid; neither is it possible there should be, in that thou hast heard in that chapter treating of the angels creation, that reason in the purest sense is but a meer desire of the enjoyment of something that is above it, so no real satisfaction in its self; therefore if the nature of God were pure reason, as Papists, Episcopal, Presbyter, Independent, Anabaptist, Ranter, Quaker, and all Atheistical opinions of the seed affirm, then I say the Creator that gave satisfaction to another is not satisfied in its self, and so in thy reason would follow, there is something above God that must give satisfaction to God, which from an unerring spirit, is cursed blasphemy; when it is written, *In him all fulness dwells, and he it is that filleth all in all**; And again it is written, *There is none like unto him, or before him, or that shall be after him*†, for a spiritual body of all divine heavenly faith, and therefore it is written, the wonderful transendent vertues of faith, in so much that there is not the least let or doubt, but whatever it believeth shall come to pass, and to faith there is nothing impossible, that its revelation moves it to do; when on the contrary, reason is such antiphathy, that it is a body of meer imaginary desires, and no reality, cloathed with fear, let, and doubts of faiths eternal power.

Now though the soul of *Adam* through the divine purity of its nature, was immortal and uncapable of any rebellion against the glorious spirit of its Creator, yet because its body was natural, and had its beginning of this dust below, his immortal soul having its being in a piece of clay, was become subject through temptation, to be transmuted from its present condition of his created innocency, for this faith knows though the soul of *Adam* was of a divine nature, yet because it was a created nature distinct to it self, it was become a Son or Servant, yea subject to its divine God; and that through deep temptation he was subject to be transmuted into a sinful condition, through which both soul and body, might not onely be subject to natural death, but also full of fear of eternal death, or casting out of the spiritual presence of a divine Majesty to bring forth his heavenly design of a more transendent, eternal glory that he had prepared

---

* Col, 2. 9.
† Isiah 43. 10.

through suffering, to be enjoyed by his divine image at the last day, with himself face to face.

Reason. I conceive if *Adam* had such divine immortal heaven life, breathed into him which thou calls his soul, that was of the same property and nature of the divine God, he might by that life have withstood all temptation whatsoever, though it was in a house of clay.

Faith. Again and again, against all thy seed I affirm, that the soul of *Adam* was onely of the divine nature in its creation, yet because it was on essence with a body that was taken out of dust, it was both probable and capable, to be thought into a condition of entering dust again, and that for these ensuing particulars:

1. First to fullfil these Scriptures, saying*, *In the day that thou eatest thereof, thou shalt die the death: And in the sweat of thy face thou shalt eat thy bread till thou return to the earth; for out of it thou wast taken; because thou art dust, and to dust thou shalt return again.*
2. Secondly, if the body of *Adam* had been immortal in his creation as well as his soul, he would not onely have been uncapable of natural generation, but also he would have been uncapable of any transmutation whatsoever, and where then had been the prerogative power of infinite wisdom and transcendent glory of the Creator ever been seen or known by angels or men? And therefore it was *Adam* knew not whether he should stand or fall from his present state or no, neither did he know what power he was indued withal in his created purity, neither did he know any greater glory, but what then at present he enjoyed; so that if *Adam* had known that he had power in his own will, to preserve himself in his present condition, thou mayest be sure that if he could have kept himself in that blessed state, he would never have lost it, for making use of all the power that was in him, to have resisted a temptation unto rebellion, in which he knew there was threatening of a loss of that created glory he enjoyed, as aforesaid.

---

* Gen. 3. 19.

CHAP. 7.

Shewing who it was that tempted Adam, *and who it Was that tempted* Eve, *whether it was the Angel aforesaid; And if so, why he is called a Serpent, a Tree, &c. and how And which way they were deceived, and what effects it hath ever since produced.*

Reason.   However, I cannot believe whatever thou hast related as touching these things; yet tell me who it was, and by what means *Adam* was deceived.

Faith.   I say, though the Soul of *Adam* was Divine, and free from all kinde of rationality, so could not possibly have any desire in him after carnal copulation with his Wife; for I know, that carnal pleasures were too low for a spiritual Soul, whose nature was variety of Divine satisfaction in it self; and therefore the woman *Eve,* through the permission of God was first guilty of the transgresssion of lust, and so tempted her innocent Husband to lye with her; if possible to cover her folly. And now from the Lord I say, that the carnal desire in her towards her Husband; proceeded not from her Divine purity, but from the rational nature of the unclean Serpent within her.

Reason.   Now I understand that thou makest Faith and Reason two contraries, as fire and water, so that from hence I understand, that Seed thou callest Faith hath no desire, but that all desire doth onely flow from Reason alone.

Faith.   Whether thou understood or no, yet this I shall reveal to thee, that God is now a body of flesh and bone glorified, with all Divine, Spiritual, Heavenly Faith, and no Reason as aforesaid, for if so, God himself would be subject to transmutation as man; and so full of unsatisfaction that all his transactions would be imperfect, and not Eternal.

Reason.   Seeing thou* sayest God had no Reason in him How comes it then that God saith, *Come now lets reason together, saith the Lord, &c*†*? Now if there were no Reason in God, How could he have reasoned with the Rulers of Israel?

Faith.   Oh! That thou could but see, how thy ignorance blinds thee from the true understanding of any Scripture, as to think that God in his person should Reason with them, when thou reads, it was

---

* The original manuscript is very unclear at this point
† Isaiah 1.

none but the Prophet *Isaiah,* who from the Revelation of Faith in his own Soul, reasoned the cause with them as from the Lord; for I tell thee, and all blind *Quakers* Reason with thee, that if God were not of a nature contrary to the nature of Angels and men, there could have been nothing created nor preserved in their form and order as now they are; and this I know, that Faith can take up the words of Reason, though not inherent in it, as Reason to take the words of Faith, though not experienced in it.

Reason.   What then was that Reason which deceived *Eve,* or was it an Apple or Serpent, for the woman said, the serpent beguiled me, and I did eat? Now if thou canst, tell me what it was that deceived *Eve.*

Faith.   Though I tell thee thou canst not believe, yet thou mayest read, *That the great Dragon, the old Serpent, called the Devil and Satan, which deceiveth the world, he was cast out into the earth**; therefore it is written, *We unto the Inhabiters of the earth, for the Devil is come down among you;* So that from my Seed-spring I say, that Angelical Serpent, which I have discoursed with thee in the 4th Chapter, was that which deceived *Eve.*

Reason.   I cannot find in Scripture that was an Angel which deceived *Eve,* though I confess the Scripture saith, there was an Angel cast down, but for what I know not, for it is written, *Thou shalt not eat of the tree of knowledge of good and evil;* and in another place it is said, *a Serpent beguiled her,* not in the least relating it was an Angel; so that I believe it was one of the beasts of the field, which the Lord God had made, and the Devil was an invisible spirit, which entered into the body of the Serpent, and spake those subtile expressions through his mouth, and so caused the woman to eat of the fruit of a natural Tree, which the Lord God had forbidden, and tempting her Husband to eat of the fruit with her, it operated that venemous evil in them and all man-kinde.

Faith.   Oh! The gross darkness that lodgeth in the spirits of the learned and unlearned of they seed, not knowing the Scriptures are generally expressed in natural terms, for the manifestation of spiritual things, and yet the learned of thy seed would perswade men exactly to understand them in the Letter, because thou measurest the glorious things of Eternity, by thy rational learning, when thou maist read that the seed of the Devil are sometimes called by the name of *Devils, Dragons, Vipers, Serpents, fruitless Trees,* and such like; so this Angelical reprobate, by whom *Eve* was deceived, was called, *the Dragon, an old Serpent, the Devil, Satan, the Deceiver,* or *the Tree of*

---

* Rev. 12. 12,13.

knowledge of good and evil, and such like names sutable to his cursed nature; so in truth I say, that Serpent that tempted *Eve,* was that Angelical Dragon-Devil aforesaid, which God from the highest Heavens cast down to this lowest earth; and it was his seeming Divine wisdom, and Angelical person, that bewitched *Eves* innocent Soul to hearken to him, and her eyes to dote upon him; for let but moderate Reason guide thee, and thou maist see it must be a person more wise and comely than *Adam* to deceive her; and therefore it is written, *When the Woman saw the Tree, it was good for food, pleasant to the eyes, and a Tree to be desired to make one wise, she took of the fruit thereof, and she did eat, and also gave to her Husband, and he did eat**.

Reason. Well, then, suppose it be granted it was the Angel that deceived her by words. What is then supposed by eating, *And she saw it was good food, and did eat?* So that the words of the Angel might entice her; But what was that she did eat?

Faith. That is when the innocent Soul of *Eve* was over-poured by the Serpents subtile Language, her spirit did consent unto him, to come in to her and take full possession of her, to be her God and guide instead of her Creator: Now by the word eating of *the Tree of knowledge of good and evil;* from the Lord of ever-living Faith I say, that the Creator called it eating.
1. First, Because none of thy seed should know the Lords secrets, until it was his pleasure he would receive honour by it.
2. Secondly, The Spirit of God called it eating, because of the civility of the Speech; for the Scripture Language is much like a modest pure Virgin, which is loath to have her secret parts mentioned in the least.
3. Thirdly, That she might beware how she hearkned to any voice that was contrary to the voice of the Seed of God in her; so that if she should hear the voice of a stranger, she should not give away, as many a Virgin since hath been deluded: So that I say, this Angelical person entered into her womb, through her secret parts, and being united to her Soul and body, his Serpentine nature dissolved it self into her pure Seed, and defiled her throughout, and so became essentially one with her, through which she naturally conceived a Serpent, Dragon, Devil into a man-child of flesh, blood and bone, and brought forth her first begotten son of the Devil, yea, the Dragon Devil himself, and called his Name, according to his nature, *Cain* or cursed, though ignorantly she said, that she had received a man from the Lord, just so on the contrary the womb of the Virgin wife *Mary,* was honoured with the Angelic God himself, through which her polluted nature was not onely cleansed while he was in her

---

* Gen 3. 6.

womb, but also by the vertue of the Divine power, she was inhabited to conceive his glorious Majesty of her Seed into a holy Babe of unspotted flesh, blood and bone, and in his season to bring forth her first begotten Son of God, yea, the true God and everlasting Father himself, and called his Name, according to his Nature, *Emanuel*, Jesus, or Blessed, as at large is disputed in the second Chapter.

Reason.   Thou sayest eating was admitting the Angels person into her body, if the Angel was of as large a compass as I am, how was it possible, and where do we read that God cursed the Angel? And how can it be proved that Angel was the first Devil?

Faith.   As Christ said unto *Nicodemus*, so say I unto thee, though the body of the Angelical Serpent in its length or breadth was as a man is, yet I know, it was not of so gross a substance as man is, for it was a spiritual body created in another World; for though the bodies of the mighty Angels are in forms like men, yet I know they shine like unto the Sun or a flame of fire, being formed in a Region of a more higher nature than this; therefore they are of a motion as swift as thought, and of a pure, thin, or bright fiery nature; so that with great ease they pierce through a narrow passage at the Divine pleasure of the Creator.

Reason.   Were it so as thou sayest, What harm or defilement could this be to her Soul or body, he being a person so glorious? I conceive it should rather endue her with more knowledge than before.

Faith.   Though the Angel was glorious in person, yet his nature was corrupt in comparison of hers, even as that blood which is defiled with the Pox or Gangreen: Now this man to enter the body of a woman whose blood is pure and free from any corrupt distemper; Is it not a defilement to her body? Even so his Serpentine Reason dissolved it self into her pure Seed of Faith, and became essentially one with her, through which she was Soul and body defiled throughout, by which she lost her Divine satisfaction and Heavenly Peace, that formerly she enjoyed in her own Soul.

Reason.   How will this stand agreeable to Scripture, when thou sayest, it was an Angel that deceived *Eve,* and the Letter faith, it was a Serpent? And besides it is written, God cursed not the Angel, but the Serpent; What then dost thou say, the Angel was the Serpent? And if so, what glory was there in a Serpent? And where was the Angel or Serpent, when cursed?

Faith.   Though I have told thee of this before, yet now I tell thee again, he was called a Serpent as unto the subtility of his nature or seed, and that Serpentine Angelical form, that by enticing words did deceive her, was wholly dissolved into seed in her womb, when the Eternal curse was passed upon him.

Reason. If the Angelical person was in the body of *Eve,* when he received his curse, How then could he be capable of understanding a Sentence denounced against him, being in the womb, and changed from his former condition, as thou hast revealed?

Faith. The curse denounced by the Creator upon the Serpent in the womb of *Eve,* was not for his satisfaction in the least, but to convince *Eve* of her deceived thoughts, of possessing such God-like happiness promised to her by the Angel; also it was to convince her of doting of her first born, but instead of rejoicing in him at his birth, her Soul would not only loath his company, but would also cast him out of her presence, least he should murther her as he did his Brother *Abel,* for her tender compassion towards him: Furthermore it was spoken for her Divine satisfaction, when the light of Redemption should shine in her deceived Soul, and shew her that her first-born son was not from the Lord, but the Angelical Serpent, cursed in her womb by the Creator.

Reason. Why should the Serpent and his generation undergo an eternal curse, and *Eve* and her generation suffer but an external curse, seeing she rebelled against a greater light than the Angel?

Faith. I know she was utterly uncapable of eternal curse, for these considerations;
    First, Because her Soul proceeded from a Heavenly Nature of Eternal Majesty himself.
    Secondly, Because that consent in her to evil, proceeded not from her own nature, but the unclean spirit of the Serpent speaking into her innocent Soul.

Reason. Seeing the Serpent before he tempted *Eve,* was called, *A Tree of knowledge of good and evil;* surely, then that good was not cursed, but the evil onely; and on the contrary, *Eve* partaking in her womb of the evil seed, must be evil also.

Faith. Though the Angel had been a Tree in his first estate, which knew nothing but good, before *Eve* or *Adam* had any sensible beings, yet being fallen from his created purity, he was become a Tree of sin or evil onely; So that he was a cursed out-cast Tree from the glorious presence of life Eternal, before his visible appearing unto *Eve;* so that he was far from repenting of rebellion against God, yea, altogether uncapable of reproof of sin, whereby he might be restored from his wretched estate, that he did utterly abhor both God and man, unless he might be Ruler over them; when on the contrary, *Eve* through temptation was overcome by the Serpent; yet she had some relenting light of life left in her after her rebellion, which occasioned a secret shame and confusion of Soul in her; so that she was capable of being made a good Tree again, yea, a Tree of more transcendent glory than she was before.

Reason. By this I understand, that the Seed of the Woman and the seed of the Angel were two contrary seeds, then tell me whether the Seed of the Woman was before, or in his fall? And the Seed of the Woman blessed before, or after his fall?

Faith. That there is two Seeds or Trees of Eternal life thou maist read, *A good Tree cannot bring forth evil fruit, nor can a corrupt tree bring forth good fruit; therefore, by their fruits they are known:* So that the Serpent angelical tree being reprobate to all manner of evil: therefore he and his seed of men and women, were not onely cursed in the womb of *Eve,* but also before the world was; but on the contrary, innocent *Eve* being a good Tree in her creation, through her proceeding from the Divine Nature of the Tree of Eternal glory; so that it was impossible that she and *Adam,* or any of their Seed should eternally perish, because they were Trees Elected to bring forth good fruit unto everlasting life and glory long before the creating of this world.

Reason. However thou seems to prove that it was no natural Tree, so no natural apple, then what dost thou say to those sayings where he is called, *A Serpent, and cursed above all cattel and every beast of the field, upon thy belly shalt thou go, and dust shalt thou eat all the dayes of thy life*;* So if it were not a natural Serpent that tempted *Eve,* Why then doth not *Cain* and all his seed, being as thou sayest of the Serpentine nature, yet men and women? I say, why do not those men go upon their belly, and lick up dust while they live in this world?

Faith. However, thou or all thy seed vainly dream of Apples pulled from woodden trees, or of a natural Serpent, or an evil spirit in the body of an ignorant horned beast, or any such like imaginary fancy concerning the deceiving of *Eve,* yet I having the Spirit of Revelation, do know that the Serpent which beguiled *Eve,* was that Angelical Reprobate, cast down from the Kingdom of glory; also I know, that the Serpentine Angel deceived *Eve,* not upon a natural account, but a spiritual account, in that she was ignorant of lusting after a man, until she had obeyed the Serpents voice. Now when the curse was denounced upon the Serpent and his seed, that Angelical

---

* Gen. 3.

Serpent was not without but within the womb of *Eve,* as aforesaid, and he was called a Serpent, because of his exceeding subtilty; Now if it had been a natural Serpent without her, what prejudice had the tenour of that curse been to *Eve* or *Adam?* It was as good to him to eat of the fruit of the Tree as the choicest things, that one being as natural to him as to the other; and also what dammage had it been to the woman, for to curse a natural serpent without her, or suppose that curse had been denounced against an evil spirit distinct from the soul and body of *Eve,* what harm would that have been to *Adam* and *Eve,* or their generation? Or who should regard a Curse upon any devil in the least, so that he himself be not that evil spirit or devil so cursed? And who is it but that serpentine nature the devil that goeth upon their belly, and lick up the dust of this world? Is it not that unclean reason, and wicked imagination that was in *Cain,* and now is in all his angels, who are the lords of this earth, or god of this world, whose spirits wholly thirst after things that perish, and are never in their proper center, but when they are licking, that is, feeding upon gold and silver, riches and honor of this world, which is no more than the dust of the earth? Which the fair Ladies and rich men of the world lick up all the days of their life?

Reason.   Suppose it should be granted, that that serpent by whom *Eve* was beguiled, was none of the trees of this creation, or an evil spirit in the body of a natural serpent, as by me is believed, but it was an absolute serpent devil, as before hath been related by thee, and that it entered into *Eve,* and in her womb was pronounced cursed by the Creator, and so naturally brought forth himself a cursed *Cain* of her seed. What was this unto *Eve,* or why should she suffer any kind of punishment for being overcome by an enemy that was too mighty for her?

Reason.   Though the soul of *Eve* was not onely purely created in its kinde like unto other creatures, but it was also of the very same nature, of his most glorious spirit that formed it, so that she could not be ignorant in the least, that all obedience was most due unto her Creators command; also the Creator by his royal will, for the manifestation of his glorious power, might give his creature a spiritual law, yea life and light in its self, and yet reserve to himself the prerogative power of it, so that the Creator might present unto the view of his image, a serpent devil for the trial of his workmanship, and yet might upon pain of death, forbid his creature for having to do with that tree, or of hearkning to it in the least, also I know the divine Creator might leave his divine image unto his present strength, through which by a subtile enemy she might be tempted and overcome to commit evil with the angel against its Creators law, and yet its sin be upon its own head, and that because it rebelled not onely against its divine light, but principally because their was no law to bind an infinite Majesty to protect *Eve* in her created purity; and whether her enemy was too potent for her, that was hid from her eyes, by the unsearchable wisdom of the Creator, so that seeing the wonderful wisdom and ways of the Lord are past finding out, then thou wouldst forbear reasoning against the Creators prerogative power, and yield thy self to be damned at his pleasure.

CHAP. 8.

Shewing whether Cain was not the first devil, and who are his seed children; and what devils those were that are so frequently spoken of in Scripture.

Reason. What then dost thou say that *Cain* was the first devil and was there no evil spirit before *Cain;* and if so, prove that *Cain* is called a devil.

Faith. From the divine spirit of the Lord of glory I affirm, as before is proved, that the angels were the first sensible living forms that ever were created, and that reprobate angel as I have said, dissolved into seed in the womb of *Eve,* and there conceived into flesh, blood and bone, her first-born *Cain,* yea the first devil and father of the damned; so that against thee and all thy seed, I say, there was no other devil before *Cain,* and that thou mayest know *Cain* is called a devil, read these Scriptures, Not as *Cain,* which was of that wicked one, and slew his brother; Again it is written, He that soweth the good seed, is the son of man, and the field is the world, and the good seed are the children of the kingdom, and the tares are the children of the wicked one, and the enemy that soweth them is the devil: Again, Ye are of your father the devil[*], and the lusts of your father ye will do, he hath been a murtherer from the beginning, and abode not in the truth, because there was no truth in him, when he speaketh a lye, he speaketh of his own, for he is a lyar and the father thereof: Now then, what sayest thou, was not *Cain* the first murthering lying man that ever was born of a woman?

Reason. I have read in Scripture that there are evil angels or devils living in the Ayr, and a devil amongst them called *Beelzebub* the prince of devils, now I judge the devil is of such an invisible spirit, that he is here, there, and everywhere, and so can infuse evil thoughts into man, and man cannot see the devils that tempts him.

---

[*] John 8. 44.

Faith.   If this be as thou sayest, what need any man trouble himself with the least fear of eternal death, whatsoever wickedness is committed by him? For I say, if any man be tempted to evil by any devil, but what is in his own nature onely, that devil or evil spirit is to be eternally damned, and the man to be set free; and if sin issued not from mans uncleane reason, or lying imagination within him, how is it possible that any man should be so tormented as thy seed are with inward burnings, through a secret fear of eternal sufferings rising in them from the guilt of former evils committed against the light of conscience: Now if it were possible for thee to know, that the subtilty of the prince of the ayr that rules in the hearts of disobedience, was thy own imaginary reason or evil spirit, that is, the prince of all airy disputes concerning God, devil, angels, heaven, hell, eternal glory; or shame to come, then thou wouldest see the truth of what I speak.

Reason.   What then dost thou say there never was, is, nor shall be no other devil but men and women; and if so, from whence comes that devilish nature in man, and whether all have not the devilish nature in them, and if so, how shall any man escape damnation?

Faith.   As unto this thy Question, I answer as aforesaid, There never was no devil till the angel became a man-child of flesh, blood and bone, and that evil nature ever since hath generated in all the sons and daughters of *Adam,* since his fall, both reason and faith lay hid in that seed that conceived in the womb: So that I say, as *Adam* and *Eve,* the womb of all living had both reason and faith in them, so of necessity it must follow that all that are begotten or generated by them, must needs partake of both natures, so that I affirm that all the righteousness as the wicked have the devils nature in them, and yet the seed of the woman shall escape damnation.

Reason.   What then dost thou say that the devils have faith in them, and yet shall be damned, and the true believers have reason in them, and yet shall be saved? Now there being both seeds in one as the other, how comes it that all are not either damned or saved? Certainly faith being as thou sayest, of the nature of God, then that faith in the devils must return to God again.

Faith.   I say *Cain* the father of all devils, had faith in him as all his children have at this day, as it is written touching the four seeds speaking of them *that hath the seed sown on a rock, when they hear, they receive the word with joy, and these having no root, which for a while believe, and in time of temptation fall away*[*]: And it is written, *the devils believe and tremble*[†]*,* so that if thou were not stone-blind

---

[*] Luke 8. 13.
[†] Jam. 2. 19.

thou mightiest see that there is no other devil but men and women, and that faith in them doth cause many secret feares of damnation, and yet that faith in them shall never return to God, nor they themselves saved; for this I know, that faith that is in the seed of the serpent shall die with them, and rise with them, for the devils shall rise all reason and no faith, or shall not be capable to ascend to glory, when on the contrary, the blessed of the Lord all their Faith in the life time out-topped reason, by which he came to the knowledge of God; so that at his death his reason shall dye with him, insomuch, that at the Resurrection he shall rise all Faith and no Reason, so shall be able to ascend to glory.

Reason.   What then shall become of natural fools and children, that understand neither Faith nor Reason, shall they all be damned, if they be of the serpents seed?

Faith.   From an unerring Spirit I speak it, there is neither child nor fool that dies uncapable of the breach of the Law, that shall be damned; so that herein the Justice and Mercy of God appears, that as he will damn whom he will, so he will damn none unjustly; therefore I say, let them be children or fools, though the seed of the Serpent, yet they shall be raised to the glory their father had before his fall, *viz.* the estate of angels.

Reason.   If there be no other Devil but *Cain* and his generation of men and women, What Devils were then those from these Scriptures, where it is written, *Then was Jesus led up of the Spirit into the Wilderness to be tempted of the Devil, which Devil taketh him up into the holy City** &c. again it is written, *Satan entered into Judas*†, &c. and it is written, *Out of Mary Magdalene Christ cast out seven Devils,* with many hundred examples more; onely one more I shall quote, which is more remarkable then those before, and then let me hear thy answer‡, and that is touching the man *that lived in the land of the Gadarenes*§, *which man had Devils a long time, and wore no cloaths, neither abode in any house but in the tombes, and no man could bind him, no not with chains, neither could any man tame him, and alwayes night and day he was in the mountains, and in the tombes, crying and cutting himself with stones, and all the Devils in him besought Christ that they might go into the Herd of Swine, which they had no sooner entered but the man was well in his right minde, and the whole Herd of Swine ran violently down a steep place, into the Sea:* Now if thou canst make it apparent, that these were no Devils besides *Cain* and his

---

* Matt 4. 1.
† Mark 5. 2.
‡ Luk 8. 27.
§ Mark 5. 4.

seed, then I shall with thee believe that there is no other Devil but man and woman.

Faith.   From Christ, the onely Lord of glory in the Revelation of his Eternal Spirit, I affirm, that those Devils so tituled from the first of Matthew to the last of the *Revelation,* were onely the Seed of Reason and the violent distempers of the imagination thereof; as first mind, that the Devil that tempted Christ, was one of the ablest Disputants, whether a Pharisee of Sadducee, I cannot by Faith finde, yet by permissions I judge him rather a Saducee, they being the wisest and subtlest Devil of the two; I say, the Pharisees and Saducees commissionate this man, which by experience they found were best versed in Scripture, to see if he could tempt the Lord Jesus, to Baptize them with the holy Ghost, and fire; so that I say, this Devil was a man, of the same seed of those where it is written, *Ye shall not tempt the Lord your God, as ye tempted him in Massah**; again it is written, *When your Fathers tempted me, proved me, and saw my works 40 years*†; as at large thou may read in a Book of mine, entituled, *Look about you, for the Devil that you fear is in you;* so that I say, these tempters of the Lord were the people of *Israel,* men and women, and no other form or Spirit whatsoever; and again it is written, *That man is tempted, when he is drawn away of his own lusts and enticed*‡; so that I affirm, that there is no other Devil but thy lustful Soul within thee, that doth tempt thee to commit any wickedness acted by thee; so that I say, the meaning of that Satan entered *Judas,* was onely this, being by Christ Jesus discovered, that he was the man that should betray him, then forthwith nature in him entered into a resolution to betray the Lord of Life, being then sealed up to a reprobate minde, went out to his Brethren the Pharasaical Devils, and sold him for thirty pieces: so that I say, there was no other Devil entered him but what was in him, no more then would enter thee, if thou wert now damned by me, onely a spirit of tormenting envy would as it did in *Judas,* so flame and burn, that if possible thou wouldst destroy me, as *Judas* did Christ.

Reason.   Notwithstanding what thou has said as touching a Devil, tempting or entering, seems to have some colour of truth in it, But then what wilt thou say of those Devils that were cast out of *Mary,* and many others? But especially of those legion that was cast out into the Herd of Swine? For it is expressed, when the Devils were cast out of the man, they went into the Herd of Swine; so that surely this was something more than Reason; otherwise, if Reason be the

---

* Deut 6. 6.
† Heb 3. 9.
‡ Jam 1. 14.

Devil, and Reason cast out, then the man had not been cloathed in his right minde, but been altogether unreasonable.

Faith.   Let me speak never so plainly, thou canst not understand me; yet however, this I shall tell thee, that those Devils which by the powerful Word of Christ Jesus, were cast out of *Mary Magdalen,* or out of that man or any other creature spoke of in holy writ, were onely all manner of filthy diseases, or violent fiery distempers that hurried that man about such desperate wickedness oftentimes increasing so powerfully, that it did not onely occasion to rend his own body, and break Iron chains, but also ready to tear any one in pieces, as many of thy seed at this day are possessed with Devils, by such as thou are believed to be Devils; and therefore it is that learned of thy seed have attempted by Conjuring Physical Medicaments, to chain up that distemper, or cast out by Vomit or Purgation, and such like deceitful means, which if thou wert not stone blind, mightest see that these supposed Devils, yet real distempers, were no other but such as thou calls Lunatick frenzy, Madness, Convulsions, or falling-sickness, & such like proceeding from melancholy is Colerick, corrupt humors of the blood, that by these Devilish distempers many of thy seed are chained up Prisoners in *Bedlum* all the dayes of their life, which if they could be cast out by Faith, being Lord over those Colerick and Melancholy distempers of the minde, then they would by the Divine knowledge of the true God, be cloathed in their right minds.

Reason.   If this were as thou sayest, onely violent distempers in that man, and so in *Mary,* what then was that which came out of the man, and entered into the Herd of Swine; and if they were onely that we call diseases, why then are they called Devils?

Faith.   From life of that Divine light in my Soul, I declare, they were no other but violent distempers aforesaid, which said diseases by the powerful Godhead in Christ, was commanded at the request of the man to enter the Herd of the Swine, which when the Swine were possessed with the same distemper, they were as mad as the man, tearing and tumbling themselves into the Sea, by reason of that violent distemper or affliction, that the swine became giddy in their heads, not able to preserve themselves through the violence of the said affliction.

Now why the said distempers are called Devils, are because none should know the true Devil, but the Heirs of glory; for thou mayest read the whole transaction of Christ were revealed in Parables, and the mystery of Truth only revealed to the true Believers of the Lord of Glory; And if thou supposest they were Devils, what then dost thou apprehend them to be? And how got they into the Herd of Swine, and not seen?

Reason. I conceive the Devils are invisible spirits that tormented the man, and so could convey themselves into the Swine without the fight of any, even as the Soul or Spirit of man at the hour of death do go forth of his body to Heaven or Hell.

Faith. Oh! Thou senseless sottish Reason, now thou discovers thy ignorance in his, as hath been in the rest, as though the Devil were an invisible spirit, and so cannot be seen by the man, how the Devil got into him, nor how this Devil or Devils went out of him, and got into the Herd of Swine, nor what become of those Devils in the Sea, whether drowned in the Sea, or no; but however, so as I have said before, so I say again, that there is no Devil without a body, that can torment another, neither can that Devil if he were not generated in man, either come in or go out of man, but he must be seen, otherwise he is no Devil at all; as for instance, the distemper of man cannot be cast out, but it may be seen and felt in the foul and stinking body, that poysoned and distempered the minde of man; And how dost thou know that the Soul of man leaveth or goeth out of the body at the hour of death?

CHAP. 9.

Shewing what the Soul is, and what it is that dieth, how that the Soul which is the life of the body can dye, and nothing else but life that dieth.

Reason. Why? I believe the Soul cannot dye, because I conceive it a thing impossible, the Soul being an Eternal Spirit, cannot be capable of death; and besides *Solomon* faith, *then shall the dust return to the earth as it was, and the Spirit shall return unto God who gave it;* So it is my believe the Soul cannot dye.

Faith. Though this Principle be fully clear in the Prophets Book, called joyful news in Heaven; yet I shall reveal the truth of it upon another account, that the Soul is mortal so capable to dye, otherwise it could not live Eternal; for as nothing but life can dye, and that life being dead, shall be made capable to live a life Eternal.

Reason. Before thou proceed any further, let me but hear how that nothing but life can dye, which it is conceived by all knowing men, that life which thou callest the Soul is immortal, and cannot dye: Now that natural life that runs in the blood may dye; and therefore it is confessed when a man is murthered or hanged, his breath is stifled, and so the natural mortal dies; yet all this while, as *Solomon* faith, *The Soul goeth to God that gave it.*

Faith. Having in our former writings made it appear that *Solomon* was the highest pitch of Reason that ever was, so what he spake was onely knowledge in nature, and not by the Revelation of Faith; therefore no Scripture: For Reason imagineth things that are not, and things that cannot be understood by any sober man, much less by a man in Revelation, as to think that an immortal Soul or Spirit, should be limited to a mortal body, which is as possible as light and darkness to dwell together, as an immortal Soul to live in a mortal body; therefore I say, that the Soul and body of man are one distinct living and dying essence, for the Soul or Spirit in the womb by degrees congeals together into a rational fire of blood and water, and so in due time become a compleat body of flesh, blood and bone; so that the life that is in man, is not Divine but natural onely.

Reason. This is strange, that the Soul or Spirit of a child should conceive in the womb, that being a breath or gift of God, and not generated in or by the seed; for I read, that God breathed into *Adam*, and he became a living Soul; so his Soul was not immortal, but mortal, and so is all man-kind.

Faith. However it is strange to thee, yet I know it is a real truth to me, that the Word by which God first created life in man, that Word or Breath is immortal, which by his fall became mortal, as at large is cleared in the seventh Chapter; and this know, God never created but male and female, and gave life but once, and since every life in its kinde hath generated bearing seed in its self; so that from my Revelation, I say, that the rational Soul or Spirit of man lyes secretely his in his seed, like unto a spark of fire; which spark doth quicken it self into a living form, like unto his nature, and so having cloathed it self with flesh, his Soul or Spirit runs invisibly through the whole body, and so is one entire substance, being both conceived into life in the womb together, and both living together upon the earth their appointed time, and being both polluted together with sin, is it not requisite that they should dye together, and turn to the dust and non-being again, until the general bodily Resurrection of all man-kind?

Reason. I know no other, but that every man hath in him a good Spirit, and a bad spirit, as it is written, *The Spirit lusteth after the flesh, and the flesh against the Spirit, and these are contrary*[*]; So that by the learned it is believed, that there is a natural life, and an Eternal life in one man, otherwise the body and Soul are both one, which in Scripture I never read, that these were both one, but two; one fleshly and the other spiritual.

---

[*] Gal 5. 17.

Faith.   Didst thou know the truth of what thou hast said, then wouldst thou know as followeth, that every man in his fallen spirit hath remaining a little light, or motion in him to justifie all the righteous proceedings of the Creator in his Conscience as the last day; yet mind what I say, he hath but one Soul or Spirit in him, for that which the Apostle calls spirit in this place, was a Divine light of life received unto the dark understanding, by vertue of a word speaking from the eternal Spirit of the Lord of glory (and not the essence of the holy Spirit) for I know, that those who do expect a glory to come in the invisible Heavens do confess that the spirit of the Divine Majesty is infinite, unchangeable, immortal & eternal; therefore how thinkest thou it possible, for men or Angels to be capable of the indwelling of the office of his Eternal Spirit? And that which the Apostle calls flesh, was mans own Spirit which consists of nothing but confused lying imagination, or cursed carnal reasoning against the Heavenly light aforesaid; Now that I may answer the last clause of thy demand, that the Soul and body is one, it is written, *All the Souls that came with* Jacob *into Egypt, which came out of his loins, were threescore and six souls**; again it is written, *Thy Fathers went down into Egypt with seventy persons*†; So that it is plain man is sometimes called Soul and sometimes is called a body or person, or Soul, Body and Spirit, and yet man is but one living essence, or substance. However the learned of thy seed pretend they know much of this, when indeed they know the least of all, as to separate a mortal soul from a mortal body, which is as possible to make light and darkness, God and Devil, one.

Reason.   This is strange, that none but thou shouldst know or discern the Soul immortal, when almost the whole world believes the Soul was never generated, but the breathings of the Spirit of God, which are immortal, and cannot dye.

Faith.   From the Revelation of Faith, I say, those conceited wise men, which through the ambition of Tongues and Languages have studied beyond all sober sense or reason, to make all the world senseless sots, as to think when the Seed is conceived in the womb, that then God must come and give it a Soul, be it a Bastard or Freeborn, the child can have no Soul till God give it; so that thou makest God not onely a partner, but a perfecter of mans base lust in that filthy act: But however, thy thoughts are unseal'd concerning God; yet this I know, that all Souls since the fall of *Adam*, are but mortal, natural, and must dye in the body, being generated to live together must dye together, in that they are both guilty of sin, cannot ascend but rot in the grave together, as it is written, *The Soul of man shall be*

---

* Gen 46.
† Deut 10.

cut off from the Land of the Living, and the Soul that sins shall dye, and that the pure Soul of Christ was poured forth unto death, and the Lord has said that Adam and Eve were but dust, and to dust they should return again; also it is written, That David is not ascended into the Heavens*, &c. Now what should ascend, if not Davids Soul? For it is written, Not this body, but such a body as pleaseth God to give it; So not the body, but the Soul thou sayest must ascend; then know, this Soul was in the dust, and not ascended; for David is not ascended, as much as if it had been said, Davids Soul is not ascended, nor no Soul without a body can ascend, and there can be no ascension till the Soul hath past through death, it can never ascend to Eternal life.

Reason. If the Soul at the hour of death, did not ascend to glory, or descend to misery, how come it then that John writes, I saw under the Altar the Souls of them that were slain for the Word of God, and for the Testimony which they held, and they cryed with a loud voice, saying, How long, O Lord, holy and true, dost thou not judge and avenge our blood on them that dwell on the earth†? So that surely John saw many Souls in Heaven crying unto the Lord to avenge their blood on their enemies, otherwise he had not declared it.

Faith. Thy ignorance hath been great, as now it is in this, as for thee to imagine that John saw Souls in Heaven without bodies, and their spirits without face, mouth and tongue, should cry, How long holy, and true? &c. When a Soul without a face and tongue cannot be seen, nor speak; therefore I tell thee, there is a greater Mystery in those words, then thou art aware of; for from thy Seed spring I say, it is no more then the blood of Abels which cryed unto the Lord from the ground; and so doth all the blood of the Saints, From the blood of Righteous Abel, unto the blood of Zacharias; and so to the end of our Commission, Do cry O Lord, holy and true, why dost thou not avenge our blood on them that dwell on the earth? This John saw by Revelation as Steven and Paul in another case did see the Heavens opened: And so John saw a wonder in Heaven, a Woman cloathed with the Sun, and the Moon under her feet, and the Stars upon her head‡; Now when John saw this great wonder, he was not in Heaven, but upon the earth; so it was the blood of the Righteous Souls that were murthered in their bodies, that John saw, not in glory, but upon this earth.

Now whereas thou art almost confident, that at the hour of death the Souls go out of the body, if so, deal plainly with thy self, and tell me what it is like; for surely, the Soul must have some form or shape and so cannot get out but it would be seen by some that stands by; for if a soul were of that form and fashion as White in his Chamber

---

* Acts 2.
† Rev 6. 10.
‡ Rev 12. 1.

at *Whithall* shewed me the picture of a soul in a Book, a dark soul, and a light soul, in form like a scoperil; I say, if the soul were as such wise Head-pieces reports, how comes it that it cannot be seen to go out of the diseased? For my part, I have been at the death of some, and yet could not discern any thing come from them but groans and flegm; so that if thou will all thy seed were not stone blinde, thou wouldst clearly see the soul dyeth within the body for want of evaquation with the body.

Reason. If it be as thou sayest, that all souls are dead in the dust, and so become dust, How, or which way shall there souls be found out, or raised at the last day?

Faith. From the Lord of glory I speak it, there is not any of the seed that doth in the least understand how to answer this Argument; therefore that Faith may be known to be Lord over thee and thy seed, I declare, that Christ Jesus being a quickning Spirit, not oneley as in relation to himself, but all man kind, as it is written, *The first man* Adam *was made a living Soul, and the second man* Adam *was made a quickning Spirit;* I say, his Soul being perfectly dead and buried in the grave, yet in death he quickned himself to life without the help of any, as in the second Chapter is clear; so as it is written, *Your life is hid in Christ with God, so that when Christ who is our life shall appear, then shall we also appear with him in glory**: therefore as he was able to quicken his own Soul so at the general account he is far more able by the word of his mouth, to quicken the Seed of Faith, that now are dust to eternal glory; also to quicken the seed of Reason to eternal misery; yea, and that from the first soul called *Adam,* to the last soul dying, he can and will in the twinkling of an eye, raise all the Seed of Faith, that hath layn so long in the dust, to meet him in the Air with bodies sutable to their natures; yea, the very appearance of Christ, who is all life, will quicken that which is dead in the grave to hear his voice, and immediately to come forth and meet him in the Air, as it is written, *The hour is coming in which all that are in the graves shall hear his voice*†.

Reason. That I understand is the raising of another body, and not the soul, for it is written, *it is sown a natural body, and is raised a spiritual body;* so that I conceive it is not the soul but that body raised another, that will be the work of the Lord at the day of Judgement.

Faith. Oh! Senseless sot, that I should thus spend my time with thee, when thou neither believes Scripture, nor can rightly interpret any Scripture, when thou mayest read in the 36th and 37th

---

* Col. 3. 3,4.
† John 5. 28.

verses these words, *Thou fool, that thou sowest is not quickned, except it dye, and that which thou sowest not, that body that shall be but bare grain, it may chance of wheat, or of some other grain**: Now consider, is not the life of the wheat grain in the body of the wheat corn when it is sowed? And doth it not in its season dissolve its body with its life into dust, and there dye, yea, perfectly dead, till such time as refreshing showers, and the heat of the Sun beams, which is the life of the earth, quicken that life which then lay dead, to a new life, by which vertue it cloaths it self, not with that old body, but a new body, and so abides not alone, but brings forth a new encrease of *sixty, seventy or an hundred fold?* Now let me speak freely to thee, as it is with the grain of wheat, so it is with the soul of man, for that is buried with the body in the earth, were both soul and body is corrupted to dust, and there lyeth as the wheat grain, perfectly dead, till such time that quickning Spirit, the Lord of all life, do appear, and quicken that mortal soul which then was become dust, to an immortal soul, which after shall become an immortal life, by which quickning it is clothed with a spiritual immortal body, all glorious like God himself; so now having a body sutable to its nature, a spiritual, powerful, swift body, like unto its Soul, is now able to ascend to meet his Redeemer in the Air, and so return with him into glory; so that from the Lord of all power, I say, if the soul were immortal in a mortal body, and could not dye, but ascend to glory, then I say, there would be no need of Resurrection, in that *this body shall not rise, though the Grave and the Sea at that day shall give up their dead,* is not intended their dead bodies, but their dead souls that hath been many years drowned, or buried, that shall arise whether out of water or earth, their souls shall arise, every seed his own body; but this I say, if the soul were in glory already without a body, as it cannot be, then it were in vain to raise a body out of the earth, to meet a spiritual Soul in Heaven, in that no body can be raised without its soul, nor a soul be anything without its body; so that if thou wert not stone blind, thou wouldst say with me, that to believe thy soul should go to Heaven without its body, neither God nor Angels could see it or take notice of it, nor the soul it self know what or where it is, and so in conclusion never be capable of glory at all.

CHAP. 10.

Shewing what Heaven is, and how many there are, with the nature and form thereof.

Reason. What Heaven is that, or where is it that these believing souls shall go to at the last day of Resurrection?

---

* 1 Cor 15. 36.

Faith. First I shall tell thee from an unerring Spirit, how many Heavens there are, and which of those three, this Heaven is, that all believing souls shall inherit eternal glory in the personal enjoyment of their God, face to face.

I find but a threefold Heaven spoken of in Scripture, whatever thy seed vainly imagine to the contrary.

The first that I shall infallibly speak of is the visible Firmamental Heaven, which is adorned with maty majestical lights above us, and a fixed earth beneath us, beautiful, in its season with variety of delights, which is natures onely desired Heaven, through the secret Decree of the most wise God, to manifest the variety of his most infinite wisdom unto Elect men and Angels, in creating such natural glory to perish, with the Angelical merciless Rulers thereof, after they have enjoyed their momentary glory, as it is written, *Thou Lord in the beginning hast established the earth, & the Heavens are the works of thy hands, they shall perish, but thou dost remain, they shall wax old, as doth a garment;* this is that visible Heaven with the glory thereof.

Reason. Which is then the next Heaven by Scripture proved, that so, if possible, I may come to know that Heaven which is Eternal, and shall never perish.

Faith. As I do not set forth these Heavens in order, so I say, thou canst no, nor none of thy sed have any Faith in what I have or shall say; but however, the next Heaven I shall treat upon, is that within the bodies of men, or the first man *Adam,* as it is written, *The Kingdom of Heaven is within you, and Christ in you the hope of glory, and know you not that Christ is in you, except ye be Reprobates?* Now this Heaven is that spiritual creation in natural bodies, and within this perishing Globe, that through its union with changeable nature, if might enter into mortality, that so after a moments tasting of silent death, as God himself did, it might quicken again through death it self spiritual bodies, full of Divine glories, by which all the Elect, as swift as thought, ascend to meet their Lord in the Air, and with his Divine person of bright burning glory, enter into that prepared Throne of Eternal pleasures, by which such a soul hath perfect peace with assurance here, that it shall enjoy what it in this world believed.

Reason. How is it possible any creature should give a description of the Kingdom of glory? Which I perceive thou wilt say, is the third and highest Heaven, seeing it is a place that by mortals cannot be seen, therefore not known; I conceive no mortal flesh is able to speak of it, according to its form and nature.

Faith. From the Lord of glory I say, what is impossible to Reason, is possible to Faith; for by the Revelation of this Faith I can see, and do know that the third Heaven is invisible, yet visible ravishing glories which are Eternal; this is that vast Kingdom, where the persons of the mighty Angels, and glorified bodies of *Moses* and *Elias* do now inhabit, beholding the Face of that most Excellent Majesty, whose Divine nature is Crowns of unutterable excellencies; this is that habitation, third Heaven, Throne, or Kingdom, that the Pen of man is not able to write, or his Tongue to speak. However, what by Revelation I have seen, I shall here declare, that the form of it is non-Globical, insomuch, that there is no end of the height of it, nor circumference thereof; insomuch, that God, his Saints and Angels, may ascend ten thousand times ten thousand, and yet no Globe to hinder, so excellent, glorious, swift, personal Majesty as God is; and as for the nature of this Heaven, it is so infinite, that there is all manner of creatures, for the contemplation of God, his elected Saints and Angels.

Reason. What dost thou believe that there is all manner of other creatures in Heaven, besides Angels and Saints, as there is here below in the same forms and shapes, as they are here in this world? If so, How are they supported, and by what means do they live?

Faith. From my Seed-spring within me, I affirm, that in the third and highest of Heavens, the Kingdom of glory, there is a perfect earth, and that is the Lords foot stool, which earth is immortal glorious, upon which there is all manner of Trees, Herbs, Plants, and all manner of four-footed beasts, all manner of Fowls; also I say, there is chrystall Sea, in which are all manner of Fishes, nay, to be shore there is nothing here but what is there, though this is to be understood, as these are mortal, those are immortal, fiery glorious of a bright shining nature, sutable for such a Majesty to solace himself withall, as also his Saints and Angels; also there is Thrones, varieties of Glory, with such Heavenly glorious Trumpetting voices, from the Divine mouth of Saints and Angels, that the Glory of Eternity doth ring again with such a sweet Divine Harmony, that the enjoyment thereof is unutterable, and the more they daily encrease with new joyes of ravishing praises and delights after all their tedious sufferings, and that without end; Oh! The Eternity, the Eternity, is that which makes it incomparable delightful, otherwise the Kingdom of Glory above would little transcend the glory here, were it not Eternal and full of variety of Divine pleasures, but in that it is so, as I know and believe; therefore I cannot but say, as touching the third and highest Heavens, Oh! The Glory, the top of Glory, yea, ravishing glories without end.

Reason. How dost thou know this, and where by Scripture canst thou prove this, that there is such variety of immortal creatures there, as there are mortal creatures here?

Faith.   Although this by Scripture could not be proved, yet by Faith it ought to be believed; for it is written, *Faith is the substance of things hoped for, and the evidence of things not seen, for through Faith we understand the worlds were framed by the Word of God; so that the things which are seen, were not made of things which do appear**: Now if thou couldst understand the truth herein contained, then thou wouldst with me conclude, that all things that are here seen with thy natural eye, were brought forth after the same plat-form of things above, which do not appear; so that from my Seed-spring, I affirm, that there is not the variety of things here, but there is the same above in the same likeness, there in glory, as here in shame; so that there is all day and no night, and that because the fiery glorious person of God being the light thereof, in which Kingdom the glorified of the Lord may stand, walk, talk, sit, lye, flye, yea, recreate themselves in whatsoever their Divine Souls moves them to, and that without the least motion of either pain, sorrow or weariness, in whatsoever it is intended to do, and that because there is no end of new springing delights, and that non fancies of the eye, but substantial realities that may be felt and embraced; so that I esteem the hardship of this present world not once to be compared to that glory that shall be revealed in my soul, and that Eternal without end, so as it is written, *We look not at things which are seen here, by the eye of Reason*†; but at the things which cannot but by the eye of Faith, *In that things which are seen, are temporal, but the things which are not seen, are Eternal;* therefore, *Our affliction, which is but for a moment, worketh for us a far more exceeding weight of Eternal Glory.*

CHAP. 11.

Shewing what Hell is, where it is, with the Form and Nature of its torment.

Reason.   What is that place called Hell, and where is it, that the unbelieving souls go to at the day of Resurrection?

Faith.   Having at large treated about this Particular in a Book of mine entituled, *Look about you, for the Devil that you fear is in you;* as touching the place of torment, as also what Hell is, and where it is; yet now I shall give thee a discovery of it upon a clearer and higher account, that Hell is the body of man, and the life, spirit or soul therein, is the Devil.

---

* Heb. 11 1, 2.
† 2 Cor. 4. 17.

Reason.　　　How can Hell be in man? When it is written, after both *Dives* and *Lazarus* was dead and buried, the *which man being in Hell**, *he lift up his eyes in torment, and seeth Abraham afar off, and* Lazarus *in his bosom, and he cryed and said, Father* Abraham *have mercy on me, and send* Lazarus *that he may dip the tip of his finger in water, and cool my tongue, for I am tormented in this flame;* so that from hence I judge no man is in Hell, till after death.

Faith.　　　In the first place thou must know, this was a parabolical speech of the Lord of Glory, in which the nature of two Seeds, *viz.* Faith and Reason are discovered; that is to say, Faith representing the poor man *Lazarus,* and Reason representing the person of the rich man *Dives,* not that the rich man was in any Hell without him, no more then thou art at this time; yet this I know, it is a true description of the state and condition of Reason, being tormented in a burning flame, with the sting of their own Conscience, and that not onely as in relation to the various doubts and fears that attends themselves; but on the contrary, the assurance that believers enjoyes in this his present being; for this I know, that those who are true heirs of *Abraham,* according to Faith, are in his bosom, that is in the same peace and perfect assurance as *Abraham* was; for this I know, that *Abrahams* Soul is rotted with his body in the grave, and can neither see, hear, speak, move or go, no more the rich Devils of this world can, till the day of Resurrection; from my Seed-spring, I declare, that the Souls of Righteous or Wicked goes neither to Heaven nor Hell, but both lyes uncapable of either joy or sorrow in silent dust, as at large is handled in the ninth Chapter; And whereas thou sayest, there is none in hell, till after death; I say, thou believes thou knows not what, for there is not onely thou, but many of thy Seed, are now in Hell tormented, that they cry unto the Seed of *Abraham,* to know what shall become of them in this their flame, crying out, they are damned, they are damned, wishing, Oh! That I had but one drop of that everliving water, to quench my flame, that runs as a Well-spring in the Souls of the Seed of Faith, by which they are freed from the unspeakable torment, that notwithstanding all thy riches and wisdeom, thy seed or generation are plugged in.

Reason.　　　However, thou would perswade me that there is no Hell without man, what then dost thou say to that place, where it is written, *Tophet is ordained of old, yea, for the king it is prepared, he hath made it deep and large, the pile thereof is fire, and much wood, with the breath of the Lord, like a flame of brimstone doth kindle it*†; So that I believe there is a hill, either in the air or under the earth reserved for the souls of all the wicked at their death, as it is written,

---

* Luk 16. 20.
† Isaiah 30. 33.

The wicked shall be turned into hell, and all the nations that forget God[*].

Faith. Whatever thou hast in this conference thought of me, yet I have not in the least gone about to perswade thee, or any of thy seed, to credit what I have revealed, in that the benefit of this discourse will onely redound to the seed of faith, and as for this Scripture that thou hast quoted, here is neither thou nor any of the seed can tell, what to make of it, yet for thy conviction and confirmation of the blessed of the Lord, I shall give thee the true interpretation thereof, which is as followeth, *Tophet is ordained of old, yea, for the king it is prepared:* Now I know this king is reason which is the God of this world, as indeed there hath been since kind *Saul* but few Kings that were of the seed of *Abraham*, according to faith, but onely reason, yet however, the king here intended is the seed of reason, whether moderate or immoderate, it is *Esau* the elder brother, as unto the Government of this world, it is the onely king, and the situation of it is deep and large, in that there is no end of reasons imagination, it is so deep in cogitation, *that it is compared to a bottomless pit;* and therefore the prophet crieth, *Hell hath enlarged her self, and opened her mouth without measure,* as all along it hath appeared by thee, so deep and so large, that faith can neither fathom thy God or thy devil, thy heaven or thy hell, they are so infinite and boundless, that there is no true account of any thing thou sayest for a true believer to build his salvation upon: Now whereas it is said, the pile thereof is fire and much wood, that is, the evil motions and wicked actions which thy deep and large seed of reason hath imagined things to be that are not, and things that are real in their being cannot be comprehended by thee, *Therefore the breath of the Lord like a stream of brimstone doth kindle it;* which breath is no other but the Law held forth by his Messengers, which will kindle thy motions and actions in a never-dying fire; for as the pile and the wood is fuel, for the external fire, so are the wicked actions of Reason fuel for the eternal fire of the Law, that shall burn throughout thy Soul and body, with an unquenchable flame; so that this soul of thine is that Hell surrounded with the wicked imagination of reason.

Reason. What then is there no place of torment to be prepared for the wicked, as there is a place of glory prepared for the Godly? And if there be a place, let me hear thy judgement, where it is to be, and the nature of it.

Faith. This in a few words I shall give thee a true description thereof, that the place where all the seed of Reason shall possess their eternal tormenting misery, shall be on this earth; for as it is in your

---

[*] Psal 9. 17.

Law, where a man commits his fact, there he must receive his penalty; so where a man commits his sin, there he must receive his torment; then know, that on this earth it shall receive its torment, which when the Lord cometh to put an end to this thy kingdom, the Sun, Moon and Stars shall be put forth as the snuff of a Candle; and then this light, glorious world shall return to a confused darkness, yea, a darkness that may be felt, and the waters for want of the Moon, will become a standing stinking Pool, and the earth for want of the Sun, will be dust or dry land, where there the seed of Reason shall be raised spiritual bodies, sutable to their souls, where therein shall flame, yea, burn, and that for ever, yea, for ever, for ever, without end.

Reason. If these that thou hast here related be truth, then I say, there can no flesh scarcely be saved; and for my part, I am no wiser in what I have heard then what I was before; neither do I know, what to make of them, nor hereafter shall much trouble my minde with them; but do really believe, that there is more blasphemous lies, then real truths in them; for all the moderate wise men of the world, do judge God a Spirit, and the Devil not man, but a spirit; and as for the Soul, is believed to be immortal, and so either to ascend to Heaven, or descend to Hell; and I verily believe, there is not one of 20 thousand, that will believe any thing contained in thy discourse, so that it causeth admiration in me, that all should be deceived; but those that believeth in these things, which if I be deceived, I must be, for I can neither believe in thee, nor thy Doctrine.

Faith. What thou hast now said, is not in the least strange to my Soul, that thou shouldst declare thy self, as how thou hast done; for I have told thee all along, that thou nor thy seed was not to understand this Doctrine, no more then the Jews were to understand Christ, as it is written, *Why do ye not understand my speech, because ye cannot hear my word, for ye are of your Father the Devil, and the lust of your Father ye will do?** &c. Even so I say unto thee, thou being according to birth the seed of Reason, so of the nature of the Devil, thou judgest the truth a lye, and a lye a truth, because it is not given to thy seed to know the Mysteries of the Kingdom of Glory; therefore I say, as *John* said, *We are of God , and the whole world lyeth in wickedness*†; so I infallibly know, that almost the whole world will perish, save those few that believed in the last spiritual Commission, and because thou hast called this a blasphemous lye, by Christ Jesus Creator of Heaven and earth, whose Revelation of Faith, the Seed of his own body, thou has judged false, and called a blasphemous lye; I say in the vertue of our Commission, that was given by a audable

---

* John 8. 43,44.
† 1 John 5. 19.

CHAP. 12.

Shewing what Authority a Commissioner hath in the vertue of his Commission; what the effects and operation thereof.

Reason. What art thou more then I, that thou dost thus assume Authority to thy self, that onely belongs to God? however, thy curse I matter not, onely I tremble to behold thy presumption for I know it is the curse of God, and not of man, that must bring a soul under condemnation.

Faith. Whatever thy thoughts are of me, I matter not; but this thou shalt finde, that I have power in the Revelation of my Commission, to curse not onely thee, but any of thy seed, that shall do as thou hast done, to call it a lye: And in the Revelation of my faith, I say, That the Sentence of Blessing and Cursing belongs onely to the Prophets and Messengers of that Commission: for I testifie unto thee, That God the giver of Commissions, never damned any but the Angelical seed in the Womb of *Eve,* who is the Father of thee, and all the damned, as all along it is recorded: That in the name of the Lord, the Prophets and Apostles pronounced Plagues, Woes and Judgements against all the despisers of their Commission, in that they were Ambassadors and Stewards in Christs stead; so we the Prophets and Messengers of God, represent the Authority of our Commission, as the Prophets and Apostles did in theirs.

Reason. If thou please, let me hear what thou intends by a Commission, and why this is a Commission more then any other Dispensation now in being; for I conceive, were it not ambition in them, that Quakers and all others, may assume the Authority to bless and curse as now thou dost.

Faith. Notwithstanding, I have sufficiently unfolded our Commission in the *Quakers Downfal;* yet that thou mayest be left excuseless, I shall in another way infallibly lay down the truth thereof in these particulars:

1. How many Commissions there was to be in this perishing world.
2. The nature and tenor of a Commission.

3. The powerful operation of a Commission.

1. As unto the first, it is writ, *There are three that bear record in heaven, the Father, the Word, and the Holy Ghost, and these three are one; and there are three that bear witness on earth; the Spirit, the Water, and the Blood, and these three agree in one**: Now as God did consist of three titles, and not three persons, as thou and thy seed vainly immagine; that is to say, Father, Son, and Holy Ghost: So from each of these issued forth a Commission upon this earth; for in the time that he bore the title of Father, *Moses* and the Prophets was in Commission: Now when that Father became Word, Flesh, so called Son or Christ, then the Apostles were in Commission; after that both Father and Son became Holy Ghost, or one entire Spiritual Body, now in Heaven glorified, the next after came forth our Commission; so that according to the titles above, there was to be three Commissions in this world, suitable to the three titles in Heaven.
2. As unto the nature of a Commission, it is not given in silence, but upon record under hand and seal, to the Messenger or Messengers therein included, with an exact charge to observe the Kings pleasure, according to the tenor and form thereof: Now in this Commission being given to thee, doth not concern another; for the names included for that Embassage, doth this Commission belong: Now for any other to counterfeit thy Commission, thou hast power by vertue thereof, to apprehend him for a Traytor against the King thy Master.

    Even so it is with a Commission from God, which is not given by private whisperings in the soul, as all counterfeits imagine, every motion, whimsey or fancy in the minde, more than ordinary, is a call from God; not knowing, yet daily reading, that all Commissions were given by laudable voyce of words, to the hearing of the ear, as to *Moses, Paul,* and now in this last to *John Reeve:* Now then, what are all these seven Dispensations, but by *Moses,* the Apostles, and this Commission, impeached for Traytors against the Christ the Lord of Glory.
3. And thirdly, the power of a Commission is so great, that it commands, yea, subjects the spirits of all that it hath to deal with: A man in Commission, represents the Authority of the great God of Heaven and Earth, that whatever he bindes, imprisons or condemns on earth, is so in Heaven; and whosoever he declares blessed or happy here, are so in Heaven; so that if thou wert not stone blinde, thou wouldst then see, that there is no Teacher publique nor private now living, that hath a Commission, but we; and therefore it is we have power over all mens spirits, yea, the judge of all spiritual things, of what sect or opinion soever.

---

* 1 Joh. 5. 7,8.

Reason.   O what a boasting dost thou make, that none but your Commission hath power over mens spirits; and that onely to you belongs blessing and cursing, when I conceive there is many able, wise Teachers, that are as true Commissioners as you, and yet dare not assume that power to themselves, as you do.

Faith.   O thou man of pretended light, yet gross darkness, bring any man now living, except this Commission, that dares say he had a Commission by voyce of words from God, as we have, thou shalt hear that I will curse them, as I have cursed thee: And where is any of your Teachers, that hath a Commission of his own, but *Moses* and the Apostles, whom they counterfeited and made merchandize for their own gain: From the Lord of Glory, I say, not any of them, no not the wisest or moderatest head-piece, dare or can in peace of conscience say, that thou are damned, and another is saved: Alas poor blinde leaders of the blinde, they know not what will become of their own souls, how then can they judge anothers, but they will be condemned for so doing; for were I not certain of the knowledge of the true God, and the right Devil, and all others that are ignorant thereof, are culpable of judgement, instead of being justified, I should be condemned; and yet what a flutter *Casars* Ministers make, in praying to a God that is no God, and preaching delusions of their own inventions, pretending thus and thus, saith the Lord, when Christ the onely God knows them not, neither did he send them; therefore from my Seedspring, I say, they are all Thieves and Robbers, yea Traytors against the God of Heaven, for do but bring any of them before me, and thou mayest take notice I have power over their blinde zeal, that if they do not for future desist in bewitching the people to believe lies, thou shalt then hear the same sentence pass upon them, as hath already passed upon thee.

Reason.   Which of them will believe the sentence of thy Commission, unless thou couldst shew some present example either without or within, as the Prophet *Elias* did, to cause fire from Heaven, and stop the rain, that it rain not: Now if thy curse be true, how comes it that I do not finde it immediately within or without.

Faith.   Thou art worse then the inhabitants of *Jerusalem and Judea, that believe in* John *that did no miracle, and yet was a Prophet, yea, I say, more then a Prophet; for as Christ said, among them that are born of women, there hath not risen a greater then* John *the Baptist*[*]; and yet thou and thy teachers will not believe unless present vengeance fall upon thee: But know this, though the Pharisees *desired a sign from Christ, and none would be given them but the sign of the*

---

[*] Mat. 11. 11.

Prophet Jonas*; yet know this, he was Christ the Eternal God for all that; and though Christ rebuked *James* and *John,* in the saying, *Lord, wilt thou that we command fire from Heaven, and consume them, even as* Elias *did*†? Yet they were not for the future freed from the Eternal fire in their souls: So let me tell thee, and yet not I, but the Revelation of the Holy Spirit within me, though not presently, yet it shall flame within thee as fire from Heaven, and that without end, till it consume all thy hopes of salvation, and thou shalt know and finde, that this sentence of thine shall shut the Heavens, and it shall rain no more showers of mercy or comfort in thy soul; so that I say though thou finde it not presently, thou shalt surely feel it after death, as Christ is God the Eternal Father. And what if miracles did belong to our Commission, as they do not, in that ours is the Commission of the Spirit, so our sentence spiritual, thou wouldst no more believe then thou dost now, but rather call us Conjurers, unless the tenor of our Commission was as the two former, to execute present vengeance; and if it were executed once or twice, and not upon every occasion, thou wouldst be as much seared up in unbelief as thou art now.

Reason. If thy Commission were as real truth as *Moses* and the Apostles, and such a power did attend thine, as was in theirs, that I should as truly believe in yours, as now I do in them.

Faith. Ah blinde Soul, thou dost not know what is truth, and what not; for if thou didst, thou wouldst as really believe in me as in them: But from my Seedspring I tell thee, That thou, nor none of thy Seed, do really believe, that the Scripture is the true Record of the Transactions of Christ; thou mayest talk of it, and preach from it, but if thou wert really perswaded in thy own soul, of the truth therein contained, then thou wouldst believe in us; for the Apostles writ of us, as *Moses* and the Prophets writ of Christ to come; and therefore if thou didst believe in them, that have nothing but a dead letter to prove them Commissioners, surely then thou wouldst believe in us that are living; and know this, if the Roman Authority had not established *Moses* and the Apostles Writings for Scripture, then it has been believed no more then ours; for thy Fathers, in the days of their lives, notwithstanding their miracles, did no more believe in them, then thou dost in us; and know this, the same power that attended them upon externals, doth belong to our Commission in spirituals; and therefore as the Apostle has power in his Commission to curse either Angel or man, that did preach any other Doctrine, so we have the same power in ours.

---

* Matt. 12. 38.
† Luke 9. 54.

Reason.   What then, doth not their Commissions belong to us in these days successively, as it did to them? What then is the meaning of those Scriptures, where it is writ, *The Scriptures aforetime are written for our learning:* and again it is writ, *Teaching them to observe all things whatsoever I have commanded you, and loe I am with you always, unto the end of the world**.

Faith.   From the Lord of Glory I tell thee, That neither of those Commissions do belong to thee, or any of thy Seed, either by succession or otherwise; for from my Seed of Faith I declare, That the Scripture was never written for the learning of any of thy Seed, though none living now present, do make it a more Idol for their own gain, then thy Seed doth: Though I have sufficiently proved this point in the *Quakers Downfal,* yet from my well-spring within me, I tell thee, That as the Scripture was written by the revelation or inspiration of Faith, so I know it was writ for the use of none, but the Believers of that Faith; which neither thou nor none of thy Seed are partakers of: For as *Paul* the great Commissioner, was the Penman of those sayings, so that Scripture that he spake of, was the writings of the first Commission; *viz. Moses* and the Prophets, which were written before his time, and so for the learning of him, and all that believed in his Doctrine, for our learning that are of the Seed of Faith, and for none of the Seed of Reason, whatsoever, but for our learning: The word *Plural* includes all the Seed of Faith with him were the Scriptures written; so the Commissions of *Moses* and the Apostles were not written for the use of any of the seven Churches, but our Commission alone; for as none understood the Commission of *Moses* and the Prophets, but the Apostles, so none now living understand either of the two former Commissions, but this our spiritual Commission now in being; and therefore from my Seedspring I tell thee, We onely are the Judges of the Scripture, whatsoever Reason, thy cursed Seed, pretend to the contrary, as now thou shalt hear an infallible Exposition of the other Scripture which thou hast quoted, which all besides our Commission, gives a false definition thereof; *Go ye therefore and teach all Nations, baptizing them in the name of the Father, Son and Holy Ghost, teaching them to observe all things whatsoever I have commanded you, and loe I am with you always, even unto the end of the world*†: Now from hence, all the seven Churches of thy Seed; *viz.* Papist, Episcopal, Presbyterian, Independent, Baptist, Ranter and Quaker, do suppose, that the extent of these words are in force to the end of this world; and therefore the Baptists have assumed the Apostles Commission as their own, when as if ye were not stone blinde, you may read as ye run, that this Commission was given to the twelve then living, and not to *Kiffin* and *Patience,*   or any other Teacher of the Baptists

---

* Matt. 28. 20.
† Matt 28. 20.

whatsoever; for ye were not born many hundred years after, when this command was expressed, *And loe I am with you always, even unto the end of the world;* with you my beloved Disciples, and none other.

Reason. I cannot conceive from this Scripture, but there was to be a continuance of the Apostles Commission to the end of this World; and though there was none of the Commissioners left to give or invest the same power by imposition of hands, yet we having the same Spirit of God in us, although not in the same measure, yet may we not lawfully follow them as our patern, and as the Apostle exhorts, *Brethren, be followers together of me, and mark them which walk so, as ye have us for an ensample*;* otherwise what should all the World have done, to have known God or Christ these many hundred years since, were not the Scripture written for our learning; and if the Scripture do not belong to all, then also the Law is void, and belongs to none; so then none would be condemned, as it is written, *I had not known sin, but by the Law,* and the Law makes sin exceeding sinful; so that if the Scripture do not belong to us, then we are freed from the Law, so then for thy curse, I shall be happy as thou.

Faith. In this last answer, I shall finish my discourse as touching the truth and variety of these three Commissions, in that I have already so infallibly treated of them in the first Chapter of the *Quakers Downfal,* I shall no longer demur with thee upon this, but shall divide the heads of thy Question into these particulars, and so exactly answer them as they lie in order.

1. That thou believes the Apostles Commission is to continue to the end of this World.
2. That though all the Commissioners were dead that had power to invest another, yet thou having the same Spirit, though, as thou faith, not the same measure, yet thou believest thou mayest pray, preach, and baptize, from the letter, as they did.
3. Thou sayest, if ye had not thus done, how should the world have come this hundred years to have known God or Christ, Hell, Heaven, or Devil.
4. Thou sayest, if the Scripture do not belong to thy Seed, then the Law doth not belong to thee, and so thou concludes all shall be happy as we.

    1. First, I declare, That the Apostles Commission was to continue to the end of the World held forth in that Commission; for this I know was the condition of thy Fathers the Jews, that did as really believe in blasphemy, for Christ or the Apostles to put an end to the Ceremonial part of the Law, as now thou dost that our Commission should put an

---

* Phil. 3. 17.

end to all Formal Worship under the Gospel: But however, I say unto thee, as Christ said to thy Fathers, *Think not that I am come to destroy the Law and the Prophets, I am not come to destroy, but fulfil;* So I am come not to destroy the revealed transactions of the Gospel, but to tell thee and thy Seed, that as there was to be three Commissions before the end of this World, so I know that every Commission is a World in it self, and to it self; and when the Commissioners dies, that commissionate World ends with them, otherwise thou mayest call God a lyar, to promise he would be with them to the end of this World, and many hundred years ago they are all dead, and yet this World remains; so that as I know the command was to none but them, and to hold no longer then the lives of them: so I know, that the beginning of one Commission here below, is the end of another; as thou art not ignorant what overturnings here hath been in your Kingdom, to the admiration of the inhabitants, so are the Commissions of God, the beginning of one was the end of another, by which the infiniteness of the Divine Revelation in the Person of God, is the more admired, to behold the seeming contrarieties of these three Commissions, that one puts a period to the other, as a greater light clouds the use of the other; not but the Moon is a true light in her self, but living in the light of the Sun, we have no need of the light of the Moon: So the Apostles light being more glorious then that of the Law, therefore no need of the Ceremonial part of the Law: So our light being far more glorious then that of the Apostles, therefore no need of the formal Worship of the Gospel.

2. Secondly, seeing the beginning of one Commission was the end of another, how then canst thou plead for a succession of the formal Worship in the Gospel, after all the Commissioners of the first or second Magnitude were put to death by the Fathers? Now if onely the Apostles had onely been put to death, yet if *Timothy* or *Titus,* who were Bishops or Messengers authorized by them, had been preserved in the continuance of that Commission, they might by the same power have continued the Bishoprick, by their imposition of hands upon another: If so, the effects thereof would not have produced such blind Lordly Bishops with lawn sleeves, caps, tippits, and such like fopperies, as ever since hath continued; so that if thou wert not stone blinde, thou mightst all along discern there was no succession, considering the Divine Knowledge, and poor mean estates of true Bishops, and the Humane knowledge, and lordly ragin of all the false Bishops ever since, as it is not many years ago since the Roman Lordly Authority had the whole power in this Nation, as in all other places, though now of late from that great Monster Bishop, the Whore of *Babylon,* there hath sprung six Sons or Generations, one from the loyns of another, yet each one refined more then his Father, as the Episcopal more than the Papist, the Presbyter more then that, and the Independent more then that, and the Baptist more then that, and the Ranter more then that, and the Quaker more then you all, insomuch, that the Father

hath disowned the childe, as the childe now doth the Father; and yet the refinest Son of them is but a Formal Worshipper in the Gospel, which when the last Son was begotten, or as it is written, *The last Angel founded, viz.* The Quaker, *then the mysterie of truth was revealed;* that is, our Commission was given by voyce of words, from the mouth of the Lord Jesus, as *Moses* and the Prophets were; which spiritual Commission of ours, doth abolish all formal Worship in the Gospel, as the Apostles did the Circumcision, with the blood of Bulls and Goats, and all such traditional Ceremonies attending the Law; and therefore as I am a Bishop or Messenger authorized in the power of my Revelation, confirmed by the Commission of this last Witness: so being in the height of Revelation with them, I say, That your Praying, Preaching, Breaking of Bread or Baptism, is now of no more value then Circumcision, or the blood of Bulls and Goats was in the Commission of the Apostles; which circumstances was of high prize and great value in the days of *Moses,* though not regarded by the Apostles; so all formal worhip of the Gospel is highly esteemed by thy seed, when by our Commission it is forbidden, and not regarded, as before I have finished my discourse with thee, thou shalt hear, so that till then, have patience, that so I may proceed to the third.

But thirdly, thou sayest, What should all thy Seed have done, had it not been for the Commission of the Apostles? As unto this I shall answer thee, As the *Disciples went all night a fishing, and caught nothing,* so thou hast all thy life time been enquiring after the true God by the light of another, and so hast not the knowledge of the true God, nor right Devil; but like a sloathful servant, hath hid thy talent in the letter of the Apostles; so that when the death summons thee to give an account of thy Stewardship, then thou begins to trim up thy lamp, and findes therein no oyl, and then cryeth unto the wise Virgins, that is, the wisdom of faith, *Give us of your oyl, for our lamps are gone out;* but then all in vain will thy doleful cries be, for the Scriptures cannot help thee, nor we cannot help thee, and therefore thou must go to thy Prayers, thy Preaching, and Pharisaical Righteousness, to buy thy salvation, and they can do thee no good; so that now thou mayest see how thou hast deluded thy soul with anothers Commission, so that now those small hopes of comfort shall be taken from thee, which then the Scripture will condemn thee, and our Commission keep thee in utter darkness without end.

But as some of the high flown of thy Seed, endued with a notional light above their fellows, have replied and said, That they will believe no report of man, but onely wait upon God for the teachings of his Spirit, supposing thereby to finde eternal satisfaction, without the revealed report of his Messenger at all; and that because they finde a saying to that purpose, as it is written, *The Anointing which ye have received of him, abideth in you, and ye need not any man teach you, but as the same Anointing teacheth you of all things;* and in another place, *Ye shall not need every man to teach his neighbor, for ye shall* *know the Lord, from the least to the greatest*;* Now there is not any of thy Seed that understandest these sayings were fulfilled in the days of the Apostles, as is confirmed by *Peter,* saying, *This is that which was spoken by the Prophet Joel†, &c.* that God would send the Comforter, which did fill them full of the Holy Ghost, as there at large is recorded; but however thou canst not believe this, yet in Revelation I tell thee, That if any such ever finde eternal happiness, it must be from the Commissioners of God, as from the mouth of *Moses* they received the Law, and by the Prophets the Rulers of *Israel* heard the Word of the Lord; and so in the two Commissions of the Apostles it is written, *How shall they call on him in whom they have not believed? And how shall they believe in him of whom they have not heard? And how shall they hear without a Preacher? And how shall they preach, except they be sent?‡* So that faith in the true God, comes by hearing the report of his true Messengers, and without them, how shall we ever know or come to God; for I infallibly declare, That the Messengers of every Commission hath *the word of Reconciliation, Salvation or Damnation, committed to them,* as it is written§, *We are Ambassadors for Christ, as though God did beseech you by us; so that we pray you in Christs stead, be ye reconciled to God, for he maketh manifest the savour of his knowledge by us in every place:* So that against all thy Seed I affirm, Whoever pretends to wait upon God, without the report of his Messengers that are sent by laudable voyce of words, they know not the true God, nor shall ever see the face of God at all; and therefore take notice, the onely Messenger of God told thee so.

Fourthly and lastly, I say, Though the Scripture doth not belong to thee yet the Law doth onely belong to thee, and thy Seed; for had it not been for thy Seed of Reason, their had been no need of a Law given; but because of the enmity of thy Seed, against the Seed of the Woman, the Law was revealed to *Moses* and by *Moses* was given to the people of *Israel,* in consideration there was a mixture of Seeds, which caused divisions and rebellion against the contrary Seed; *viz. Moses,* and that Generation, therefore that obedience might be required of them by the grand Commissioners, to that end of the Law was given to the universal body of *Israel,* that all *Israel* that was according to the flesh, and not the Spirit, might be made subject by the Law; that so upon their transgression, they might receive the penalty of the Law; and therefore it is written, *The Law is not made for a righteous man, but for the lawless and disobedient**;* for the ungodly and such like, which none of the Seed of faith once called are guilty of, but it is the daily practice of thy Seed, Reason the Devil; and therefore the Law

---

* 1 John 2. 27.
† Joel 2. 27, 28.
‡ Rom 10. 14,15,16.
§ 2 Cor 5. 19,20. 2 Cor 2. 14.
** 1 Tim 1. 9.

was given to the Devil, which thou mayest read in *Chap.* 8 recorded at large what his form and nature is, how compleat and beautiful, how learnedly wise he is in naturals, that this is his Kingdom, and the Devil the King thereof.

CHAP. 13.

Shewing what the Law is at large, and in short, and whether any can keep the Law, and when his is said to keep the Law, and when not.

Reason. Thou seemest to affirm, That the Law was given to the Seed of Reason, which thou all along hath said is the Devil; and if there had been no such Seed as Reason, there had been no need of a Law; by what rule then doth the Seed of Faith walk by, if the Law was not given to them as well as to our Seed, seeing both Seeds inhabits together, and those of that Seed have been as wicked as Reason.

Faith. As before thou hast heard me prove it, so now I affirm it, That the Law Moral, or the ten Commandments, was given to none but the Devil, that proud majestical Seed, the God of this World; for I must tell thee, if that wise rich Devil had not a curb to bridle them, there had been no living for the poor Devil of thy Seed, much less for the Seed of Faith to pass quietly by thee in the streets; were it not the Law doth say, *Thou shalt not kill,* thou wouldst murther me for declaring the truth to thee[*]: But in that *the Law makes sin to be sin, yea, and that exceeding sinful,* not onely the Gentile, but the Jew Devils also do, yea, are afraid to execute their cruelty beyond their bounds; though many of thy Seed do exceed it, yet the moderate Devil is fearful of it, saying, have a care what ye do to these men; as *Pilate* said, *I finde no fault in him, nor no cause of death*[†]*;* and so the Law wrought a terror in *Pilates* wife, saying *Have thou nothing to do with that just man,* &c. insomuch that *Pilate* took water and washed his hands before the multitude, saying, *I am innocent of the blood of this just person, see ye to it;* and therefore it is written, *That we may be delivered from unreasonable and wicked men*[‡]*,* that live without a Law, of which many of the Gentile Devils are guilty of, onely a word and a stab; when as the Jew Devil is subject to the Law, he is unreasonable, in that he will moderately try the innocent by the Law; so that God saw good, the Devils should have a Law to curb them, yea, torment them, and condemn them for ever.

---

[*] Rom 7. 7.
[†] Matt. 27. 19.
[‡] 2 Thes 3. 2.

Now the rule that the Seed of Faith doth walk by, is, not by the Law, but by Faith, as it is written, *The Law of faith hath freed us from the Law of sin and death**; though most of thy Seed do conclude themselves believers, yet I say, that freedom onely belongs to a Commission, and the believers thereof; as the Apostle includes all believers with him are free from the Law, and none other; *For Christ is the end of the Law for righteousness, to every one that believeth*†; And what though I have been a great sinner, yea so great (murther excepted) that there was few beyond me; yet now being *washed, sanctified, yea justified,* that I am now no longer *under the Law, but under Grace,* which none of thy Seed shall ever attain too, notwithstanding they seek it with tears.

Reason.   What then, do all believers of thy Commission keep the Law, and not any of the seven Churches keep the Law as well as thou? What then dost thou say of the Quakers, and many others, that are very moderate just men, insomuch that none can tax them with the breach of any of the ten Commandments?

Faith. I say, in the experience of my Revelation, there is not any keeps the Law, but those that are freed from the Law as aforesaid; and sure I am, there is none in the perfect Law of Liberty, but the Seed of the Woman; which Seed of Faith, doth run in the line of one Commission to another; so that I can speak for no more then I finde in the publique profession thereof, not denying, but there may be here one, and there on scattered up and down, which if the report of our Commission came but to the hearing of their ear, they would embrace it, as the rest of our believers do: But truly, I speak it, there are so few known, and not known, that there is not a hundred to ten millions of the contrary Seed, that will or can believe the report of a Commissioner as touching the true God; and therefore we may say with the Prophet, *Who hath believed our report, or to whom is the Arm of the Lord revealed*‡; that is, the arm of Faith revealed: So few there was in every Commission, that they were but a little, yea, and that a very little flock, in comparison of the non-commissionate Churches: And whereas thou supposeth by the moderate carriage, and just dealing betwixt man and man, the Quakers, with many other of thy Priesthood generation, may keep the Law as well as the believer of a Commission; I shall moderately answer thee in that saying of *James, That whosoever shall keep the whole Law, and yet offend in one point, is guilty of all*§: So that I say, though the Quakers of all the seven Churches, do nearest keep the Law, yet in that they offend in the first

---

* Rom 8. 2.
† Rom 10.4.
‡ Isa 53. 1.
§ Jam 2. 10.

command, they are guilty of all; for it is written, *Thou shalt have no other Gods but me**: Now, as aforesaid, thou hast heard me in the first and second Chapters, that there is none of your seven Churches, Sons of Generations, but you have other gods, besides Christ the onely God, some of you saying, God is a Spirit without form, and this Spirit God is within you; and other of you, will have no God but Nature onely; and the rest of thy Babylonish brood, will have one Spirit to have three persons: So that from the knowledge of the true God I tell you, all are guilty of the Law, though I acknowledge the Quakers exact walking, and therefore I love them, yet in that they are ignorant of the knowledge of the true God, which is life Eternal: I say, your Directories, forms of Prayer, the Creed, Baptism, breaking of Bread, and set days of Fasts and Thanksgiving, and such like stuff, are not onely a breach of the first, but second Commandment, all which have a *form of godliness, but not the power:* So that I say, they are no less then Idols, and graven Images of thy own invention, and therefore it matters not, though some of you keep all the rest of the Commands, and not know the true God, thou art guilty of all.

Reason. Then if a man come to the knowledge of the true God, that is sufficient, notwithstanding he break all the rest of the Commands; because thou faith, Thet keeping of all the rest is nothing, without he know that God which thou hast revealed.

Faith. However, it is thy pleasure to misconstrue me, in that thou knowest not the indwelling of truth in me; yet this is the thing I said unto thee, That though any of thy Seed keep all the Commands but the first, in that they keep not all, they are guilty of all; for this I know, the knowledge of the true God, leads forth a soul to keep all the Commandments of God; for in that I know him, therefore I love him, and so keep his Commandments, as it is written, *If ye love me, keep my Commandments.*

Reason. What then, dost not thou sin, because thou knowest the true God, and keeps his Commands? Then I must say, thou art more righteous and perfect then any man upon earth; for it is written, *If we say that we have no sin, we deceive our selves, and the truth is not in us*†, with such like places.

Faith. Let me tell thee, if I sin, I do not keep the Law, as it is written, *Whosoever commiteth sin, transgresseth the Law, for sin is the transgression of the Law*‡: But in that I have known the true God, which Seed of God remaining in me, I cannot sin, because I am

---

* Exo 20. 3.
† 1 John. 8.
‡ 1 Joh. 3. 4.

partaker of the Divine Nature of God: Now if I should say, that I have no motions to sin, I should deceive my self, and the truth is not in me; for I know there is a great difference betwixt a motion and an act; for it is to be understood, not he that thinketh a sin, *but he that committeth sin is of the Devil;* as all thy Seed are at a loss as touching the mysterie of this secret, not understanding a motion from an act, and therefore thousands of thy Seed perish for want of knowledge in that saying of Christ, *That whosoever looketh upon a Woman, to lust after her, hath committed adultery with her already in his heart*[*]: from hence concluding, that if thou dost but lust after her, thou mightst as well lie with her, and soo too too many of thy seed do commit the act indeed; when if thou hadst a discerning betwixt a thought and an act, thou hadst not defiled thy soul, as it is written, *When lust hath conceived, it bringeth forth sin, and sin when it is finished, bringeth forth death*[†]: Now while thy lust is a tempting, by which means, that thou hadst intended, is not conceived (so no sin) indeed lust was burning in thy heart, but in that it came not to perfection, the law hath quenched the flame; for what hath the Law to do with a heart-adultery, no, no, it is no thought, but an act that breaks the Law, and what comes not within the bounds of the Law, be it adultery, nay be it murther, if it lie onely in the heart, and be not acted, there can no Law condemn thee.

Reason.   What is thy thoughts as touching the fourth Commandment, as being changed from *Saturday* to *Sunday?* and what is the reason why this Command was changed above all the rest? and whether this Sabbath, called, *The first day of the week,* is not according to the judgement of the Assembly of Divines, to continue to the end of the World, without any alteration thereof?

Faith. It matters not me, what grounds or principles of Religion your Assembly of Divines holds forth, as a Catechism to thy Seed, for this by Faith I know, and against men and Angels affirm, That as the Commission of *Moses* ended in the Commission of the Apostles, so the Jewish Sabbath, with the rites thereof, ended in the Sabbath, or first day of the week of the Apostles: then know, as the Commission of the Apostles ends in our ours, so we have power as the Apostles, to erect you a Sabbath suitable to our Commission, for know this that one Commission is not tied in point of Revelation, to observe the former; but each Commission, according to its title and place, hath power in it self, to direct you what manner of Sabbath you are to keep; therefore observe the Sabbath of *Moses* Commission was in this nature as followeth; *viz.*

---

[*] Matt 5. 28.
[†] Jam 1. 15.

Remember the Sabbath day, to keep it holy, six day shalt thou labour, and do all thy work, but the seventh day is the Sabbath of the Lord thy God, in it thou shalt not do any work, thou, nor thy son, nor thy daughter, thy man servant, nor thy maid servant, nor thy cattel, nor thy stranger that is within thy gate; for in six days the Lord made heaven and earth, the sea, and all that in them is, and rested the seventh day: wherefore the Lord blessed the Sabbath day, and hallowed it.

Now this Sabbath thou wilt now own, but the First day, or Sabbath of the Apostles, which hath no such form in it, as the Sabbath of the Jews hath: And why the Sabbath of the Jews was altered, I tell thee, in that Christ the onely God, by his own power that day, had quickned death into life, as it is written, *In the end of the Sabbath, as it began to dawn towards the first day of the week, came Mary Magdalen, and the other Mary, to see the Sepulchre, and behold there was an earthquake; for the Angel of the Lord descended from Heaven, and came and rolled back the stone from the door, and sate upon it*[*]: So this being the first day of Christs Resurrection, was a day of joy and gladness to the Apostles, in that it brought peace and rest to their souls, confirmed in their faith, that he was Christ the Son of God: Whereupon the Revelation of their faith led them forth to keep the first day of their Saviours Triumph over sin, hell and death, to be a day set apart to assemble together, and contribute their benevolence for the refreshment of the poor members of that faith, as it is written, *And upon the first day of the week, when the Disciples came together to break bread*[†], *Paul preached unto them, ready to depart on the morrow, and continued his speech until midnight;* also, *Upon the first day of the week let every one of you lay by him in store, as God haht prospered him, that there be no gathering when I come*[‡]: Now this Command being a day set apart in point of Worship; therefore as the Commission changed, so the Worship changed, and so the necessity it will follow, that the day must be changed: Therefore take notice, as this Commission was not to hold to the end of the World, no more ought that First day; for as I said before, every Commission hast power in it self in the vertue of its Revelation, to change its Worship suitable to its Commission; so a Commission hath power to change a day for that Worship: Now our Commission being spiritual, doth hold forth no manner or forms of Worship, *but the worshipping of God is Spirit and truth:* Therefore, I say, not onely the Jews Sabbath, but also the Apostles First day, in our Commission are void, and of no effect, as it is written, *He spake on a certain place of the seventh day on this wise, and God did rest the seventh day from all his works*[§]: So the

---

[*] Matt 28. 1,2.
[†] Acts 20. 7.
[‡] 1 Cor. 16, 2.
[§] Heb 4. 4.

blessed of the Lord believing Christ to be God the Father, Creator of Heaven and earth, are entered into the perfect liberty of faith, which frees them from the lusts of the flesh, and so entered into peace and rest; by which not onely the Jews Sabbath, nor the Apostles First day, but every day is a Sabbath to the Elect of the Lord*: Now in that the Priests of this World do know, that if the first should be as another day, then they would loss their hearers, and so in conclusion lose their tythes; therefore as Christ and the Apostles by the Jews were accused for breaking their Sabbath, so the Pharisaical Teachers of thy Seed, will condemn us for repealing the First day of the Week: But however, in the Authority of our Commission I declare, That every soul which knoweth Christ in his Form and Nature, the Devil in his Form and Nature, hath entered unto his eternal Sabbath of perfect rest without end.

Reason. Let me but hear thy judgement as touching that saying of the Lawyer to Christ, *Master, which is the great Commandment in the Law?* Now Christs answer was, *That thou shouldst love the Lord thy God with all thy heart, and with all thy soul, and with all thy minde: this is the first and great Commandment*[†].

And the second is like unto it, Thou shalt love thy neighbour as thy self: on these two Commandments hang all the Law and the Prophets: Now what manner of love is this, with which if we love the Lord and our Neighbour as our self, we keep the whole Law; but for my part, I know not the man that can love his neighbour as himself, and so none can truly love God.

Faith. My judgement is, That all the ten Commandments are according to the sequel of these words, reduced into two heads; and these two are comprehended, yea, fulfilled in this word *Love,* as it is written, *Owe no man anything, but to love one another; for he that loveth another hath fulfilled the Law*‡: And true it is, when rightly considered, the efficacy of spiritual love, it is of so pure and holy a nature, that it cannot possibly do any impure or unholy thing, when it is moved to manifest it self according to its Divine Property, it naturally produceth all Heavenly excellency in the Elect of the Lord: Love delights to Lord over none, but be servant to all, and gives every one preheminence before it self; and therefore it truly *Honors its Parents*: Love is so far from envy, that instead of killing of any, it lieth down and envies feet to be killed of him, yea, it stayeth envy by its patience and meekness; and therefore saith *Paul, Our weapons are not carnal, but spiritual*§: Not a sword of steel, but a sword of love. Oh! The

---

* Matt 12, 1,10.
† Matt. 22. 36, 37, 38.
‡ Rom 13. 8.
§ 2 Cor. 10 3,4.

Revelation of faith teacheth his to slay none, but with love; nay, love is that Divine balsom, that it cureth all wounds made by envies weapons: Love is so sincere, *That it will not do that to another, that would not another should do to it:* And therefore it will not *commit adultery,* nor wrong any, though it might have many an opportunity to defraud and cozen another; it will rather want, before it will *steal:* Is this love there is no equivocation, it will not backbite, or stain anothers reputation, as it is written, *Love worketh no ill to its neighbour*,* and therefore would rather die than *bear false witness against* either friend or enemy: Also this love is generous, full of pity and mercie, *That it cloathes the naked, feeds the hungry, visiteth the sick in prison, and out of prison:* Nay this love is so pure, that it enjoys it self no longer then it is doing good to others; and therefore it will not *covet his neighbours house, his neighbours wife, his man servant, or maid servant, his ox, or his ass, or any thing that is his neighbours:* so that I tell thee, there is none of thy seed, but for want of this love, breaks the Laws (and in some thing therein confirms it by authority;) so that by this I love my neighbor as my self: Now my neighbours are the Believers of our Commission, that hath faith in our Revelation, as it is written, *Brethren, ye have been called unto liberty†, onely use not liberty for an occasion to the flesh, but by love serve one another; for all the Law is fulfilled in one word, even in this, Thou shalt love thy neighbour as thy self:* For love is the fruit of the Spirit, so that all believers are neighbours, and therefore it is written, *Let brotherly love continue, love the brotherhood, love as brethren:* This loving our neighbour as our self, is life in death, as *John* saith, *We know that we have passed from death unto life, because we love our neighbours or our brethren‡:* Now the great Commandment is, *To love God with all thy heart, and with all thy soul:* Now if thou canst not love God thou never sawest: *For what I have seen and heard I declare unto thee,* that without knowledge their can be no love, and yet what vain repetitions thy Seed makes to a God ye know not: As I said before, so I say again, Though some of thy Seed keeps some of the Commandments, nay, if possible, keep all, yet in that thou art ignorant of the true God, and so Worship another God, thou art guilty of all.

CHAP. 15.

---

* Rom. 13. 9.
† Gal. 5. 13.
‡ 1 John 3. 14.

Shewing whether Prayer doth not belong to all, and that by Prayer we may come to the knowledge of God, and whether it is our duty to make use of the Lords Prayer, or no.

Reason. Thou seemest to say in thy last, That without the knowledge of God, no man can love God, and so all that he doth is sin: What then, shall not a man that is ignorant of God, pray unto God for knowledge of him? Otherwise, how shall a soul love God[*]? and to that end, there are many Exhortations to prayer, and that especially the Lords prayer, which there we are taught the form and manner thereof, as it is written.

Our Father which art in Heaven, hallowed by thy name, thy Kingdom come, thy will be done, in earth as it is in Heaven[†]*: Give us this day our daily bread, and forgive us our debts, as we forgive our debtors, and lead us not into temptation, but deliver us from evil, for thine is the Kingdom, the Power, and the Glory for ever. Amen*

As I have said before concerning the Sabbath, That every Commission in its time and place is to be considered, That according to their Revelation, so was their Worship; but I know the Revelation of the Apostles led them forth to prayer, and therefore in their Commission it was requisite, and their duty so to do: Also, the form of these words was directed to the Disciples, but none of thy Seed whatsoever, for I should blaspheme to say, That Christ uttered these sayings for the instruction of thy Seed, when he saith, your Father is the Devil, as it is written, *Ye are of your Father the Devil*[‡], *and the lust of your Father ye will do:* so that this Prayer belongs to none but the Disciples; *After this manner therefore pray ye*[§]; yea, ye the beloved of the Lord, and sons of the Father, as it is written, *Because ye are sons, God hath sent forth the Spirit of his Son, by which you cry, Abba Father:* Now were this set form to be used in these day, as I cannot finde, that to them to whom it was spoken, never made use of that form after; yet, I say, if it were, it onely belongs to sons, who are believers of a Commission; so that I say, it belonged to none but us, in that by the Revelation of our faith, we know the Father that is in Heaven, both in form and nature, and none but we; and therefore as we are sons, and not servants, we can with joy and peace of conscience say, *Our Father which art in Heaven;* whereas your Seed being but servants, and no sons, may take shame and confusion of face: as for a man of quality to have another mans childe in the market-place as him blessing, and call him Father; What would his friends think of him? Judge thou: So your Seed, that are bastards,

---

[*] Mat. 6. 9.
[†] Luk. 11. 2.
[‡] Joh. 8. 44.
[§] Gal. 4. 6.

and not sons, when you come in your publique Worships, what a babling you make, *thinking to be heard for your much speaking**, when he hears you not, nor knows you not, neither doth he in the least take notice of your fasts, nor your tears, they are all vain repetitions, of no more account then the barking of a Dog, or the wallowing of the Sow in the mire: From the Lord I speak it, they are not.

Reason. What then, must we not pray at all, though we use not those form of words? Yet I believe, as occasion is offered, and as we are moved in our hearts, so we ought to pray: To that end, the Scripture holds forth a thousand examples, of which I shall but instance one or two, *viz. Call upon me in the day of trouble*[†], *and I will deliver thee, and thou shalt glorifie me. Elias was a man subject to like passions as we are*[‡], *and he prayed earnestly that it might not rain, and it rained not on the earth for the space of three years and six months.*

Faith. Ah blinde soul! What a hodge podge thou makest of Scripture, as to think that the sayings of *David,* and the prophesie of *Elias* and the Apostles belongs to thee, when I know thee the son of *Belial,* the Seed of the Serpent; and they are the true Prophets and Messengers of the Lord, so had a command for what they did do, but thou has no command *to declare the Statutes of the Lord, or take his Covenant in thy mouth;* for all thy prayers are abomination, and such as thee God will not hear; and yet you cry that you are sent of the Lord, and thus and thus saith the Lord, when ye know not the Lord in his form and nature, and yet you would have his *Kingdom come,* when you neither know the nature of it, nor where it is, supposing his Kingdom is in this World, and yet he saith, *My Kingdom is not of this world;* then you pray, that his *will may be done on earth as it is in heaven,* and yet what in you lieth, you pray, that all the Seed of Reason shall be damned, and none but the Seed of Faith saved, and yet you pray; that all may be saved, when it is written, *He will have mercy, on whom he will have mercy, and whom he will, he will damn*[§]*:* So that you pray you know not for what; and then you desire God *to forgive you your trespasses as you do forgive them that trespass against you.* Oh friend, were God as thou sayest, and that he should hear thee, then this I tell thee, instead of forgiving thee, he must of necessitie consume the best of you in a moment: As do but observe the transactions of thy Seed in these daies, you pray, fast, and weep, that God would forgive you, as you forgive another; well, according to your prayer, so it shall be, for instead of forgiving, you backbite, persecute,

---

[*] Isa. 1. 15.
[†] Psa. 50. 15.
[‡] Jam. 5. 17.
[§] Rom. 8. 13

imprison, and put to death, even so shall ye be dealt withal; nay, you are of such a cursed Seed, that you will not shew mercie to them that have shewn mercie to you, you will not give the libertie, that when others had the day over you, they gave you your libertie: I speak this to the shame of thee and all thy Seed; and then you pray and cheat, you pray and tyrannize; you pray with your tongues, and murther with your hand; and yet such Hypocrites as thy Seed are most professors, and supposed most believers, and most pretended Saints, and most of you hopes to be saved; and yet, as I have said, ye are all of the Seed of the damned, and have no knowledge of the true God at all: So that from my Seed-spring I speak it, There is neither thou, nor the wisest Gifted head-piece of thy Seed, that can experimentallie say, that God ever heard any of your prayers[*]; recollect your thoughts, either in publique or private, that ever God gave thee an answer to any petition thou requested of him: It may be thou hast found in the soul more satisfaction one time then another, insomuch, that thou hast wept for joy; but deal plainly, didst thou ever hear God verbally speak with thee, as he did to the two former Commissions, and now in this our last (sure I am thou never didst;) and therefore minde what I say, all whisperings or inward movings of the Spirit, as thou callest it, are nothing else but Reasons imagination, that God hears thee, and answers thee; for alas, poor soul, though I know it is the Seed of Faith at certain times springing up, ravishing joys in believing the true God, not within me, but without me; yet this I know, God hears me not, and sure I am, if God every heard any, he would hear me: but when I consider how vainly you are acted forth, to make use of an Infinite nothing, to do all things for you, it discovers what you are, *even blinde leaders of the blinde:* just as a horse in a mill goes round, even so do ye, beating the aire, as though ye had done something, when indeed ye have done nothing at all, as at the hour of death doth manifest; What praying and crying out, Lord save me, when in your health ye pretended assurance of salvation, and now at the point of death, ye know not what shall become of your souls; so that in truth I speak it, you are ever praying, and yet have never perfect assurance of what you pray for; as it is written, *ever learning, and never able to come to the knowledge of the truth:* Now though I never pray, yet my faith being in continual prayer, I have nothing to do at death, but yield up my Soul to the power thereof for a moment, knowing that when *he appears, I shall appear with him in endless Glory,* without the least let or doubt whatsoever; at which time, thou being in doubts and fears, calls upon a God that is no God; neither hast thou faith in what thou sayest, but a meer tradition that moves thee, when thou neither knowest what thou sayest, nor to whom thou speakest; but at the very time of prayer, thy heart is either plotting mischief, or coveting the riches, honour and glory of this world; and so contents thy self with

---

[*] Isa. 1. 15.

vain lip-labour; as it is written, *These people honour me with their lips, but their hearts is far from me**.

CHAP. 16.

Shewing whether there be any truth in the Faith of the Church of England, expressed in the Creeds or Articles recorded.

Reason. What doest thou conceive, or what is thy thoughts concerning the Faith of the Church of *England,* expressed in their Creeds, but especially that of *Athenasius?*

Faith. I shall in brief tell thee, That they are a rapsido of nonsense, yea, that which thy Seed calls blasphemy, as shall in these ensuing words appear: And that I may not be over tedious, I shall reduce them into three heads *verbatim* as they lie, provided thou wilt from the first of them, shew what is thy faith in them.

Reason. My Faith is this, *That we worship one God in Trinity, and Trinity in Unity, neither confounding the Persons, nor dividing the Substance; for there is one Person of the Father, another of the Son, another of the Holy Ghost, yet the Godhead of the Father, of the Son, and of the Holy Ghost is all one, the glory equal, the majestie co-eternal; such as the Father is, such is the Son, and such is the Holy Ghost, the Father uncreate, the Son uncreate, and the Holy Ghost uncreate; the Father incomprehensible, the Son incomprehensible, and the Holy Ghost incomprehensible; the Father eternal, the Son eternal, and the Holy Ghost eternal, and yet they are not three eternals, but one eternal, &c. so the Father is God, the Son is God, and the Holy Ghost is God, and yet they are not three Gods, but one God, &c. and so we are to acknowledge every Person by himself to be God and Lord, without which no man can be saved.*

Faith. Before we proceed any further, let me give answer to what thou hast already declared, and the remarkablest confusion therein contained, I shall pitch my discourse upon, which is, *Neither confounding the Persons, nor dividing the Substance;* for thou sayest, there are *three Persons, and but one God; their glory equal, their majestie co-eternal, all uncreate, all incomprehensible, all eternal, and yet not three, but one eternal;* Now let the wisest head-piece of thy Seed answer me from these words, Whether thou intends *the Father is God, the Son is God, and the Holy Ghost is God,* as in relation to their Persons, or their Natures; for let me tell thee, if thou believe them, as

---
* Isa 29. 13.

touching their persons, then know thou hast divided the Substance; as for instance, the potter of one substance, matter or earth, makes three vessels; now though these be of one and the self same substance, yet they are divided, so not one, but really three, distinct in each for the one from the other: As thus, here is three ☉☉☉, distinct in themselves, yet one like another, not onely in form, but nature also, in that they are all of one matter, so cannot disagree, though three, yet let thy Reason work which way it will, thou canst not make of these three one ☉, in which single face or person, that intire nature that is unity in trinity, must be comprehended and contained in one single person alone, onely bearing the name of three titles, *viz. Father in the Creation, the Son in Redemption, and the Holy Ghost in Justification:* Without the true knowledge of what I have said, from my Revelation, I tell thee, thy faith shall perish eternally.

Reason. *I acknowledge every Person by himself to be God and Lord, and yet I say there are not three Gods, and three Lords; as thus, the Father is made of one neither created nor begotten, the Son is of the Father alone, not made nor created but begotten, the Holy Ghost is of the Father, and of the Son, neither made, nor created, nor begotten, but proceeding, c. and in this Trinity, none is afore nor after another, none is greater, nor less another; but the whole three Persons be co eternal together, and co equal: So thus the Unity in Trinity, and the Trinity in Unity is to be Worshipped; he therefore that will be saved, must thus think of the Trinity.*

Faith. O senseless sot! As were thy Teachers, so art thou, as to imagine that one God should have three Persons, which is as unpossible, as for a mortal King to have three persons, and but one King; for this I know, though a King by generation may beget a son, yet that childe is not a father, but a son, so not one, but two; neither is the son equal with the father, though the next heir to the Crown: But however, this by Faith I know, the Son was the Father, neither made, created, nor begotten, as in the second Chapter is proved at large; for this know, if Christ was begotten, then he was created, so made; and if begotten, tell me who begot him, and where, and by what means Christ was begotten.

Reason. *I know no otherwise, but as in the Creed I believe Christ Jesus to be the onely Son of God, begotten of his Father before all worlds, God of God, Light of Light, very God of very God, begotten, not made, being of one substance with the Father, by whom all things were made for us, and for our salvation came down from heaven, and was incarnate by the Holy Ghost of the Virgin Mary, and was made man, and was crucified under* Pontius Pilate; *he suffered, and was buried, and the third day rose again and ascended into Heaven, and sitteth on the right hand of the Father; and I believe, as in the other Creed, Christ was God of the Substance of the Father, begotten before the Worlds; and man of the Substance of his mother born in the worlds; and man of the substance of his mother born in the world, perfect God, and perfect man, of a reasonable soul, and humane flesh, subsisting equal with the Father, as touching his Godhead, and inferiour to his Father, as touching his Manhood; one altogether, not by confusion of substance, but by unity of person: for as the reasonable soul and flesh is one man, so God and man is one Christ, who shall come again with glory to judge both the quick and the dead, which Kingdom shall have no end: And I believe in the holy Ghost, the Lord and giver of life, which proceedeth from the Father, and the Son, who with the Father and the Son together, is worshipped and glorified, who spake by the Prophets, &c.*

Faith. What a knotty, gouty thred hath thy Seed spun insomuch, that therewith they have woven a web of linsey-woolsey stuff, sufficient to cloath the Devil; as have but patience, and thou shalt hear what confused blasphemy there is in these Creeds, held forth to be the Faith of the Church of *England*, without which thou sayest, no flesh can be saved. That thou mayest for the future take notice of thy ignorance, I shall reduce them into three heads, and so answer them directly, as I shall quote them in their order:
1. First, *Thou believest as thou hast expressed, That Christ was God of the substance of the Father, begotten before the Worlds; and Man of the Substance of his mother born in this World.*
  If this by thee were rightly understood, I should not need to expound them any other then *verbatim* as they lie; but in that I know thou intends the Father, as he was a Person, got his Son a person also; therefore from the Authority of our Commission, I say, Thou knowest not how the Father came in being to be God, much less then, how this Son was begot by the Father; for the word *Begotten* doth imply, first the Father begetting. 2. The matter conceived. 3. The formation of this conception into a person like his Father; for this I know, no childe can be begotten, without a dissolution of seed, which seed must first dye, before it can quicken to a new life, which life will produce a form like its seed, now this could not be in the Father, didst thou but with me, know what the Nature and Person of the Father was before the World; *That as the Godhead was offered unto death, through the Eternal Spirit**: So from my Revelation of Faith, I say, The Eternal Spirit, according to its own word and pleasure cloathed it self with a Divine Heavenly Substance, in the proportion and linaments of a man, whose person was more bright and glorious then the Sun, softer then Doun, and swifter then thought: So that I say, this was the substance the Fathers person then consisted of; and against men and Angels I affirm, that there was no person before the world, but the Father onely, neither could he beget a Son, until he dissolved his

---

* Heb. 9. 14.

Divine substance into seed in the womb of *Mary;* by which dissolution, the Father begot or conceived himself into a Son of flesh, blood and bone: For this by faith I know, that the person of the Father was capable of transmutation into the form of flesh, though now he is not, having taken upon him the form of flesh, in fulfilling that promise: saying, *The seed of the woman shall bruise the head of the Serpent***; which was no other, but the Eternal Father was to be born of a woman, with flesh, blood and bones; so that it was not the Father begot a Son, but the Father became a Son as the Prophet *Eliah* by Revelation clearly unfolds, saying unto us, *A childe is born, unto us a Son is given, and the Government shall be upon his shoulder, and his name shall be called Wonderful, Counsellour, the mighty God, the everlasting Father, the Prince of peace*†*;* and then it is written, that I that Word or Eternal Spirit that formed it self as aforesaid, *that Word became flesh, and dwelt among us;* and saith *Paul, The Godhead dwelt in Christ bodily*‡*;* so that it is clear, as in the second Chapter is infallibly proved, that the Father begot no Son before the Worlds, but the Father in time became a Son himself, and that not in two persons, but one person alone.

Reason.   But then what wilt thou do with these Scriptures, where it is written,

Thou art my Son, this day have I begotten thee; also it is said, *We beheld his glory, the glory as of the onely begotten of the Father*§*;* and again it is said, *Unto which of the Angels said he at any time****, Thou art my Son, this day have I begotten thee;* and again, *No man hath seen God at any time, the onely begotten Son, which is in the bosom of the Father*††*:* He that declared him also, it is written, *I will be to him a Father, and he shall be to me a Son*‡‡*:* Now if Christ was not begotten of his Father, why or wherefore should the Apostles Revelation declare, that Christ had a Father, and was begotten by him?

Faith.   As I have often told thee, so I say again, What hast thou to do with Scripture, our Commission being the onely Interpreter thereof, thou not believing the report therein, was damned: Yet for the further satisfaction of the hearers that shall believe this, I shall declare, that the Apostles in their Commission was not to know Christ any further or otherwise, then onely a Son begotten by his Father, and

---

* Gen. 3. 15.
† Isa. 9. 6.
‡ Joh. 1. 14.
§ Psal. 2. 7.
** Joh 1. 14.
†† Heb. 1. 5.
‡‡ Joh. 1. 17.

that for them in their time was sufficient, as the Son himself expresseth, *All things that the Father hat made known to me, I have made known unto you**; also Paul declares, *He that confesseth with his tongue, and believeth with his heart that Christ is the Son of God, shall be saved:* Though now in our Commission it is not sufficient, in that our Revelation leads us infallibly to believe Christ was and is the Everlasting Father, Creator of Heaven and earth, as by Scripture is confirmed, *All things were made by him, and without him was not any thing made that was made:* So that Christ as he was the Father, was the Creator of all things, whether in Heaven or earth; as is manifest in that intricate Revelation of *Paul,* which he wrought in Christ, when he raised him from the dead &c. Who can tell but our Commission, who raised Christ from the dead[†], was there any other God or Father, but what was within him, that raised him from the dead; as he saith, *I have power to lay down my life, and I have power to take it again[‡],* as in the third Chapter is shewed at large: And who should set him at the right hand of the Father, but the Godhead power within him, that enthroned him *far above all principality, and power, and might, and dominion, and every name that is named, not onely in this world, but that which is to come;* insomuch, that Christ by his death hath conquered himself, to be head over all things: And what is that which so highly promoted him above all, even his Spiritual body, *the fulness in which was that which filled all in all:* So that I say, That Father which Christ so often called upon when he was on earth, I say, if it had not been his creature *Elias* commissionated in Glory, then Christ could have made nothing nor by his own power have quickned himself to life again: Nay, I say, if Christ had a real Father that had begotten him, then Christ could not have had the preheminence in power, name, and been the chief head, in that the Father is above the Son: But however, let blinde Reason think what it will, from an infallible Spirit I say, that *Elias* was his Deputy-Father, and so at Christs ascension was to give up his Authority and Commission to Christ the Eternal Father, from whence he received it.

2. Secondly, *Thou believest God a reasonable soul, perfect God, and perfect man,* &c.

In answer to which, from the Revelation of Faith, I tell thee, is the greatest blasphemy that by man can be imagined, as to consider the nature of the two Seed; *viz.* Faith and Reason: First, as in relation to their Satisfaction. Secondly, their power.

    First, What Divine satisfaction could there be in God, if there were the least spark of Reason in him. I knowing in Reason, there is no real satisfaction whatever, it being a seed, though as pure as in the Angels, yet it is altogether unsatisfactory in it self, as hath been

---

* John 15. 16.
† Eph. 1. 20
‡ John 10. 18.

proved in the Reprobate Angel, he being left to his pure Reason alone, was brought to aspiring confusion, if possible to unthrone God, and all creatures made by him, as at large in the fourth Chapter is proved; which if the nature of God were but pure Reason, then might the Reprobate Angel have kept his standing, and the rest of the Angels have had full satisfaction in themselves, without any supply from God at all, which in the fourth Chapter thou hast heard to the contrary: And therefore if the Nature of God were pure Reason, he could have no satisfaction in himself, but from another, and so in conclusion, there must be some above God, to satisfie God: Therefore from that God who is a body of living Faith, I say, Cursed is that soul who believes God to have the least motion of Reason in him; nay further, in the power of our Commission, I say, there is no creature believing God a reasonable soul, that shall have true peace here, or glory hereafter; as is confirmed in these Scriptures, *Being justified by faith, we have peace in God*[*]; and again, *Let us draw near with a true heart, in full assurance of faith; and without faith it is umpossible to please God*[†]: I say, if God had but a reasonable soul, what matter for faith; for by reason we may have peace in God, and in reasons belief thou mayest please God: But alas, poor blinde souls, for want of this precious seed of faith, thou canst not know God in form and nature, so not believe him as he is.

2. Secondly, as there is no satisfaction, so there is no power in reason, as there is in faith; as it is written[‡], *I say unto you, if ye have faith as a grain of mustard seed, ye shall say unto this Mountain, Remove hence to yonder place, and it shall remove, and nothing shall be unpossible to you: By faith God framed the Worlds, by faith Abels sacrifice was accepted with God, by faith* Noah *was warned of God*[§], *by faith* Sarah *believed, by faith* Abraham *offered up his son* Isaac, *by faith* Moses *refused to be called the son of* Pharoah, *by faith fire was quenched, the Lyons mouthes stopped, the prison doors opened.* So by faith I know, that Christ is the Everlasting Father; by faith I know the soul of Christ is all faith, and no reason; by faith I know, it was his pure Soul, or Godhead Father in Christ that dyed, and by his own power quickned himself again by faith. I know, that God in this our last Commission, spake to *John Reeve,* as he spake to *Moses* and *Paul:* Oh what a powerful Seed is faith! that kills sin, kills the Devil, yea, kills death, nay, what a high gloss doth the Lord of glory stamp upon faith, and not so much as taking notice of reason at all; and yet blinde reason the Devil, will have God a reasonable soul: O if not for fear, yet for shame, desist thy damned belief, and from me observe, the Soul of Christ is all Divine Heavenly faith, which none shall know

---

[*] Rom. 5. 1.
[†] Hebr. 10. 22. Heb. 11.6.
[‡] Matt. 17. 20.
[§] Heb 11

that God in his Form and Nature is, but he whose faith is Lord over reason in this life.

Reason. If the Soul or Nature of God be not pure reason, how comes it then that God saith, *Come now, let us reason together, saith the Lord?* &c*. which if his Nature, as thou saith, were all Divine, Heavenly faith, and not reason, I conceive God could not have reasoned the case with them.

Faith. O the gross darkness of reason, that cannot understand, that it was not the Lord from his own mouth that reasoned the case with them, but the Prophet *Isaiah;* for this by faith I know, that God never reasoned with any, but the Commissionate Prophets, whose Seed is of his own Nature, and in the vertue of that Commission, are Ambassadors in Gods stead, to reason the case with them; for this I know, that faith can take up the words of faith, though faith speaks powerfully and infallibly, when as reason speaks but dubiously and doubtfully.

Reason. Is it not strange, that reason should be the Governour of this World, as thou hast formerly expressed, and hath by its wisdom erected things in such glorious form and order, as now they are, and yet should not be a Seed satisfactory in it self? How comes it then, that the Governours thereof taketh so much delight and pleasure in this World, if man were not satisfied in the affairs of his life? Surely I cannot see, but there is as much satisfaction in reason, as in faith; for I conceive, men endued with reason, have more content then men endued with faith.

Faith. Now thou hast raised an Objection, that thy experience may silence thee, in the various transactions of this bloody World, that the mutability thereof floweth from the nature of that Seed reason; as instance, the grand mutations of thy Kingdom: Why you had a King before, you were not therewith satisfied, but cryed out, no Bishop, no King and through much bloodshed, you attained reason desire (for know this, faith will shed no blood.) and therefore observe, it is the Seed of reason divided against it self; and then reason hunted the King like a Patridge, till you had your desire accomplished; and when you got victory over the Kings Army, then the Bells rung, and Bonfires made, yea, days of thanksgiving kept for joy, and now you are unsatisfied for a King again, and reason improved all it subtilty to attain its desire, and then for joy of that which formerly it killed, the bells rung, the fire flamed, oathes were sworn, and healths were drunk, till you could not stand, to the destruction of your own souls; and therefore, I say, there is no satisfaction in reason, let it be never

---
* Isa. 1. 18.

so rich or great in this its Kingdom, that it is cloathed with crowns of Gold, and deckt with Pearls and Diamonds, and attendee with variety of Servants, yet in all this reason is not satisfied, but sometimes it would enjoy more honour and joys of this World, and then it is afraid it shall lose all its honour, pleasure and delight that it formerly enjoyed: So that I say, there is not from the King upon his Throne, to the Beggar in the straw, whose reason is Lord over faith, that hath any true satisfaction at all: For alas *Solomon,* the greatest of all, found no real content, but cryed out, all that he had enjoyed was vanity: So that reason in the purest sense, is compared to *the bottomless pit,* that hath no end of its imagination; and yet such Devils as thee, will have God a reasonable Soul, when in my Revelation thou hast heard, there is no durable satisfaction at all in reason, but faith alone: for faith hath a foundation, and can limit it self to a small compass, yet be really contented without the glory of the World at all, knowing this is but mortal, and must perish in the desire thereof; and therefore faith is satisfied in that it lays holds on that which is Immortal, Eternal, and shall never perish, no more then God himself: so that for all thy Kingdom, with the glory here below, my faith will have nothing to do with thy powers, thy trading, thy great joy and delight, in that they must all vanish as the smoak in the ayre, for the delight of my soul is in that glory and riches on the other side of death, which is eternal, and shall never perish world without end, which neither thou nor none of thy Seed shall never see, nor in the least measure enjoy. But then,

3. Thirdly, *Thou believest in the Holy Ghost, the Lord and giver of life which proceedeth from the Father, and the Son, who with the Father and the Son, is worshipped and glorified, &c.*

Answer. As unto this, I know thou hast no ground in Scripture to prove the Holy Ghost a person, though they are recorded in your Creed three persons, and one God: Yet by faith, I say, as I said before, there never was, is or shall be, but one Personal God, even Christ Jesus alone, blessed for ever, as onely those who believe my Revelation*, can with me understand, that the Holy Ghost was the Eternal Spirit, or invisible Soul of Christ, as it is written, *The Holy Ghost shall come upon thee, and the power of the highest shall overshadow thee*†; yea, that was the Holy Ghost, or invisible Soul of Christ, which dissolved into seed, there dyed in the womb of *Mary,* and quickned it self into a son of flesh, blood and bone; yea, the Holy Ghost remained with him, and in him all the time he was upon earth; yea, that was the Holy Ghost, or Eternal Spirit, that dyed in the grave, for they signifie both one and the self same thing, as it is written, *The Spirit of God descended upon him like a Dove, so the Holy Ghost descended upon him like a Dove:* So that take it which way thou

---

* Isa. 43. 10, 11.
† Luke 1. 35.

pleaseth, the Holy Ghost, or Eternal Spirit, which is the Godhead Father, was in no Person of its own, but the Person of Christ onely.

Reason. From those Scriptures thou hast quoted, I understand, that the Holy Ghost was not in the person of Christ, but in Heaven a Person of its own; as it is clearly recorded, and the *Holy Ghost descended in a bodily shape like a Dove upon him, and a voyce came from Heaven, which said, Thou art my beloved Son, in whom I am well pleased:* And so in the rest of the Evangelists it is written, *That the Heavens were opened unto him, and he saw the Spirit of God descending like a Dove, and lighting upon him**: So that I do not deny, but that the Spirit and the Holy Ghost is both one, yet, I cannot believe, but that the Holy Ghost is in a form or shape of its own, and that in Heaven, when Christ was upon earth, as it written, *The Holy Ghost descended from Heaven upon him;* And besides, it is clear, that Christ had a Father then in Heaven, that sent the Holy Ghost, and said, *Thou art my beloved Son, in whom I am well pleased?*

Faith In answer to this I shall unfold this deep secret which none of thy seed can ever understand; yet that it may be recorded for the blessed seed of faith, that shall hereafter believe in our commission, I infallibly declare, That there is a Holy Ghost, as also a gift of the Holy Ghost.

Reason But before thou speakest of this, I desire, if thou canst, remove this great stumbling block, What father this was that said, *Thou art my beloved Son in whom I am well pleased?* and if *Elias,* as thou hast at large treaaed with me in the third Chapter, then tell me by what Authority could *Elias* call Christ his beloved Son; and why did Christ make use of his Creature, to call his Creator Son? Surely it cannot be *Elias,* that should assume such a prerogative to call Christ Son, but it must be God the Creator of all things, that did call Christ his beloved Son, otherwise Christ would never have so seriously and confidently have called *Elias* his Father.

Faith. As I have formerly said, so I say again, That herein consists the infiniteness of Eternity, that he could become time, yea, so far deny and abase himself, as to be protected by his Creature; for as it is written, *In all things he became like unto us, sin onely excepted:* not like unto the seed of reason, but the seed of faith; yea, he was like unto his Prophets and Messengers in point of Commission; for though Christ, as he was God the Father, gave all Commissions, yet now from *Elias* he took his journey in the flesh, as in the third Chapter I have declared, wherefore he took up *Elias,* that he might present the very place and authority of God, as when God was there himself, *Elias*

---

* Luk. 3. 21.

being the Seed of his own body, he could trust him, when he could trust none of the Angels, and *therefore he took upon him the seed of Abraham**, *and not the nature of the Angels:* Now having taken him up into glory, in that his time was nigh that he must fulfil his promise to the seed of *Adam;* I say, he commissionates *Elias* with Authority, Power, and Majestie like himself (creating excepted) to take care of Christ the onely God, in this his difficult journey, by which Authority, *Elias* had full power to protect Christ in his infancy, and confirm his Revelation, both in Doctrine and Miracle, and to call him his Son, as Christ was to call *Elias* his God and Father, as at his death he acknowledgeth, *Elias, Elias, my God, my God, why hast thou forsaken me*†*?* Which some of them that stood by, understanding his language, said, *behold, he calleth Elias;* which none but the true believers of our Commission can understand, and therefore must perish for want of the true knowledge of this: So that from the Revelation of faith, I say, herein was the infinite wisdom of the Godhead made manifest, in Christs Humility, that although he was the Creator, *yet he took upon him the form of a servant,* and in the place of his glory, authorized his Creature *Elias* as a Father: Though the Scripture intricately prove this, yet who but the Elect of the Lord can believe this, that *Elias* had power to send down gifts of the Holy Ghost, in what form he pleased, to commissionate Christ the giver of all Commissions, and yet the Eternal Spirit or Holy Ghost was in the Person of Christ alone.

Reason. Let me but ask thee this once, and I shall trouble thee no longer; that is, let me hear thee discover thy thoughts, betwixt the Holy Ghost, and the gifts of the Holy Ghost, whether it be a Person of its own, or onely in the Person of Christ alone.

Faith. As I said before, so I say again, That if the Holy Ghost had a person of its own, so the Lord and giver of life, then its Person must be in the form of a man, suitable to the person of Christ, in that it is the very nature of Christ, so every Nature hath its own form, so the form of Christ; but that which descended upon Christ, was not the Holy Ghost, but the gift of the Holy Ghost; for, as I have said before, Christ who had the Holy Ghost in him, invested the gift thereof upon *Elias,* that so *Elias* might protect and preserve Christ in his non-age, as aforesaid; so that I say, the essence of the Holy Ghost is inherent in Christ alone, from whence the gifts or influence of the Holy Ghost flows; for by my Revelation I know, that when Christ ascended to his Majestie on high, he sate down on the right hand, which signifies, that *Elias'* power and authority was surrendered into the Person of Christ alone; so that after that, all the gifts or influence of the Holy Ghost came from Christ, as it is written, when Christ was ascended to glory,

---

* Heb. 2 16.
† Mark 16. 34, 35.

then he fills the Apostles full of the Holy Ghost, which then appeared in the form of a Cloven Tongue, and not in the form of a Dove: So that it is clear, though the Holy Ghost be one intire Divine invisible life in Christ, yet take notice, the gifts thereof are divers, so that the gifts of the Holy Ghost hath various forms, though the Holy Ghost hath no form but man, and that Christ alone: And therefore minde the gross darkness of all thy Seed in their Creeds, as though the Holy Ghost had a Person of its own, so the Lord and giver of life, when it is written in divers places, *That Christ is the way, the truth, and the life: I am that bread of life, he that believeth on me, hath everlasting life**; and in his saying to the woman of *Samaria, But the water that I shall give him, shall be in him a well of water, springing up to everlasting life:* So that the Holy Ghost must needs be in Christ, in that Christ is the giver of life; and yet such blinde reason as thee, will have the Holy Ghost in a Person distinct from Christ, the Lord and giver of life, when to thy shame thou hearest, that Christ alone is *the Resurrection and the Life, insomuch, that he that believeth in Christ, though he were dead, yet shall he live*†: So that much in confutation to the authors and believers of those Creeds: Yea, from the Revelation of my Faith I infallibly against Angels, and all thy Seed of Reason conclude, That so many of them so living, and so dying in the belief thereof, shall with thee perish eternally; Yea, in the Vertue of our Commission, I say, there is no God that can or will deliver thee or them to all Eternity.

---

* John 4.
† John 11. 25

A
DIVINE PROSPECT

For the Elect of the Lord, that after our departure, shall come to the belief of this our last Commission, though ye knew us not in our life time, yet you have the Revelation of faith left upon record, by which you will be supported, in believing *John Reeve* and *Ledowick Mugglton,* the last Commissioners that ever shall appear in Reasons Kingdom; as also, that I am the onely Bishop or Messenger in Revelation, bearing witness against all Gain-sayers, to the truth of this Spiritual Commission now in being, and so to remain till time be no more on this side of death; then, and at which day it shall be made manifest, that we, and onely we, were the last Messengers of Jesus Christ, who at the day of Resurrection shall ascend to glory in the publique view of our Enemies, as also all other believers who credited our report, not weighing their lives unto death: Which when we, and all that knew us, are in silent dust; then I say, our Revelation will be in great esteem by the next generation of faith succeeding: And therefore that there may be no division among you, from the Lord of Glory, I reminde you of these ensuing Propositions, they being a breviate of all the chief heads that my Revelation hath reduced from the Commission:

1. You are to believe, There was to be three Commissions before the end of this world, thus recorded, *The Spirit water and Blood, and these are the three that beareth witness upon earth.* I John 5.8.
2. It is to be believed, That a Commission is given forth by laudible voyce of words, to the hearing of the ear, from the mouth of the Lord Jesus in the highest Heavens.
3. It is to be believed, That who ever pretends a Commission, not being one of these, are real whimsies, notions, yea, lies, and no truth.
4. It is to be believed, That though a Commission consist of few words, without encrease, yet their Revelations are various, and encreaseth daily.
5. It is to be observed, That the two last Commissions are not to offend or defend in point of Externals, but either active or passive to yield due obedience to King, Governor, or any other Magistrate whatsoever.
6. It is to be believed, That no Commission ought to be obedient to any formal Dispensation, but in their time or place, hath power to curse either Angel or man, that in opposition thereof shall hold forth other Doctrine.

7. It is to be believed, That neither of the two former Commissions, was to understand what God in his Form and Nature was in the Creation, as this our Commission doth.
8. It is to be believed, That our Commission alone doth understand how this God and Father, after intelligence given to *Mary* by the Angel, descended from heaven as swift as thought, into the womb of *Mary,* and there dissolved his immortal body into seed, and from thence quickned himself into a mortal body of flesh, blood and bone so called a Son.
9. It is to be believed, That the Eternal Father, now become a Son, had the Supreme power within him, that quickned his Godhead, being perfectly dead in the grave, to life again, without the help of either Father, God, or Spirit, without him whatsoever.
10. It is to be believed, That the Prophet *Elias* in his transmutation, that nature of faith in him became a chariot of fire, so struck out the gross Elements, *viz.* Water, Earth, and Aire, and in that fiery faith of his own, ascended to glory, to represent the Person of God, while he took his journey in the flesh.
11. Also it is to be believed, That our Commission alone, in the Revelation thereof, hath the true knowledge of these things, as also, what the form and nature of the Angels are, of what they were created, and wherefore created, and what was the cause of the Angelical fall above the rest, and why, and wherefore he was cast into this world in the presence of *Adam* and *Eve.*
12. It is to be believed, that never any but our Commission, knew that it was that said Angel, that in his whole form entred the womb of *Eve,* and there dissolved into Seed, and conceived into flesh, blood, and bone, by which *Eve* was deceived, so called a Beast, Serpent, Tree of Knowledge of good and evil, that so none of that Seed might understand, what it was, and how it was *Eve* was deceived.
13. It is to be understood, That none but our Commission knows, that this dissolution of the Angel in the womb of *Eve,* became *Cain* the first Devil, and the Father of all the damned.
14. It is to be believed, That there never was, is, or shall be any other Devil but men and women, and that for the most part he is the comeliest of all other of that form.
15. It is to be believed, That none but our Commission knows, that the souls of both Faith and Reason, are mortal ever since the fall of *Adam*, and shall dye and rot in the grave till the day of Resurrection; and that though dead five thousand three hundred years ago, yet at the day of our glorious Gods appearance, each seed or soul shall arise with bodies suitable to their natures; that soul or seed of faith that believed in our Commission, shall ascend to meet its Saviour in the ayre; and

that soul or seed of Reason that despised our Commission, shall arise a spiritual body upon this earth, tormented to all Eternity.

16. It is to be believed, That the Kingdom of glory, where Christ the onely God, his Elect, Saints and Angels, doth and shall inhabit to all eternity, is non-globical, where God and his mighty Angels can at their pleasure with their bodies, fly as swift as thought, ten thousand miles in a moment, and when he pleaseth, God can stand, sit, lie, in as narrow a compass as my self, for none but our Revelation knows, that there is an immortal Earth, Sea, Fish, Fouls, Beasts, Hearbs, Trees, yea, all things immortal, glorious there, as they are mortal, deformed here, and all this for the contemplation of God, his Elect, Saints and Angels, to whom let all ye that have, or shall have belief in our Commission, so living, and so dying in the truth of our Revelation, sing praise, glory, and honour, that ye shall see and enjoy what now ye do believe, as touching our Commission.

17. It is to be believed, that certain men and women have, and will, seeingly come to the belief of our Commission insomuch that they have rejoyced in it, contended for it, yea, have said, they desired to depart this life in the belief of it; and yet being according to birth, the seed of Reason, and not the seed of Faith, in time of persecutions, riches, glory, and honour of this world, fell away to their eternal perdition; as I could name some, but wo, wo, for as sure as Christ is God, they shall never see that glorious Kingdom aforesaid.

18. And lastly, it is seriously by you to be observed, That by believing the truth of what I write, you will finde great satisfaction when I am taken from you, that as this is the last Commission, so the, the, the truth (yea, the onely truth) that shall remain to the end of this bloody, unbelieving world, to reminde you of this one thing, that it is not to be expected many to come to believe a Commission, as to a notional dispensation; for in the two former Commissions, they cryed out, *Two of a Tribe, one of a City;* so few in their Commissions, that the Prophet *Elijah* said, *I, even I onely am left, and they seek my life to take it away;* and then saith *Isaiah, Who hath believed our report, and to whom is the arm of the Lord revealed?* So few, that in the time of Christ, at his sayings, they were so hard to be understood, that there fell away 70 at one time, nay, none stuck to him but the Apostles, and a few more: And then in the second Commission there was so few that really believed, that sometimes *Paul* had but two or three stood by him in the faith: And now in this our last, they are so few, that they are not worth the numbering, among the multitude of notional Churches, and therefore forget not that

saying of Christ, *Strait is the gate, and narrow is the way that leadeth unto life, and few there be that finde it:* But herein comfort your selves, that those few of you that really enters in, shall feel, yea, see and behold your God face to face; yea, sing out triumphing voyces of joy, with eternal harmonies of divine musick for ever, yea for ever, in that glorious Kingdom aforesaid, prepared for Christ your God, and you his Elect Saints, with the Elected Angels world without end; so that ye shall sit, stand, lie, walk, go, flie, at your pleasure, having nothing to say, but glory here, is the height of glory in the presence of our Saviour, yea, an endless glory, without end.

These twenty particulars underneath, asserted in the *Quakers Downfal* by Scripture proved, and in that Revelation infallibly confirmed that *Law. Claxton,* the onely Bishop, and true Messenger of our last Commission, doth in the death of his soul seal them a real truth, in confutation to the Quakers blinde Reasons imagination, which are as followeth:

1. *That faith shall dye in the heel, and reason in the head.*
2. *That the Angel did descend into the womb of* Eve.
3. *That a Spirit cannot live without a body.*
4. *That we and our God are cursed to all eternity.*
5. *That Christ our God is above the Stars, with a body of flesh and bones.*
6. *That God, that Christ said was a spirit, the meaning of his Revelation was, that his invisible soul was that God or spirit abiding onely in his person.*
7. *That Reason is the seed of the Serpent.*
8. *That by faith, reason shall be kept in eternal death.*
9. *That God gave Faith, Reason and Sense but once.*
10. *And that Faith, Reason and Sense have in all generated, in its kinde, form and nature.*
11. *That the Devils Kingdom and Reasons Kingdom are one.*
12. *That God doth damn as well as save, and that not for any evil thing done, as he hath asserted.*
13. *That we acknowledge no other God but what was within us.*
14. *And that we conceive this God was an infinite nothing, and so made all things of nothing.*
15. *That the light in us is darkness.*
16. *That an Infinite Spirit without a body is nothing.*
17. *That we say God hath no form.*
18. *That all the time* Paul *was cloathed with a corrupt, persecuting spirit, he was a vessel of honour in the account of God.*
19. *That God is all Faith, and no Reason, and that Reason I of the Nature of the Devil*

20. *That it was the wisdom of the flesh that made a chief Magistrate*

In the next place, I return as the Majestie of Christ, the onely God, in condemnation of your Diabolical, perjured lies against the holy Spirit, of the nature of the most high God, now revealed in us his last powerful, infallible Prophets and Messengers of his eternal Majestie in the highest Heavens, brought upon record in our Revelation, as in your Reasons libel, *verbatim,* are asserted by that son of perdition *J. Harwood.*

1. L.C. said, *He would prove God to be a man, flesh and bones as we are.*

Now ye the Believers of our Commission take notice, that of which of these twelve particulares before quoted, you by my pen finde silence, we own as eternal truth; but the rest that I set my pen against, was not our words, but Reason the Devil-lying imagination, by those aforesaid Quakers; as do but observe, and thou mayest discern how I binde them hand and foot from their supposed light, yet real darkness, as seriously minde the first forged lie.

4. L.C. said, *He had nothing of God in him, and many other places, nought of God in him.*

Answ. That you the blessed of the Lord my know, this was forged by their own lying imagination, do but read the third affirmation in p. 37 of the *Quakers Downfal,* and there you shall read the nature of God in all men more or less &c.

5. L.C. said, *The Devil was the author of this light in the world.*

Answ. Now the words that was then said, were, That Reason, the Devil, was the light within them; but in the *Quakers Downfal* you shall finde all along that Christ as he was Creator of Heaven and earth, by his word of Faith created this light now in being.

8 L.C. said, *He had damned the Lord Mayor seven or eight years ago, and a thousand within this eight years, and that he had justified forty or fifty.*

Ans. Now ye of the seed of Faith may discern of what seed or spirit these men are of, when it is not unknown to you, it is not above two years and a half since I first heard of this Commission: Now indeed *Ledowich Mugleton* said some of those words, that the Lord Mayor, with Recorder *Steel,* and the whole Jury, with thousands more, had by them been damned.

9. *He pronounced damnation to* George Fox *junior, and to* John Harwood, *and said several times, he would speak no more to them, yet after did; and said he would answer no queston, but after did.*

Ans. Had but any discerning soul been there, he might have beheld the spirit of *Cain* in them, so cruel, so tempting, that they pull'd us by the Coats, and with diabolical speech said, they would ensnare us; so that I could not but tell them, I did not think there had been such a violent spirit in them, &c. Now after their condemnation, charging them with their blasphemy and witchcraft carriage, this they esteemed an error or weakness in us.

12. One of them said, *That a Spirit hath flesh, blood and bones contrary to Christs words.*

Answ. Now do but read their first particular, and compare it with this last, and then judge, of what a dark, formal hypocritical, *Rabsheca* nature, the chief heads of these Quakers are of; insomuch, that I say, were it not that I know ye are all the seed of the Serpent, so in darkness, I might admire ye should say this or that is blasphemy when as we have told you, we onely are the Judge of the Scripture, and what we judge is blaspemy, heresie, or a lye, is so (and no other:) For this I infallibly say, the first Commission was onely understood by the second Commission; and the first and second Commissions are onely understood by our Commission; so that the notional Churches have nothing to do with Scripture much less to say the two first Commissions were truth, and the last Commission a lye: From the Lord of Glory, I say, that as theirs were truth in their time and place, so now is ours the onely commissionate truth now in being; and therefore let me but tell you this once, that your Pharasaical preaching and praying with your moderate, civill walking, are all but as dirt, or the dunghil, yea, as a menstrous cloth, not knowing the true God: So that from the seed of Gods own body, I say, ye had better been generated a Snake, or a Toad, then a rational, understanding man, as in the day of account, when it is too late, you will acknowledge, but then in vain.

FINIS

ERRATA

Page 106. line 25 for that faith can take up the words of faith; read, *that faith can take up the words of reason, as reason can take up the words of faith.*

The Lost Sheep
FOUND:
OR,
The Prodigal returned to his Fathers house, after many a sad and weary Journey through many Religious Countreys,

Where now, notwithstanding all his former Transgressions, and breach of his Fathers Commands, he is received in an eternal Favor, and all the righteous and wicked Sons that he hath left behind, reserved for eternal misery;

As all along every Church or Dispensation may read in his Travels, their Portion after this Life.

Written by Laur. Claxton, *the onely true converted Messenger of Christ Jesus, Creator of Heaven and Earth.*

LONDON:
Printed for the Author. 1660.

The Lost Sheep
FOUND:
OR,
The Prodigal returned to his Fathers house, after many a sad and weary Journey through many Religious Countreys.

Having published several Writings in confirmation of this spiritual last Commission that ever shall appear in this unbelieving World, a Well-wisher to this Commission, yea a man of no mean parts nor Parentage in this Reasons kingdom, much importuned me to publish to this perishing world, the various leadings forth of my faith through each Dispensation, from the year 1630, to this year 1660. and that for no other end, than that Reason, or the Devils mouth might be stopped, with the hypocrisie of his heart laid naked, and the tongues of Faith with praises opened, to consider what variety of By-paths, and multiplicity of seeming realities, yet absolute notions, the souls of the Elect may wander or travel through, seeking rest, and yet find none till the day expected, that Soul as a brand be plucked out of the fire of his own righteousness, or professed wickedness, unto the true belief of a real Commission which quencheth all the fiery darts of sin, that Dispensations have left cankering in his soul, [minde this] as have patience, and thou shalt hear the more I labored for perfect cure and peace in my soul, the further I was from it, insomuch that I resolved to seek forth no more, supposing my self in as perfect health and liberty in my spirit, as any then professing an unknown God whatsoever.

As do but seriously minde this ensuing Epistle, and thou mayest in me read thy own hypocrisie and dissimulation in point of Worship all along; as in that year 1630. being of the Age of fifteen yeares, and living with my Parents in the town of *Preston* in *Amounderness,* where I was born, and educated in the Form and Worship of the Church of *England,* then established in the Title of the *Episcopal,* or Bishops Government; then, in that year, my heart began to enquire after the purest Ministery held forth under that form, not being altogether void of some small discerning, who preached Christ more truly and powerfully, as I thought, than another, and unto them was I onely resolved to follow their Doctrine above any other, and to that end my brethren being more gifted in the knowledge of the Scriptures than my self, and very zealous in what they knew, that they did prevail with Mr. *Hudson* our Town-Lecturer, to admit of such Ministers as we judged were true laborious Ministers of Christ, who when they came, would thunder against Superstition, and sharply reprove Sin, and prophaning the Lords-day; which to hear, tears would run down my cheeks for joy: so having a pitiful superstitious fellow the Minister of our Town, I spared no pains to travel to *Standish,* and other places, where we could hear of a Godly Minister, as several times I have gone ten miles, more or less, fasting all the day, when my Parents never knew of it, and though I have been weary and hungry, yet I came home rejoycing. Then the Ministers had an Order, that none should receive the Sacrament, but such as would take it at the rayled Altar kneeling, which I could not do, and therefore went to such Ministers in the Countrey that gave it sitting: Now a while after Mr. *Starby* the Minister of our Town, taking notice of leaving our Parish, informed our father the danger of his children going into Heresie, and the trouble that would ensue upon our father and his children, besides the disgrace of all good Church-men, which did much incense our father, but all to no purpose, for I thought it conscience to obey God before man; however I being under my fathers tuition, he cast a strict eye over me, and would force me to read over the prayers in the book of *Common-prayer* and *Practice of Piety,* which I have done, till they have fallen asleep and my self, this was our devotion in those days; but increasing in knowledge, I judged to pray another mans form, was vaine babling, and not aceptable to God: and then the next thing I scrupled, was asking my parents blessing, that often times in the winter mornings, after I have been out of my bed, I have stood freezing above, and durst not come down till my father was gone abroad, and the reason I was satisfied, the blessing or prayers of a wicked man God would not hear, and so should offend God to ask him blessing; for either of these two ways I must, down on my knees, and say, Father pray to God to bless me, or give me your blessing for Gods sake, either of which I durst not use with my lips, but was in me refrained; and I improved my knowledge in the Doctrine of those men I judged was the true Ministers of God, so that with teares many times I have privately sought the Lord as I thought, whether those things that the puritanical Priests preached, was my own, and the more I was troubled, that I could not pray without a Book as my brethren did, fain would I have been judged a Professor with them, but wanted parts, yet often times have had motions to tender my self to prayer amongst them, but durst not, and to that end I might be admitted to pray with them, I have prayed alone to try how I could pray, but could not utter my self as I knew they did: so I remember their was a day of Humiliation to be set apart by the Puritans so called, to seek God by prayer and expounding of Scriptures, against which day I took my pen, and writ a pretty form of words, so got them by heart, and when the day came I was called to improve my gifts, at which I was glad, yet in a trembling condition lest I should be soyled; however, to Prayer I went, with a devotion as though I had known the true God, but alas, when I was in the midst of that Prayer, I left my form of words, and so was all in a sweat as though I had been sick, and so came off like a hypocrite as I was, which so seized on my soul, that I thought for my hypocrisie damnation would be my portion; however it humbled me, that I was glad to become one of the meanest of the number, still full of fears that when I died, I should go to hell; in which time I writ all the hypocrisie of my heart in a Letter to send to Mr. *Hudson* our Lecturer, to know his judgement whether such a soul as there related might be saved? in the interim comes a motion within me, saying, *A fool, why dost thou send to a man that knows not what will become of his own soul? burn it, and wait upon me:* which Letter I did burn, and not many weeks after I had a gift of Prayer that was not inferior to my brethren, for which I was glad for the goodness of God to my soul; and as I increased in knowledge, so was my zeal, that I have many times privately prayed with rough hard Sinders under my bare knees, that so God might hear me; and when I could not end my Prayers with tears running down my cheeks, I was afraid some sin shut the attention of God from me: and thus did I do for a few years, in which time the Bishops began to totter and shake, yea, for their cruelty and superstition, was totally routed.

Now if then you had asked me what I thought God was, the Devil was, what the Angels nature was, what Heaven and Hell was, and what would become of my soul after death?

My answer had plainly bin this: That my God was a grave, ancient, holy, old man, as I supposed sat in Heaven in a chair of gold, but as for his nature I knew no more than a childe: and as for the Devil, I really believed was some deformed person out of man, and that he could where, when, and how, in what shape appear he pleased; and therefore the devil was a Scar-croe, in so much that every black thing I saw in the night, I thought was the devil: But as for the Angels, I knew nothing at all; and for Heaven I thought was a glorious place, with variety of rooms suitable for Himself, and his Son Christ, and the Holy Ghost: and Hell, where it was I knew not, but judged it a local place, all dark, fire and brimstone, which the devils did torment the wicked in, and that forever; but for the soul at the hour of death, I believed was either by an Angel or a Devil fetcht immediately to Heaven or Hell. This was the height of my knowledge under the Bishops Government, and I am perswaded was the height of all Episcopal Ministers then living; so that surely if they shall be established for a National Ministery, they will not impose such Ceremonies as then they did, but are grown wiser about God and Devil; for they will finde the major part of *England* is grown wiser, so cannot stoop to an inferiour Light; and therefore if ye now begin to stand, take heed lest ye fall.

Secondly, After this I travelled into the Church of the Presbyterians, where still I made Brick of straw and clay, nay there I found my soul the more oppressed, and further ensnared in the land of *Egypt,* burning Brick all the day; but I knowing no further light, I was willing to bear their yoke, and sometimes I found it pleasant; for herein consisted the difference of the Presbyterian and Episcopal, onely in a few superstitious Rites and Ceremonies, as also their Doctrine was more lively than the Episcopal, for they would thunder the Pulpit with an unknown God, which then I thought was true, and sharply reprove sin, though since I saw we were the greatest sinners; but however their Doctrine I liked, it being the highest I then heard of: So war being begun betwixt the Episcopal and the Presbyterian, I came for *London,* where I found them more precise than in our Popish Countrey of *Lancashire;* for with us the Lords-day was highly profaned by the toleration of May-poles, Dancing and Rioting, which the Presbyterians hated, and in their Doctrine cryed out against, which thing my soul also hated, though yet I was not clear but the Steeple was the house of God, from that saying of *David,* Psalm 84.10. saying, *For a day in thy Courts is better than a thousand: I had rather be a Door-keeper in the house of my God, than to dwell in the tents of wickedness;* so that I finding out the ablest Teachers in *London,* as then I judged was Mr. *Calamy, Case, Brooks,* and such like, unto whom I daily resorted, if possible, to get assurance of Salvation, not neglecting to receive the Ordinance of Breaking of Bread from them, judging in so doing, *I shewed forth the Lords death till he came.* Now the persecution of the Bishops fell so heavy upon the Presbyterian Ministers, that some fled for *New-England;* and *Hooker* had left several Books in print, which so tormented my soul, that I thought it unpossible to be saved; however, I labored what in me lay, to finde those signs and marks in my own soul, and to that end neglected all things that might hinder it; and thus for a certain time I remained a hearer of them till such time that Wars began to be hot, and they pressed the people to send out their husbands and servants to help the Lord against the Mighty, by which many a poor soul knowing no better, was murthered, and murthered other, taking the Bible in their Pockets, and the Covenant in their Hats, by me was esteemed the work and command of the Lord, not at all minding the command of the second Commission to the contrary, as in 2 Cor. 10.4. saying, *We do not war after the flesh, for the weapons of our warfare are not carnal, but mighty through God to the pulling down of strong hold, &c.* This was not by me understood, but as they did in the old time in *Moses* his Commission, so I thought we might do then; in which time the Presbyterians began to be a great people, and in high esteem, and at that time there was a great slaughter of the Protestants in *Ireland,* that *London* was thronged with their Ministers and people, and several

Collections was gathered for them: but this I observed, that as the Presbyterians got power, so their pride and cruelty increased against such as was contrary to them, so that

Thirdly I left them, and travelled to the Church of the Independents; for this I observed as wars increased, so variety of Judgements increased: and coming to them, of which was Mr. *Goodwin,* and some others, I discerned their Doctrine clearer, and of a more moderate spirit: Now the greatest difference betwixt them, was about baptizing of infants, pleading by Scripture, that none but the infants or children of Believers ought to be baptized; and that none of them must receive the Sacrament, as then it was called, but such as was Church-members, judging all that was not congregated into fellowship, were not of God, but the world: So that about these things I was searching the truth thereof, and labored in the letter of the Scripture to satisfie my judgement; in the interim hearing of one Doctor *Crisp,* to him I went, and he held forth against all the aforesaid Churches, That let his people be in society or no, though walked all alone, yet if he believed that Christ Jesus died for him, God beheld no iniquity in him: and to that end I seriously perused his Bookes, and found it proved by Scripture, as it is written *Number 23.21. He hath not beheld iniquity in Jacob, neither hath he seen perverseness in* Israel. This was confirmed by other Scriptures, that I conceived whose sins Christ died for, their sin was to be required no more; for thus thinking when the debt was paid, the Creditor would not look upon him as indebted to him, yet this I ever thought Christ never died for all, though the Scripture was fluent to that purpose, yet I found Scriptures to the contrary, and was ever as touching that satisfied, that as Christ prayed for none but such as was given him out of the world, *I pray for them, I pray not for the world,* so that I thought he did not die for them he would not pray for, which thought now I know is true, and have by pen, and can by tongue make good the same: But I must return to the time then under Doctor *Crisp's* Doctrine, in which I did endeavor to become one of those that God saw no sin, and in some measure I began to be comforted therewith, but how, or which way to continue in the same I could not tell; having as yet but little understanding in the Scripture I was silent, only still enquiring after the highest pitch of Light then held forth in *London,* in which time Mr. *Randel* appeared, with Mr. *Simpson,* with such a Doctrine as Doctor *Crisp,* onely higher and clearer, which then was called *Antinomians,* or against the Law, so that I left all Church-fellowship, and burning of Brick in *Egypt,* and travelled with them up and down the borders, past *Egypt,* and part Wilderness.

Fourthly, take notice in the Sect I continued a certain time, for Church it was none, in that it was but part form, and part none; in which progress I had a great sort of professors acquainted with me, so began to be some body amongst them, and having a notable gift in Prayer, we often assembled in private, improving my gifts, judging then the best thing of this world was onely prepared for the Saints, of which then I judged my self one, not knowing any other but that God was a Spirit, and did motion in and out into his Saints, and that this was Gods Kingdom, and we his people; and therefore I judged God did fight for us against our enemies, that so we might enjoy him in liberty: At which time *Paul Hobson* brake forth with such expression of the incomes and out-goes of God, that my soul much desired such a gift of preaching, which after a while *Hobson* and I being acquainted, he had a Captains place under Colonel *Fleetwood* for *Yarmouth,* so that thither with him I went and there tarried a soldier with them, at which time I had a small gift of Preaching, and so by degrees increased in method, that I attempted the Pul, it at Mr. *Wardels* Parish in *Suffolk,* and so acquainted my gifts more and more in publick, that having got acquaintance at *Norwich,* I left Company at *Yarmouth;* so after a few dayes I was admitted into a Pulpit two or three times: so coming a man from *Pulom* side in *Norfolk* and hearing of me, was greatly affected with my Doctrine, but especially my Prayer, and was very urgent with me to go to their Parish of *Russel.* which within two weeks after I assented to be there such a day, which was against the Fast-day; for at that time the Parliament had established a Monethly Fast, which was the last wednesday of the moneth: at the set time I came to the place appointed, where this man had given notice to the best affected people in those parts, what a rare man was to preach that day, which thing I was ambitious of, as also to get some silver: Well, to the matter I went, and as was my Doctrine, so was their understanding, though I say't as young as I was, yet was not I inferior to any Priest in those days: So in conclusion of my days work there came several in the Church-yard to me, and gave me thanks for my paines, yea, hoped the Lord would settle me among them, which news I was glad to hear; so for the next Lords-Day by Goodman *Mays* and *Burton* was I invited to preach at *Pulom,* which was a great Parish; so upon liking I went, and was well approved of by all the Godly, so there for a time I was settled for twenty shillings a week, and very gallantly was provided for, so that I thought I was in Heaven upon earth judging the Priests had a brave time in this world, to have a house built for them, and means provided for them, to tell the people stories of other mens works. Now after I had continued half a year, more or less, the Ministers began to envy me for my Doctrine, it being free Grace, so contrary to theirs, and that the more, their people came from their own Parish to hear me, so that they called me *Sheep-stealer* for robbing them of their flock, and to that end came to catch and trap me at several Lectures where I was called, that at last they prevailed with the Heads of the Parish to turn me out, so I slighting them as they could me, we patted, and then having many friends, I was importuned to come and live with them, so above all I chose *Robert Marchants* house my Lodging place, because his Daughter I loved; and for a certain time preached up and down in several Churches, both of

Suffolk and *Norfolk,* and many times in private, that I had a great company. Now in the interim there was one *John Tyler* a *Colchester* man frequented those parts where then I inhabited, who was a Teacher of the Baptists, and had a few scattered up and down the Countrey, which several times we had meetings and converse about a lawful Minister: now I knowing no other but that those sayings, *Go ye teach all Nations, baptizing them, and lo I am with you to the end of the world;* that continuance to the end of the world, was the Load-stone that brought me to believe that the Baptism of the Apostles was as much in force now, as in their days, and that Command did as really belong to me as to them; so being convinced for *London* I went to be further satisfied, so that after a little discourse with *Patience,* I was by him baptized in the water that runneth about the *Tower,* after which I stayed in *London* about a week.

Fiftly, then for *Suffolk* again I travelled through the Church of the Baptists, and was of *Robert Marchants* family received with joy, for I had the love of all the family; and though he had four Daughters marriageable, yet there was one I loved above any in that Countrey, though I was beloved of other friends daughters far beyond her in estate, yet for her knowledge and moderation in spirit, I loved her; so there up and down a certain time I continued preaching the Gospel, and very zealous I was for obedience to the Commands of Christ Jesus; which Doctrine of mine converted many of my former friends and others to be baptized, and so into a Church-fellowship was gathered to officiate the order of the Apostles, so that really I thought if ever I was in a true happy condition, then I was, knowing no other but as aforesaid, that this Command of Christ did as really belong to me as to them; and we having the very same rule, as Elders and Deacons, with Dipping, and Breaking of bread in the same manner as they, I was satisfied we onely were the Church of Christ in this world.

Thus having a great company, and baptizing of many into that Faith, there was no small stir among the priests what to do with me, which afterwards they got a Warrant from the Parliament, to apprehend Mr. *Knowles* and my self, for then *Knowles* was about *Ipswich* preaching that doctrine, and baptizing certain people into that Faith; now the apprehended Mr. *Knowles* in *Ipswich* Goal, and from thence with their Warrant they came to secure me, so in the week day being privately assembled in a friends house, within three miles of *Ay,* there came in an Officer from the Parliament with certain Soldiers, and two Constables, with some of the parish, having clubs and staves surrounded the house, I being earnest in my doctrine, and at that time was very much pressing the people, that without submitting to Baptism all their profession was nothing, proving by Scripture that as Christ was our patern, so we must follow him as ensample, which could not be unless we kept his commandments, as it is written, *If ye love me, keep my commandments:* Now dipping being a command of Christ, and not submit their bodies to the Ordinance of Christ, and that Christ requires obedience from none but such as was capable of being taught, and therefore no children, but men and women, ought to receive the Ordinance of Baptism, in which time some of the Officers hearing me, interrupted me in my doctrine, and told me I must leave off, and go along with them, shewing me the Authority they had from the Parliament; however, some of our friends would have opposed them, but I saw it was in vain, and so desired our friends to be quiet, and said, we must not onely profess Christ, but also suffer for him; so it being in the winter time, and almost night, they hasted me for *Ay*, though I, with our friends, desired but so much liberty as to go to my wifes father house for linnen and other necessaries, and they would engage for my appearance before the Committee at *Bury*; but all in vain, then my wife told them they should provide a house for her, for whither ever I went, she would go: at which they were very much incensed, but all to no purpose, so at last a Trooper would have her to ride behind him, but she with scorn refused, then they got her furniture to ride behind me, so taking leave with our friends, to *Ay* that night we were carried; now one of them went before to provide Lodging, so the Town having intelligence they had taken a great Anabaptist, there was no small waiting for my coming, that when I came into the entering of the town, the inhabitants had beset both sides of the streets to see my person, supposing an Anabaptist had bin a strange creature, but when they beheld me, with my wife, they said one to another, He is like one of us, yea, they are a very pretty couple, it is pity I should suffer: so to the Inne I came, where a great company was in the yard to behold me; so being unhorsed, they guarded me to our Lodging, and great provision was made for supper, where many a pot was spent that night to see my face; so to bed we went, and in the next room by Soldiers guarded, so in the morning we were hasted for *St. Edmonds Bury,* which that morning Captain *Harvey* gave out many sad and grievous words what the Committee would do with me, but the devil was deceived; however I said little: so they came to me with a Bill what I had to pay for Beer, Wine, and Meat; unto which I said, I had none, but if I had, I would pay none, it was sufficient I was wrongfully deprived of my freedom, and not to pay for their rioting; however they told me, I must before I go; then keep me here still: surely, said I, your Masters that set you on work, are able to pay you your Wages: Well, they said before I came out of prison, if I were not hanged, I should pay for it; then said I, rest your selves contented till that day: so towards *Bury* we took our Journey, and one was gone before to inform the Committee I was taken; against my appearance they were assembled in a full Committee, of which as I take it, Captain *Bloyes* of *Woodbridge* was then Chair-man, who asked my name? To which I replied, this was strange that you had a Warrant to take me, and know not my name: Well, that was no matter, do you tell us your name: so I told them: What countrey are you? I said *Lancashire*. What made you travel so far off into these parts? The like notions that moved others, moved me. How long have you professed this way of dipping? Not so long as I ought to have done, had my understanding been enlightened. What then, you approve of what you do? Otherwise I should not do it. How many have you dipped in these parts? I being a free born subject of this Nation ought not to accuse my self; but you are to prove your charge, by sufficient witness against me; but however I being brought before you for my obedience to the Commands of Christ, I am neither afraid nor ashamed to tell you what I have done: but to give you an account how many I have dipped, that I cannot tell. Then you have dipped some? Yea, that I have. After what manner do you dip them? After a decent order. We are informed you dip both men and women naked? As unto that you are not rightly informed. Where is your *Jordan* you dip them in? Though it is not *Jordan,* yet there are several places convenient. Do you not dip them in the night? Yea. And why do you not dip them in the day, it being an Ordinance of Christ as you say? Because such as you are not able to bear the truth. Then said Sir *William Spring* but Mr. *Claxton,* have not you forced some in the water against their will? That is contrary to Scripture. Did you not one time, being on horsback, with a switch force some into the water? Let them that so informed you, affirm it before you to my face. But Mr. *Claxton* who were those that you dipped about *Framingham?* At this time I cannot remember, but several I have dipped there aways. Did not you dip six Sisters there about at one time? I never dipped six at one time. Then said Sir *John Rowse,* we are informed you dipped six Sisters one night naked. That is nothing to me what you are informed, for I never did such a thing; Nay further, it is reported, that which of them you liked best, you lay with her in the water? Surely your experience teacheth you the contrary, that nature has small desire to copulation in water, at which they laughed; But, said I, you have more cause to weep for the unclean thoughts of your heart. Mr. *Claxton* have not you a wife? One that brought me, said she is in town. Where is she? Fetch her hither: she being without the door, came in quickly, and took me by the hand. Well, said the Chair-man, you are a loving woman, is this your husband? Yes, he is my husband. How long have you been married? About two moneths. Where were you married? At *Waybread* in my fathers house. Who married you? My husband, with the consent of my parents, and the Church. At that there was a great laughter, and said, your husband marry you to himself, that is against the law; I being vexed at their folly, answered, Marriage is no other, but a free consent in love to the other before God, and who was sufficient to publish the Contract as my self? Nay but Mr. *Claxton,* you are not rightly informed as touching true Marriage. I say I was married according to truth: then if your Marriage be lawful, we are not lawfully married. I question not yours, look ye to that; but this I know, and can prove, I am married according to the word of God; neither can your law repeal the contract of that couple, that hath their parents

The Lost Sheep Found

consent, and the Church confirming the same. Well, well, we shall give you the hearing, but how many was present when you took her to your wife? About twelve. What did you say to her and the Church? First, I sought the Lord by prayer for a blessing upon that Ordinance, and then I declared unto her parents and the Church what had passed betwixt she and I, and that before them all I took her by the hand, and asked her if she was not willing to take me for her husband during life? To which she assented, as also her parents approved of it, and gave her to me with the confirmation of the Church. Then said the Chair-man, What think you Gentlemen, of this Marriage? They said it was a strange Marriage. What then Mrs. *Claxton*, would you look upon this man your lawful husband? Yea, I deny all other men in the world. Then you have lain with him? I ought to ly with no other. But Mrs. *Claxton*, did your husband dip you before, or after he became your husband? Before I was contracted in publick? How or what manner did your husband dip you? in your clothes or naked? Sir, we defie any undecent cariage, if you dipped in your clothes you would spoil them, and besides it might endanger your life with cold, we have clothes for both men and women provided for that purpose. What were you plunged over head and ears? So saith the Scripture. What Mr. *Claxton*, did you go with her into the water? No I stood on the bank side. Mrs. *Claxton,* were not you amazed, or almost drowned? No Sir, the obedience to the Command of God did shut out all fear and cold. What did not you go to bed after dipped? I had a warm bed with dry linnen provided? Did not your husband lodge with you that night? There is no such wickedness among us. Why what matter, you were married before God. Till we were publickly before witness, we had no such custom, and let me tell you, if it be the practice of your Church, it is not so in ours. Nay woman, be not angry, I do not say you did so, for truly I am as much against sin as you are. But Mrs. *Claxton,* we have an Order to secure your husband, and there to endure the pleasure of the Parliament, what will you do? we have no Order to stay you. If you stay my husband, you must stay me also. Why, are you willing to go to Goal with your husband? For the cause of Christ I am willing to suffer imprisonment. Then you are resolved yours is the way of Truth. Then said I, for the present I know no Truth but this. Well Mr. *Claxton,* after a while you will be otherwise informed. Never to turn back again. We are to commit you to custody, that so you may seduce no more people. Sir, I must obey your pleasure, but I shall not deny to be obedient to the Command of Christ. Well, we shall talk with you another time: so they ordered to make my *Mittimus,* and in my presence gave it Captain *Poe* my keeper, and said, Mr. *Claxton,* you may take notice that the Parliament is favorable to you, that they will not send you to the common Goal, but to a house where none but men of Quality are kept in custody. Then said *Poe,* who was my Goaler, what shall his wife do? Then said my wife, Where ever my husband is, there will I be, then the Committee

Ordered her with me: so coming hither, there was none but two Papist Knights and a Sea Captain, so after we had supped, we were directed to our Chamber, which was a large chamber, and pretty good Furniture. Now under a week I told Captain *Poe* that I was not able to board at half a crown a meal. Then, saith he, you must go to the common Goal: Thither would I go, for I am not ashamed to sit in the stocks in the Market-place, for the name of Christ. So he informed the Committee, but they would not remove me, and said, he must agree for the chamber, and I finde my self Diet: At this *Poe* was vexed, and sent up his Handmaid Mistriss *Tuck*, to agree with me for the chamber at four shillings a week, which for the space of half a year I gave her, in which time our people increased, there being *William Muly* and some others of this way in *Bury*, I had oftentimes money from the Army, and the Churches at *London* and *Colchester,* so that I wanted for nothing; and some came to my chamber, and there I preached unto them; in so much that the Keeper informed the Committee, who that Sunday at night assembled, to consider what to do with me: in conclusion they shut me close prisoner, and kept my wife from me, which was more grief to me then the rest. Well, against the next Lords-day I appointed our friends to stand before my window on the *Argel-hill,* that being the way for all the great Ones of the Town to go to their worship, so at the very instant time putting my head forth of the Window, I did boldly exhort the people to beware of the priests, and while it is the time of your health, submit your souls and bodies in obedience to the true Baptism, and be no longer deluded to think that your infants are commanded to obey, or capable of an Ordinance imposed upon them. Oh for shame, if not for fear, stand still and hear the truth related by his true and lawful Minister, otherwise turn back again; At which a great sort of people gave attention, which did enrage the Priest and Magistrate, yet they knew not what to do with me, but charged me to do so no more. Then said I, take heed how you keep my wife from me: is this to do as you would be done unto? so they forthwith took off the Pad-lock, and let me friends come to me. After this I had the liberty of the whole house, nay, to sit at the street-door; for he had no prisoners but such as gave in great security for their safe imprisonment; and as for me, and *Westrop* my fellow-prisoner, they feared not our going away, onely they were afraid I should dip some. So a little after, Spring coming on, I got liberty, not being well, to go abroad with a Keeper, and Captain *Gray,* who was called Captain *Drink-water,* was to go with me: Now above all the rest, I desired Captain *Gray* to go with me to a Wood a mile distant from me; it having rained over night, the Brook was up, so a man coming with a Pole, I desired him to lay it over, which he did, so I went over first, and the Captain followed me, and shaking the Pole, he fell in to the middle in water, and in a trembling condition he was, lest the Committee should hear of it; so to the Wood we went, and there he dried his Hose and Stockings, so after we came to prison again, the Committee hearing of it, questioned Captain *Gray,* but he told them the truth, at which they laughed. After I had lain there a long time, Mr. *Sedgewick,* and Mr. *Erbery* came to visit me with whom I had great discourse, and after they were gone, I had a great contest in my minde, as touching the succession of Baptism, which I could not see but in the death of the Apostles, there was never since no true Administrator; for I could not read there was ever any that had power by imposition of hands, to give the Holy Ghost, and work miracles as they did; so that in the death of them I concluded Baptism to either young or old, was ceased. Now observe, I could discern this, but could not by the same tale see that preaching and prayer was to cease: for this now I know, as in the death of the Apostles, and them commissionated by them, the Commission was ceased, as unto all their Form and Worship: So finding I was but still in *Egypt* burning Brick, I was minded to travel into the Wilderness; so seeing the vanity of the Baptists, I renounced them and had my freedom. Then

Sixthly, I took my journey into the society of those people called *Seekers,* who worshipped God onely by prayer and preaching, therefore to *Ely* I went, to look for *Sedgwick* and *Erbery* but found them not, onely their people were assembled: with whom I had discourse, but found little satisfaction; so after that for *London* I went to finde *Seekers* there, which when I came, there was divers fallen from the Baptists as I had done, so coming to *Horn* in *Fleet lane,* and *Fleten* in *Seacoullane,* they informed me that several had left the Church of *Patience,* in seeing the vanity of *Kiffin* and others, how highly they took it upon them, and yet could not prove their Call successively; so glad was I there was a people to have society withal; then was I moved to put forth a book which was the first that I ever write, bearing this Title, *The pilgrimage of Saints, by church cast out, in Christ found, seeking truth,* this being a sutable peece of work in those days, that it wounded the Churches; which book *Randel* owned, and sold many for me. Now as I was going over *London-bridge,* I met with *Thomas Gun* a teacher of the Baptists, who was a man of a very humble, moderate spirit, who asked me if I own'd the *Pilgrimage of Saints?* I told him yea: then said he, you have writ against the church of Christ, and have discovered your self an enemy to Christ. Then I said, it is better be a hypocrite to man then to God, for I finde as much dissimulation, covetousness, back-biting and envy, yea as filthy wickedness among some of them, as any people I know: and notwithstanding your heaven-like carriage, if all your fault were written in your forehead, for ought I know, you are a hypocrite as well as I; which afterwards it was found out he had lain with his Landlady many times; and that he might satisfie his Lust, upon flighty erands, he sent her husband into the country, that so he might lodge with his wife all night; which being found out, so smote his conscience, that he privately took a Pistol and shot himself to death in *Georges-fields.* As all along in this my travel I was subject to that sin, and yet as saint-like, as though sin were a burden to me, so that the fall of this *Gun* did so seize on my soul, that I concluded there was none could live without sin in this world; for notwithstanding I had great knowledge in the things of God, yet I found my heart was not right to what I pretended, but full of lust and vain-glory of this world, finding no truth in sincerity that I had gone through, but meerly the vain pride and conceit of Reasons imagination, finding my heart with the rest, seeking nothing but the praise of men in the heighth of my prayer and preaching, yet in my doctrine through all these opinions, pleading the contrary, yea abasing my self, and exalting a Christ that then I knew not. Now after this I return'd to my wife in *Suffolk,* and wholly bent my mind to travel up & down the country, preaching for monies, which then I intended for *London,* so coming to *Colchester* where I had *John Aplewhit, Purkis,* and some other friends, I preached in publick; so going for *London,* a mile from *Colchester,* I met my Cane upright upon the ground, and which way it fell, that way would I go; so falling towards *Kent,* I was at a stand what I should do there, having no acquaintance, and but little money, yet whatever hardship I met withal, I was resolved for *Gravesend,* so with much a do I got that night to a town called *Bilrekey,* it being in the height of Summer, and in that town then having no friends, and I think but six pence, I lodged in the Church porch all night, so when day appeared, I took my journey for *Gravesend,* and in the way I spent a groat of my six pence, and the other two pence carried me over the water; so being in the town, I enquired for some strange opinionated people in the town, not in the least owning any of them, but seemingly to ensnare them, which they directed me to one *Rugg* a Victualler, so coming in, though having no monies, yet I called for a pot of Ale, so after a few words uttered by me, the man was greatly taken with my sayings, in so much that he brought me some bread and cheese, with which I was refreshed, and bid me take no care, for I should want for nothing, you being the man that writ *The Pilgrimage of Saints,* I have had a great desire to see you, with some soldiers and others, so for the present he left me, and informed Cornet *Lokier* and the rest, that I was in town, who forthwith came to me, and kindly received me, and made way for me to preach in the *Blockhouse;* so affecting my doctrine, they quatered me in the Officers lodging, and two days after they carried me to *Dartford,* where there I preached; so against the next Lords-day came for *Gravesend,* and there preached in the Market-place, which was such a wonder to the town and countrey, that some for love, and others for envy, came to hear, that the Priest of the town had almost none to hear him, that if the Magistrate durst, he would have apprehended me, for I boldly told them God dwelled not in the Temple made with hands, neither was any place more holy then another, proving by Scripture, that where two or three were gathered in his name, God was in the midst of them, and that every Believer was the Temple of God, as it is written, *God dwelleth with a humble and contrite spirit;* So after this we went to *Maidstone,* and *Town-maulin,* and there I preached up and down, so at last having given me about five pounds, I went to my wife and promised in two weekes to return again, which I did, but I found not *Lokier* nor the rest so affectionate as before, for he had a gift of preaching, & therein did seek honor, so suspicious of my blasting his reputation, slighted and persecuted me, so that I left them, and towards *Maidston* travelled, so one *Bulfinch* of *Town-maulin* having friends towards *Canterbury,* perswaded me to go with him, and so against the next Lords-day, having no steeple free, we had a Gentlemans barn free, where a great company was assembled: then for *Sandwich* I went, and up and down found friends, so coming to *Canterbury* there was some six of this way, amongst whom as a maid of pretty knowledge, who with my Doctrine was affected, and I affected to lye with her, so that night prevailed, and satisfied my lust, afterwards the mayd was highly in love with me, and as gladly would I have been shut of her, lest some danger ensued, so not knowing I had a wife she was in hopes to marry me, and so would have me lodge with her again, which fain I would, but durst not, then she was afraid I would deceive her, and would travel with me, but by subtilty of reason I perswaded her to have patience, while I went into *Suffolk,* and setled my occasions, then I would come and marry her, so for the present we parted, and full glad was I that I was from her delivered, so to *Maidston* I came, and having got some six pounds, returned to my wife, which a while after I went for *Kent* again, but found none of the people so zealous as formerly, so that my journey was but a small advantage to me, and then I heard the maid had been in those parts to seek me, but not hearing of me, returned home again, and not long after was married to one of that sect, and so there was an end of any further progress into *Kent.* Then not long after I went for *London,* and some while remained preaching at *Bow* in Mr. *Sterry's* place, and *London-stone,* but got nothing; so to *Suffolk* I went, and having but one childe, put it to nurse, intending to go to my Parents in *Lancashire:* So leaving my Wife at my cousin *Andertons,* I hearing of *Seekers* in *Hartfordshire,* went thither, and at last was hired by Mr. *Hickman* to preach at *Peters* in *St. Albans,* so being liked, I was hired for a moneth longer, so fetcht my Wife, and there continued till such time the Town of *Sanderidge* took me for their Minister, and setled me in the Vicaridge, where Sir *John Garret,* Colonel *Cox,* and Justice *Robotom* came constantly to hear me, and gave me several Gifts, so that in heaven I was again; for I had a high pitch of free Grace, and mightily flown in the sweet Discoveries of God, and yet not at knowing what God was, onely an infinite Spirit, which when he pleased did glance into his people the sweet breathings of his Spirit; and therefore preached, it was not sufficient to be a professor, but a possessor of Christ, the possession of which would cause a profession of him, with many such high flown notions, which at that time I knew no better, nay, and in truth I speak it, there was few of the Clergy able to reach me in Doctrine or Prayer; yet notwithstanding, not being an University man, I was very often turned out of employment, that truly I speak it, I think there was not any poor soul so tossed in judgement, and for a poor livelihood, as then I was. Now in this my prosperity I continued not a year, but the Patron being a superstitious Cavelier, got an Order from the Assembly of Divines to call me in question for my Doctrine, and so put in a drunken fellow in my room: and thus was I displaced from my heaven upon earth, for I was dearly beloved of *Smiths* and *Thrales,* the chief of the Parish. Well there was no other way but for *London* again, and after a while sent my Goods for *Suffolk* by water: now at this I concluded all was a cheat, yea preaching it self, and so with this apprehension went up and down *Hartfordshire, Bedford,* and *Buckinghamshire,* and my subtilty of reason got monies more or less; as of one at *Barton,* I had twelve pounds for the printing of a book against the Commonalty of *England,* impeaching them for traytors, for suffering the Parliament their servants, to usurp over them, judging the Common-wealth was to cut out the form, and the shape of their grievances, and send it up to their servants the Parliament to finish, shewing, as the Common-wealth gave the Parliament power, so they were greater then the Parliament, with matter to the effect. And then being presented to a small parish in *Lincolnshire,* thither I went, but finding no society to hear, I grew weary thereof, and stayd with some friends at *Oford,* so with a little monies went home again, and not long after going into *Lincolnshire,* I preached in several places, that at last Captain *Cambridge* hearing of me, and was much affected with me, and made me teacher to their Company, and said I should have all necessities provided me, and a man alowed me; then I was well recruited and horsed, so that I judged it was the mercy of God to me, my distress being great, and my care for my family. Now after a while our Regiment went for *London,* so though I had preached in *Lincoln, Horncastle, Spilsby,* and many other places, yet they would excuse me for two moneths, having no need of preaching in *London,* so with monies I had I went to my wife, and staid there a while, and so came for *London:* Now our Reigment being *Twistons,* Quartered in *Smithfield,* but I Quartered in a private-house, who was a former friend of mine, asked me if I heard no of a people called *My one flesh?* I said no, what was their opinion, and how should I speak with any of them? Then she directed me to *Giles Calvert.* So that now friends, I am travelling further into the *Wilderness,* having now done burning of Brick, I must still wander in the mountains and deserts; so coming to *Calvert,* and making enquiry after such a people, he was a fraid I came to betray them, but exchanging a few words in the height of my language, he was much affected, and satisfied I was a friend of theirs, so he writ me a Note to Mr. *Brush,* and the effect thereof was, the bearer hereof is a man of the greatest light I ever yet heard speak, and for ought I know indeed of receiving of him you may receive an Angel, so to Mr. *Brush* I went, and presented this Note, which he perused, so bid me come in, and told me if I had come a little sooner, I might have seen Mr. *Copp,* who then had lately appeared in a most dreadful manner; so their being *Mary Lake,* we had some discourse, but nothing to what was in me, however they told me, if next sunday I would come to Mr. *Melu* in *Trinity-lane,* there would that day some friends meet. Now observe at this time my judgment was this: that there was no man could be free'd from sin, till he had acted that so called sin, as no sin, this a certain time had been burning within me, yet durst not reveal it to any, in that I thought none was able to receive it, and a great desire I had to make trial, whether I should be troubled or satisfied therein: so that

Seventhly, I took my progress into the *Wilderness,* and according to the day appointed, I found Mr. *Brush,* Mr. *Rawlinson,* Mr. *Goldsmith,* with *Mary Lake,* and some four more: now *Mary Lake* was the chief speaker, which in her discourse was some thing agreeable, but not so high as was in me experienced, and what I then knew with boldness declared, in so much that *Mary Lake* being blind, asked what that was that spake? *Brush* said the man that *Giles Calvert* sent to us, so with many more words I affirmed that there was no sin, but as man esteemed it sin, and therefore none can be free from sin, till in purity it be acted as no sin, for I judged that pure to me, which to a dark understanding was impure, for to the pure all things, yea all acts were pure: thus making the Scripture a writing of wax, I pleaded the words of *Paul, That I know and am perswaded by the Lord Jesus, that there was nothing unclean, but as man esteemed it,* unfolding that was intended all acts, as well as meats and drinks, and therefore till you can lie with all women as one woman, and not judge it sin, you can do nothing but sin: now in Scripture I found a perfection spoken of, so that I understood no man could attain perfection but this way, at which Mr. *Rawlinson* was much taken, and *Sarah Kullin* being present, did invite me to take trial of what I had expected, so as I take it, after we parted, she invited me to Mr. *Wats* in *Rood-lane,* where was one or two more like her self, and as I take it, lay with me that night: now against next sunday it was noised abroad what a rare man of knowledge was to speak at Mr. *Brushes*: at which day there was a great company of men and women, both young and old; and so from day to day increased, that now I had choice of what before aspired after, insomuch that it came to our Officers ears; but having got my pay I left them, and lodged in *Rood-lane,* where I had Clients many, that I was not able to answer all desires, yet none knew our actions but our selves; however I was careful with whom I had to do. This lustful principle encreased so much, that the Lord Mayor with his Officers came at midnight to take me, but knowing thereof, he was prevented. Now *Copp* was by himself with a company ranting and swearing, which I was seldom addicted to, onely proving by Scripture the truth of what I acted; and indeed *Solomons* Writings was the original of my filthy lust, supposing I might take the same liberty as he did, not then understanding his Writings was no Scripture, that I was move to write to the world what my Principle was, so brought to publick view a Book called *The Single Eye,* so that men and women came from many parts to see my face, and hear my knowledge in these things, being restless till they were made free, as then we called it. Now I being as they said, *Captain of the Raut,* I had most of the principle women came to my lodging for knowledge, which then was called *The Head-quarters.* Now in the height of this ranting, I was made still careful for moneys for my Wife, onely my body was given to other women: so our Company encreased, I wanted for nothing that heart could desire, but at last it became a trade so common, that all the froth and scum broke forth into the height of this wickedness, yea began to be a publick reproach, that I broke up my Quarters, and went into the countrey to my Wife, where I had by the way disciples plenty, which then Major *Rainsborough,* and Doctor *Barker* was minded for Mr. *Walis* of *Elford,* so there I met them, where was no small pleasure and delight in praising of a God that was an infinite nothing, what great and glorious things the Lord had done, in bringing us out of bondage, to the perfect liberty of the sons of God, and yet then the very notion of my heart was to all manner of theft, cheat, wrong, or injury that privately could be acted, though in tongue I professed the contrary, not considering I brake the Law in all points (murther excepted:) and the ground of this my judgment was, God had made all things good, so nothing evil but as man judged it; for I apprehended there was no such thing as theft, cheat, or a lie, but as man made it so: for if the creature had brought this world into no propriety, as *Mine* and *Thine,* there had been no such title as theft, cheat, or a lie; for the prevention hereof *Everard* and *Gerrard Winstanley* did dig up the Common, that so all might have to live of themselves, then there had been no need of defrauding, but unity one with another, not then knowing this was the devils kingdom, and Reason lord thereof, and that Reason was naturally enclined to love it self above any other, and to gather to it self what riches and honor it could, that so it might bear sway over its fellow creature; for I made it appear to *Gerrard Winstanley* there was a self-love and vain-glory nursed in his heart, that if possible, by digging to have gained people to him, by which his name might become great among the poor Commonalty of the Nation, as afterwards in him appeared a most shameful retreat from *Georges-bill,* with a spirit of pretended universality, to become a real Tithe-gatherer of propriety; so what by these things in others, and the experience of my own heart, I saw all that men spake or acted, was a lye and therefore my thought was, I had no good cheat for something among them, and that so I might live in prosperity with them, and not come under the last of the Law; for here was the thought of my heart from that saying of *Solomon,* Eccles. 3.19. *For that which befalleth the soul of men, befalleth beasts, even one thing befalleth them; as the one dieth, so dieth the other, yea, they have all one breath, so that a man hath no preheminance above a beast; for all is vanity, all go into one place, all are of the dust, and all turn to dust again.* So that the 18th and 19th verses of *Ecclesiastes* was the rule and direction of my spirit, to eat and to drink, and to delight my soul in the labor of my minde all the days of my life, which I thought God gave me as my portion, yea to rejoyce in it as the gift of God, as said that wise Head-piece *Solomon;* for this was then, and ever after, till I came to hear of a Commission, was the thought of my heart, that in the grave there was no more remembrance of either joy or sorrow after. for this I conceived, as I knew not what I was before I came in being, so for ever after I should know nothing after this my being was dissolved; but even as a stream from the Ocean was distinct in it self while it was a stream, but when returned to the Ocean, was therein swallowed and become one with the Ocean; so the spirit of man while in the body, was distinct from God, but when death came it returned to God, and so became one with God, yea God it self; yet notwithstanding this, I had sometimes a relenting light in my soul, fearing this should not be so, as indeed it was contrary; but however, then a cup of Wine would wash away this doubt.

But now to return to my progress, I came for *London* again, to visit my old society; when then *Mary Midleton* of *Chelsford,* and Mrs. *Star* was deeply in love with me, so having parted with Mrs. *Mildeton,* Mrs. *Star* and I went up and down the countries as man and wife, spending our time in feasting and drinking, so that Tavernes I called the house of God; and the Drawers, Messengers; and Sack, Divinity; reading in *Solomons* writings it must be so, in that it make glad the heart of God; which before, and that some, we had several meetings of great company, and that some, no mean ones neither, where then, and at that time, they improved their liberty, where Doctor *Pagets* maid stripped her self naked, and skipped among them, but being in a Cooks shop, there was no hunger, so that I kept my self to Mrs. *Star,* pleading the lawfulness of our doings as aforesaid, concluding with *Solomon* all was vanity. In the interim the Parliament had issued forth several Warrants into the hands of Church-members, which knew me not by person, but by name, so could not take me, though several times met with me, that at last the Parliament to him that could bring me before them, would give a hundred pounds, so that one *Jones* for lucre of mony, knowing me, got a Warrant to apprehend me, who meeting me in the four swans within *Bishopsgate,* told me he had a Warrant from the High Court of Parliament to take me: Let me see it, said I, you have no power to serve it without an Officer, and so would have escaped, but could not the people so thronged about me, and a great tumult there was, some fighting with him for an Informer, but being a City Trooper, and some more of his company with him, they carried me, as I take it, to Alderman *Andrews,* where they searched my Pockets; but having dropped an Almanack that had the names of such as sold my books for me, they found it, and carried it to the Parliament, so informed the House I was taken, and likewise desired to know what they should do with me, who gave Order to bring me by water to *Whitehall*-staires, and deliver me to *Barkstead's* Soldiers, where after a while a messenger was sent to take me into custody, where I was lodged in *Whitehall* over against the *Dial,* and two soldiers guarded me night and day, for which I was to pay; but some being of my principle, they would guard me for nothing, and a Captain of theirs would give me moneys; so after two days I was sent for before the Committee of the Parliament to be examined: so being called in, they asked me my Name, my Countrey, with many such frivolous things; so coming in business in hand, Mr. *Weaver* being the Charman, asked me if I lodged in *Rood-lane?* To which I answered, Once I did. Wherefore did you lodge there? Because I had a friend there of whom I hired a chamber. What company of men and women were those that came to you? To instance their names I cannot, but some came as they had business with me. Who were those women in black Bags that came to you? As now I know not. But Mr. *Claxton,* we are informed, you have both wives and maids that lodgeth with you there? Those that informed you, let them appear face to face, for I never lay with any but my own wife. No: for you call every woman your wife? I say I lye with none but my wife, according to Law, though in the unity of the spirit, I lye with all the creation. That is your sophistication, but deal plainly before God and man, did not you lye with none in *Rood-lane,* and others places, besides your wife? I do deal plainly as you, but I being a free born subject ought not to accuse my self, in that you are to prove your charge. Mr. *Claxton* confess the truth it, will be better for you: for we assure you shall suffer no wrong. What I know is trueth, I have, and shall speak. What did you at Mrs. *Croes* in *Rederiff?* I had conference with the people. As you were preaching, you took a pipe of Tobacco, and women came and saluted you, and other above was committing Adultery. This is more then remember? No, you will not remember any thing against you: but surely you cannot but remember this *Almanack* is yours, and these mens names your own hand writing. Yea I did write them, was not these men your disciples? They were not mine, but their own. Did not Major *Rainsborough,* and the rest lye with other women? Not as I know. But Mr. *Claxton* do you remember this book is yours? I never saw that before, but may be some of the like nature I have. Why did not you write this Book? That you are to prove. Here is the two first Letters of your name. What is that to me? it may serve for other names as well as mine. Did not Major *Rainsborough* and these men give you monies to print this Book? How should they give me monies to print that which neither I nor they knew of. This Book must be yours, for it speaks your language, suitable to your practice. Though you will confess nothing, yet we have witness to prove it. Let them by examined in my presence: So calling *Jones* that betrayed me, did you never see Mr. *Claxton* lye with no woman? I have heard him talk of such things, but say no act. Though you cannot, there is some will, therefore Mr. *Claxton* deal plainly, that though you lay with none, yet did not you alow it none others? I saw no evil in them to disallow; And Gentlemen let me speak freely to you, Suppose I were your servant, entrusted with your secrets, and knew that you were Traitors against this present Power, would you take it well for me to impeach you, and bear witness against you? At which, either the Earl of *Denby,* or the Earl of *Salisbury* said, No: Such a servant deserved to be hang'd; at which they laughed and said, this was a case of another nature. I say as it is in the one, so it is in the other. Well then, Mr. *Claxton,* you will not confess the trueth. You say you have witness to prove it. However the trueth I have confessed, and no more can be expected. Do no you know one *Copp?* Yea I know him, and that is all, for I have not seen him above two or three times. Then they said, this is a sad principle, which if not routed, all honest men will have their wives deluded. One of them said, he feared not his wife she was too old, so they dismissed me to the place from whence I came, and said we shall report it to the House, that so with speed you may have your trial, but I think it was about fourteen weeks before I received the Sentence of the House, which took up the House a day and half work, as *John Lilborn* said, stood the Nation in a Thousand pounds: And thus they sate spending the Common-wealths monies, about frivolous things. Now having past some votes, at last they carried the day for my banishment, which vote that day was printed, and pasted upon many posts about the City of *London, That* Lawrence Claxton *should remain in* New bridwel *a moneth and a day, and then the High Sheriffe of* London *to conduct him to the High Sheriffe in* Kent, *and so to be banish* England, Scotland, and Ireland, *and in the Territories thereof during life, and Major* Rainsborough *to be no longer Justice during his life.* Now when my moneth was expired, their Vote was not executed, so after a while I came forth of prison, and then took my journey with my wife to my house in *Stainfeild,* and from thence I took my progress into Cambrigdeshire, to the towns of *Foxin* and *Orwel* where still I continued my Ranting principle, with a high hand.

 Now in the interim I attempted the art of Astrology and Physics, which in a short time I gained and therewith travelled up and down Cambridgeshire and *Essex,* as *Linton* and *Saffron-waldon,* and other countrey towns, improving my skill to the utmost, that I had clients many, yet could not be therewith contended, but aspired to the art of Magick, so finding some of Doctor *Wards* and *Woolerds* Manuscripts, I improved my genius to fetch Goods back that were stoln, yea to raise spirits, and fetch treasure out of the earth, with many such diabolical actions, as a woman of *Sudbury* in *Suffolk* assisted me, pretending she could do by her witch-craft whatever she pleased; now something was done, but nothing to what I pretended, however monies I gained, and was up and down looked upon as a dangerous man, that the ignorant and religious people was afraid to come near me, yet this I may say, and speak the truth, that I have cured many desperate Diseases, and one time brought from *Glenford* to a village town wide of *Lanham* to Doctor *Clark,* two women and one man that had bewitched his daughter, who came in a frosty cold night, tormented in what then *Clark* was a doing, and so after that his daughter was in perfect health, with many such like things, that it puffed up my spirit, and made many fools believe in me, for at that time I looked upon all was good, and God the author of all, and therefore have several times attempted to raise the devil, that so I might see what he was, but all in vain, so that I judged all was a lie, and that there was no devil at all, nor indeed no God but onely nature, for when I have perused the Scriptures I have found so much contradiction as then I conceived, that I had no faith in it at all, no more then a history, though I would talk of it, and speak from it for my own advantage, but if I had really then related my thoughts, I neither believed that *Adam* was the first Creature, but that there was a Creation before him, which world I thought was eternal, judging that land of *Nod* where *Cain* took his wife, was inhabited a long time before *Cain,* not considering that *Moses* was the first Writer of Scripture, and that we were to look no further than what there was written; but I really believed no *Moses,* Prophets, Christ, or Apostles, nor no resurrection at all: for I understood that which was life in man, went into that infinite Bulk and Bigness, so called *God,* as a drop into the Ocean, and the body rotted in the grave, and for ever so to remain.

In the interim came forth a people called *Quakers,* with whom I had some discourse, from whence I discerned that they were no further than burning brick in *Egypt,* though in a more purer way than their fathers before them; also their God, their devil, and their resurrection and mine, was all one, onely they had a righteousness of the Law which I had not; which righteousness I then judged was to be destroyed, as well as my unrighteousness, and so kept on my trade of Preaching, not minding any thing after death, but as aforesaid, as also that great cheat of Astrology and Physick I practiced, which not long after I was beneficed in *Merstand,* at *Terington* and St. *Johns,* and from thence went to *Snetsham* in *Norfolk,* where I was by all the Town received, and had most of their hands for the Presentation, that for *London* I went, and going to visit *Chetwood* my former acquaintance, she, with the wife of *Midleton,* related to me the two Witnesses; so having some conference with *Reeve* the prophet, and reading his Writings, I was in a trembling condition; the nature thereof you may read in the *Introduction* of that Book [*Look about you, for the devil that you fear is in you*] considering how sadly I had these many years spent my time, and that in none of these seven Churches could I finde the true God, or right devil; for indeed that is not in the least desired, onely to prate of him, and pray to him we knew not, though it is written, *It is life eternal to know the true God,* yet that none of them minds, but from education believeth him to be an eternal, infinite Spirit, here, there, and every where; which after I was fully perswaded, that there was to be three Commissions upon this earth, to bear record to the three Titles above, and that this was the last of those three: upon the belief of this I came to the knowledge of the two Seeds, by which I knew the nature and form of the true God, and the right devil, which in all my travels through the seven Churches I could never finde, in that now I see, it was onely from the revelation of this Commission to make it known.

Now being at my Journey end, as in point of notional worship, I came to see the vast difference of Faith from Reason, which before I conclude, you shall hear, and how that from Faiths royal Prerogative all its seed in *Adam* was saved, and all Reason in the fallen Angel was damned, from whence I came to know my election and pardon of all my former transgressions; after which my revelation growing, moved me to publish to the world, what my Father was, where he liveth, and the glory of his house, as is confirmed by my writings now in publick; so that now I can say, of all my formal righteousness, and professed wickedness, I am stripped naked, and in room thereof clothed with innocency of life, perfect assurance, and seed of discerning with the spirit of revelation. I shall proceed to answer some Objections that may be raised, as unto what I have already afferred.

First, *What had become of me if I had died before I heard of this spiritual last Commission?*

Answ. I infallibly against angels and men, that is, against all the seed of Reason whatsoever, declare, That if I had dyed in my time of wickedness, I had been damned. But then, you may say, How can this can be that I should have been damned then, and not now, when the determinate will of God stands sure, *that who before of old ordained to condemnation,* or salvation, so shall election stand. As unto this, it is to be seriously minded, that while I was travelling through *Egypt,* or the wilderness, I knew now more than *Paul* when he was a blasphemer, that I was elected as I do now, and at that time had no perfect peace, nor fully perswaded of my salvation at all; for alas, what comfort is it to a man that is ready to be turned over the ladder, and knoweth of no pardon, no more than a man that dieth in ignorance knoweth his election; so that you may behold what a sad journey most part of the world do travel in, even betwixt hope and despair; for it is unpossible that a soul in unbelief should know whether he be elected, or no: and therefore that Determination or Decree, doth product a means to effect the end of that mans salvation, springing in the Well of Faith, the knowledge of his election, with a protection or preservation of its own seed from the breach of the Law; or if that soul have transgressed the Law, he shall not die till a Commission come in being; so that I being elected, and yet having broken the Law, there was a necessity I should live till this last came in being, for the Law would have condemned me, and God would have disowned me, so that there was no other way but the belief of this Commission, to free me from the law of sin and death, into eternal life.

But you may say, *What became of all the Seed of Faith since the Apostles to this day, that had not a Commission to believe in, and lived in wickedness as I have done?*

As unto this I say, all the seed of *Adam* that lived till capable of a Law, did not commit wickedness, but was kept innocent from breaking the Law; which innocency of life, though not knowing any other, but Jesus Christ the Son of God, shall be raised to glory. For this is to be understood, that till within these thirty years, there hath no angels sounded above the Baptist, and therefore no such provocation to tempt the Seed of Faith to commit sin, as hath been in my days; for the sixth angel sounding forth, the Ranting principle broke forth all maner of wickednesss with a high hand, that did tempt such as I to break the Law as themselves: So that I say, the Seed of Faith that was not to live till this Commission came in being, had no such provocation, there being no such tempting Dispensations then apparent as they are now, so that they were all kept innocent in their lives from committing of sin, [minde this] not from thinking or speaking, but from acting sin, without which act the Law will not condemn thee; for the Law hath nothing to do with the heart, but an act, as it is written, not he that thinketh, *but he that committeth sin, is of the devil;* therefore blame not my revelation that it frees you from looks or thoughts upon a woman, but rather rejoyce escaping the act, [otherwise none] no not the Seed of Faith would be free from sin, and then how will you blot out that saving, *I John 3.9. Whosoever is born of God doth commit sin, for his seed remaineth in him, and he cannot sin;* and all the account is given, *because he is born of God.* Then in the first of *John 1.8. if we say we have no sin we deceive our selves, and the truth is no in us,* shall your blinde learned Reason that never spake this, or shall I in the height of revelation of the same Seed interpret this? that he that is born of God, as I am now, cannot sin to act; but if I, that am according to birth, of the Royal Seed, should say I have no motion to sin, I should be a liar like unto the seed of Reason: will ye believe this, or believe your lying imagination? however for your further satisfaction, read the thirteenth Chapter of my *Paradisical Dialogue;* so that I shall return to the next *Query,* where you may say,

Shall all the Seed of Faith now living believe in this Commission, or shall not the innocency of life as well save them now, as when there was no Commission in being?

Answer. There is not any of the seed of Faith now living, but if he hear the report of our Commission sound in his ears, though never see our faces, but he will believe; though all the seed of reason hear or read never so often, they cannot believe; but so many of the seed of *Adam* now living in this our day, that do not hear of us, nor see our writings, and so die in the ignorance of it, through their innocency of life, shall be happy on the other side of death, though not so happy here; for this I know, the real belief of a Commission, gives perfect peace and full assurance here, which the other wants, and therefore I infallibly say it is seven times more happy to be saved by a Commission, then by innocency of life; so that O the freedom, O the freedom that attends a Commission!

Again, you may say, may a man receive your Commission with joy in the belief of it, and afterwards fall away to eternal perdition?

Answer. Yea, a soul may come to believe the glorious person of our Lord Jesus, to be the onely God, and no other in finite spirit besides him, and that he is now with the same person that was crucified, in heaven glorified; as unto this I have known some in *London,* and elsewhere, that have rejoiced in it, and contended for it; and yet not being rooted in the right seed, it hath in time withered and turned back to *Egypt* again. Now the main thing of such a ones falling away, in plains tearmes, is, because they are according to birth the seed of reason, which may go very far with a believer in this Commission, as *Judas* with the twelve, before it be betrayed, which at one time or another, it is found out and so condemned; as the devil *Langly* exceeded most of you in this nature, yet now believing a prerogative, fell off and despised, for which, is now eternally damned.

Again one thing more is required to be *answered,* whether one that hath received the truth in the power and love thereof, whether such a real believer, may be left over to break the law? and if, how delivered?

Answer. As unto this I say, a Commission changeth not the nature of man, but according as he was in unbelief subject to passion, wanton carriage, or foolish language, and such like, [as it too much apparent in some] will now and then be tempting that soul sutable to its nature that hangs about him; but as to action in breach of the law, a Commission doth change the power of corruption, that though he is not free from motions to sin, yet he is freed from the act of sin, this I finde in my own soul the truth of what I write, but whether an elected vessel in the real belief of this may once slip into act, as Adultery and such like, and by returning with faith in the Commission may be recovered, this I cannot gain-say but it may be so, as I could instance: but let it be a warning to all others hereafter, and remember I told thee so.

Secondly, *whether ever any, let him be of what Church soever, had a Call, or were sent by voice of words, but a Commission onely?*

Answer. As I am endued with the height of revelation, that hath begot most of you into the belief of this Commission, let me tell you that I write not now as I have done formerly, when I was in *Egypt* or the *Wilderness,* but I write infalibly, without the help of any, as it flows by inspiration or revelation from my Royal seed-spring, otherways it were no other but reasons imagination, and so it may be true or it may be false, as all your Philosophical Histories are dubious to the writer, and indeed the Reader thereof doth approve of no other language, but what is written with a provisio, under correction to better judgements, and more learned Fathers, and so like a Schoolboy that writes by direction of his Tutor, so do ye write the Commissioners revelation and form of worship contained in *Moses*, the Prophets, and Apostles, and not from any revelation of your own, though you write you have a call from God, & are sent of God, when you shall hear to the contrary; as suffer me but to instance the vain deceit and judgling carriage of the *Quakers*, in their pretended Errands and Messages to Kings and Rulers of this kingdom, publishing they are sent of God, to tell them, that for their pride, their vain-glory, oppression, and cruelty, they shall have their kingdom rent from them, as it was from *Oliver* before them; with these and such like delusion their souls are possest withal, that they are sent, and by the Lord commanded, when in the revelation from my seed-spring I know they are liars, as in these particulars appear:

First, That God did never speak to any of you, as he spake to *Moses, Paul* and *John Reeve,* if you can deal plainly, and tell me if ever Christ from the Throne of glory, did ever audibly to the hearing of the ear, say: *George Fox, Francis Howgil,* or *John Harwood,* or any of you, behold I send you forth as my onely true and last Messenger to the King of *England,* or any other, to reprove them of sin whatsoever, and therefore ye go beyond the seas to other Nations, saying the Lord sent you, when from that spirit of divine voyce that spake to *John Reeve* I tell you, you go forth in the strength of Reasons lying imagination, which you call your light within you, and so receive the reward of your deceit upon you, as in the day of account you shall know that you run before you were sent.

Secondly, Do but observe the nature and form of words you deliver, are they any other but borrowed from the Prophets and Apostles, and so ye run up and down with their Commission, and their Doctrine, repeating what they said to Kings and Rulers, who were truly and really sent forth to deliver what they spake: now you in the vertue of anothers Commission, busie yourselves like the seven sons of *Sceva a* Jew, *who were vagabond exorcists, that took upon them to call over them which had evil spirits, in the name of the Lord Jesus, saying, we adjure you by Jesus whom* Paul *preacheth;* So ye *Baptists, Ranters,* but especially the *Quakers* like vagabonds run with the letter and doctrine of *Moses,* the Prophets and Apostles, saying, *Hear this I pray you, ye heads of the house of* Jacob, *and princes of* Israel, *that abhor judgement and pervert all equity, they build up* Sion *with blood, and* Jerusalem *with iniquity, the heads thereof judge for reward, the Priests thereof teach for hire, and the Prophets thereof divine for money, and yet they will lean upon the Lord, and say, is not the Lord among us, none evil can come unto us?* With these and such like sayings ye go to the Magistrate and Ministery, and bid them remember what judgements the Prophets threatned against such Magistrates and Ministers, not in the least having any call or command from God in your selves, without doubt and confidence, saying, I *George Fox* by vertue of my Commission that was given by voice of words from the mouth of the Lord Jesus in the highest heavens, do infallibly against Angels and Men, tell thee O King, the Parliament, and Clergy of *England,* if ye establish superstition, and blind mens consciences to your form of worship, then know this O King, that the God that bid me tell thee, contrary to thy expectation, will rayse up an Army against thee, that will blast the proceedings of thee and thy Councel for ever, I say were ye thus called, and sent forth, as ye were true Messengers, so would your Message take effect, and prove as ye have published.

But poor blind Creatures! as really & truly as I know Christ Jesus the onely God, and the Prophets and Apostles commissioned, and sent forth by God, so I as really believe ye neither know God, nor were sent forth by God, but are meer dissemblers, and liars against the true Commissioners of God; therefore I tell thee O King, and all powers under thee, that this last Commission of the eternal spirit, hath no Messages to Kings or Rulers touching the Affairs of their Government, and therefore as we have none, (thou shalt not need to credit any other,) onely this by permission I say, if thou so far retain the Prerogative in thy own hand, that no Councel, Bishop, or Minister, may molest or persecute any Opinion, Church, or Dispensation, much our Commission, that is contrary to them in matter of worship, provided they be obedient to thy Government in just civil things, I say, if this be really performed by thee, thou and thy posterity, after thee may in safety reign during this perishing world: This being done, let him be of what Church soever, that shall not without Hipocrysi of heart, be free from writing or fighting against thee, be punished.

Now ye being false, and not sent, notwithstanding all your woes, plagues, and judgements you threaten against a Kingdom (if they do but repent) though they punish with death, they be happy as well as you, not knowing your own happiness, you cannot discern anothers (when it is not so in ours) you having no discerning of the two seeds, *viz.* Faith and Reason, you make no differences, but wraps up all together, not knowing but Gods nature, Reason and Mans the same, and so if man do but hearken to the light of Reason within him, he shall be as happy as the Seed of Faith, *and thus ye are blind leaders of the blind,* pretending a Call, and sent of God, and yet you know not the form of God, nor his nature, thinking that in *Adam* both Seeds die, and so in Christ both shall be made alive, not at all that Reason was damned in the Angelical Serpent, and Faith saved in *Adam,* as in the *Quakers Downfal,* and the *Dialogue* is opened at large.

Now had you been Commissionated by voice of words, or were it possible to think of an inward Commission by the Spirit, as some of your fine-spun Professors do imagine, and to me was confirmed by one *Laine,* but especially by one *Tomlinson* a very moderate Brother of yours, that would prove a Call from God, so sent of God by the succession of the Spirit, not understanding that the Apostles, who were the Stewards and Shepherds of Christ, and in his stead had the power of salvation and condemnation committed to them, were all put to death, with every Believer of them: than how do you think they, being the conduct of the Spirit, that you should receive the influence of their Authority from a dead letter, and that conveyed to you by the Roman power that put the true Commissioners to death, it is like there should be a succession, either by voice of words, or the Spirit, when you have neither of them both, but the light or learning of Reasons imaginations onely.

And then, if ye had a Commission by voice of words, so sent of God, your language and your worship would speak for you, that you were the true and last Messenger of the third and last Commission; but alas, poor deluded creatures, you are the last angel that ever shall sound a pretended truth, yet real lying notion that every shall appear in this world; concerning which both the Ministers and Hearers are ignorant, that the Teachers of the *Quakers* are the last angel spoken of in the tenth of *Revelation,* the seventh verse, saying, *In the days of the voice of the seventh angel, when he shall begin to sound, the mystery of God should be finished,* &c. Now ye angels or teachers of the *Quakers,* do ye send forth any other doctrine or worship, but what is recorded in the Commission of others, even what they said, and did do, as near as you can do ye; which if ye had a discerning spirit, you would without censure or envy, read our revelation flowing from a Commission, doth far transcend the language or worship of either of the two Commissions before us; but ye being of the angels natures, so the seed of the Serpent, ye know not the voice of a Commission from a Dispensation from a Dispensation: As touching which, I shall open in the third Objection or Query, thus stated.

Whether there ever was more then one truth at a time, and whether there be more than our way to this truth? and if but one way, which is the true and onely way to the truth.

Answer. Truth was never known till a Commissioner was chosen, so that till *Moses* there was nothing made manifest what was truth, and what not, and therefore from thence it must be enquired, whether there was more then one truth, he being the first writer of truth that ever was, doth all along tell you in his days, there was but one truth, the knowledge of which consisted in the true God, as in the first Command it is written, *thou shalt have no other Gods before me,* so that this was the onely true God; and therefore saith *Moses, there is none like unto the Lord our God:* and again it is written, *thou art the God, even thou alone;* and so all along the Prophets do declare no other God, but what before by *Moses* was revealed, crying, *I am God, and there is none also, I am God, and there is none like unto me, therefore look unto me, for I am God, and there is none besides me.*

Then, and at that time, this was truth, yea the onely truth, and no truth besides it, though then most part of the world worshipped idols, yea a lie of their own invention, yet in the Commission of *Moses* was truth onely maintained, under the title of God the Father.

Secondly, After this God became flesh, as it is written, *The word was with God, yea the word was God, which word was made flesh, and dwelt among men,* now called a Son, or Christ the Savior, which none but the Apostles Commission believed, as from their saying, *there is no other name under heaven given among men whereby we must be saved,* with many sayings to that purpose, proving that Christ was the Son of God.

Then, and at that time, this was truth, yea the onely truth, and no truth besides it, though then there were both Saducees and Pharisees, yea most part of the Jews, and almost all the Gentiles worshipped a God besides Christ, yet in the Commission of the Apostles, was truth onely revealed under the title of Christ the Son.

Thirdly, After this, yea in this instant time, both Father and Son are in this our third and last Commission made manifest to be the holy Ghost, or one entire spiritual body, yea the same body, and no other body but what the cross suffered, is now in heaven glorified, both Father and Son, one spiritual form, Creator of heaven and earth, so called the Lord Jesus.

Now, and at this time, this is the truth, yea the onely truth, and no truth besides it, though all the Seven Churches pretends to know truth, and so by their professions holds forth seven truths, yet I infalibly say in this our last Commission, this is the truth onely revealed under the title of Christ, as he is a spiritual person not in us, but above us, in his own kingdom of glory, blessed for ever.

And yet they are not three truths, but one truth, as in respect of God the Father, God the Son, and God the holy Ghost, which three are not persons, but titles comprehended in the single person of Christ alone; but as in relation to their Commissions in time, they are three Commissions, in three distinct persons, though they all three acknowledge themselves to have their authority from one and the same person; for that person which spake to *Moses,* spake to *Paul,* and spake to *John Reeve:* the truth of this is clearly revealed in my *Dialogue,* the second and twelfth chapters, so that I shall omit to speake any further, onely leave you to that saying of *Paul, he that descended, is the same also that ascended,* so that still it is but one, and the same person, even Jesus alone, but:

Secondly, As there is but one truth, so there is but one way to this truth, and that must needs flow from them that are the publishers of truth; for it is ridiculous to think that man or men which knowes not truth, should be the way of truth, [therefore take notice and do not forget,] as there is no truth but in a Commission, so there is none, let them be never so wise or eloquent, yea righteous, or heaven-like, if he be not a Commissioner sent by voyce of words, and that audibly to the hearing of the ears, from the spirit of divine faith that cannot lie, I tell thee thou art no shepherd, but an hireling; no son, but a bastard; no true Commissioner, but a counterfeit: as deal plainly, can any of you the Angels or Teachers of the seven Churches, infalibly say, that God by voyce of words, sent you as he did *Moses,* the Apostles, and *John Reeve?* certain I am without doubt ye cannot. O then what do you think will be the end of all your profound lies, that you have preached in publick and private, by taking upon you successively to be Prophets, Apostles, and Ministers from anothers Authority, and thereby you cavel and rayle one brother against another, saying the Papist, Episcopal, Presbyterian, and Independent, are false Prophets and hirelings, and they say, you Baptists, Ranter, and Quakers are false Prophets and deluders, and who shall be judge of your pretended Commissions, and railing accusations, shall the Scripture that is a dead letter? or shall I that have the spirit of revelation? can any of you tell me, who made you Ministers and Teachers over others? the Apostles and their Bishops disowns you, their writings say your fathers murthered all of them, so that there was not one left alive to continue their succession, by imposition of hands or otherways, so that what can you say for yourselves, but that the Pope, who was made the supream head over the dead letter, and that Roman power establishing it, by its supream authority, you have your ordination from Ministers, and from no other God or Spirit, but the dead letter onely: now let me tell you all, and yet not I, but the spirit of revelation, flowing from my seed-spring, [mind what I say,] that I am as truly sent now, as *Timothy* and *Titus* were in their Commission, and therefore I can without fear, and with a real undoubted confidence say, that you are all but the Messengers of men, and therefore the next time ye read or preach from the tenth of *John,* remember that you read your selves the false Prophets and Hirelings there quoted, as in the day of eternal account you shall finde that truth of what I say, but then too late, and in vain will your doleful cries be.

But you may object and say from those words of Christ, saying, *I am the good shepherd, and know my sheep, and am known of mine,* from hence you may cavel, and say there is no mortal man a true shepherd, but Christ alone, and that because he saith, *I am the way, and the truth, and the life.*

Answer. I grant that Christ is the great shepherd of the sheep, and was the onely Prophet then living, yea then and at that time, he was the onely way to eternal life, and all that believed in him were his sheep and followed him, for then the Apostles were but sheep, and Christ their shepherd, but after that our Lord and good shepherd, had by his blood purchased eternal happiness for his sheep, then he Commissionated his Apostles to be shepherds in his place, as before he was ascended he bid Peter *feed his sheep,* which after they were indued with power from on high, they went forth in the strength of their Commission, and declared themselves to be Ambassadors and Stewards in Christs stead, yea the way and life of their salvation; and therefore saith Paul, *bretheren be followers together of me,* knowing assuredly if they believed in their Doctrine, they should be as happy, as when they believed the words of Christ from his own mouth, so that this know there is no going to God, but by Commissioners, for who they curse are cursed, and who they bless are blessed, in that the revelation thereof hath an infallible discerning who are the seed of *Adam,* and who are the seed of the Serpent.

And therefore take notice if Christ be the way now, and teacheth you by his spirit, why are you not therewith contented, and keep every man at home, but run up and down the City, some to publick and some to private, neglecting waiting upon God, and teachings of his spirits, to wait upon men and their vain teaching? and so the priests tells them they must wait upon God, in the use of means, imitating a true authority saying the Lord sent them, when they neither know the Lord nor their Message, so being but mans Ministers, they compel men to go the broad way with them to destruction.

4. Again, you read but of two ways, a true and a false, the narrow way, and the broad way, that is, the way of Faith, and the way of Reason, so unless you deny Scripture, you cannot but confess, that as truth is onely in a Commission, so then of necessity it must follow, that the true Commissioners are the narrow way, and way of Faith to eternal Truth. So that ye seven Churches what do you say for your selves? are you right, or are you wrong? are you true, or are you false? Sure I am you do all say, that you are in the truth, and the ways of truth: if ye will not believe me, enquire of *Moses* and the Apostles, and see if they do not say that there was no truth but in a Commission, and ask them if truth were ever established by Authority? [minde this] sure I am you will finde it recorded, that truth was onely contained in one Commission to another, and that truth was ever persecuted by Authority. Have you not read this? do ye not believe this? then from the letter I shall prove this, that the hypocritical *Scribes and Pharisees did build the tombs of the Prophets, and garnish the sepulchers of the righteous, and say, if we had been in the days of our fathers, we would not have been partakers with them in the blood of the Prophets:* So your fathers murthered Christ and all his Apostles, and since their children have established the Ordinance of the Apostles, and with tradition and learned Philosophy, have garnished the letter of the Scriptures with a penalty, that if any one do speak against *Moses,* Christ, or the Apostles, they shall be punished; so that ye be witnesses unto your selves that you seven Churches are the onely heires of them that killed the Apostles.

As now the last and highest truth is held forth in this our last Commission, as in my writings I have told you again and again, that there is no truth but what is revealed by us, and no way to eternal happiness without us, so that when you have established that so called *Religion* I then expect no other dealings at your hands, than our brethren the Apostles found from your fore-Fathers; and then your sons in the next generation, will say of you as now ye say of your fathers; but wo, wo, if not for fear, yet for shame leave off your tearming your selves the Churches of Christ, and that your traditioned notional Forms are the true ways of Christ, that so you may be more excusable in the eternal Account of the Lord. Do but enquire whether the way of *Moses* and the Prophets be your rule now, when it was not the Apostles in their time? and shall you that belong neither to *Moses,* nor the Apostles, by succession of voice of words, or inspiration of the spirit, ordain your selves Bishops and Ministers by the dead letter of the Apostles, and then you fetch your garb and attire from the dead letter of *Moses?* all which was abolished in the death of Christ, [and by the Apostles detested against as beggarly rudiments] so no examples for any mortals now living to imitate, [minde that] unless you do wilfully shut your eyes against what the Apostles say, and what I now write; for the glory of this perishing world hath so bewitched you to believe a lye, that you wrest the Scripture into an image of wax, framing it according to Reasons imagination, your onely idol, god, and savior, when from an infallible spirit I say, there is not one sentence in the letter of Scripture to warrant any of you seven Churches in your Forms of Worship, nor can you from any grounds of reason make *England* believe that you are the true Bishops and Ministers of God, unless you could make it apparent that you were all Jewes, and all the world besides you Heathen Gentiles, that worshipped gods of stocks and stones, then you might have some colour to practice the Rites and Ceremonies of the Law; which if you could, you must not only wear *Aarons* holy garments, but your male, both yong and old, must be circumcised, and have your peace-offerings and burnt-offerings of the blood of bulls and goats, with all other Ceremonies thereunto belonging, that so the ignorant might have some faith in you; but in that most of your Churches knows that the Jews and the Gentiles are by mixture of seeds become one Nation, they can tell you there was no Bishops, Elders, or Deacons in *Moses* or the Prophets time, and therefore ye pretending a succession from *Timothy* and *Titus,* your younger brethren, *viz.* Presbyterian and Independent, &c. can inform you, if ye were true Bishops, instead of the holy garments of *Aaron,* you must with *Timothy* and *Titus* wear a mean garb, as plain habits and such like, and not to go with long Gowns and Sircingles; and in stead of variety of Dainties, you must eat with no gentile, but suffer want and hunger; and in stead of a Coach and six horses, you must go on foot; yea, in room of many Attendance to sere and wait upon you, you must wait and serve your flock: if you had believed Scripture, as ye pretend to make it your rule, why do ye not imitate the true and great Bishop Christ Jesus? who saith, he that is the greatest, and will bear rule, must be a servant to others, saying, though I be the son of God, nay God himself, yet I washed my disciples feet, and there was no room for me in an Inn, but a manger, and I never ride but once, and that was upon an Ass, thus was I humbled, and abased my self; and though ye pretend a

Commission successively, yet ye altogether exalt and honor your selves, in contempt of me and my true Commissioners; So that as I am the true and onely Bishop now living, seeing ye boast of things that was *Moses* and the Apostles labors, and like School-boys, vaunt your tongues in other mens rules of things made ready to your hands, [minde what I say] yet whether ye do or not, I infallibly tell you from that spirit of divine voice, in the person of the Lord Jesus, that spake to *Moses, Paul* and *John Reeve,* that you have now no goard to shadow you from that dreadful sentence of this our spiritual and last Commission of the most high and mighty God, the Man Jesus.

Now having sufficiently shewen you, that all Churches, Dispensations, Gifts, or Ways are false, not proceeding from a Commission, and that from a Commission then in force and being; but all the seven Sons, or Churches, have all proceeded from no Commission, but from Reasons invention to establish others revelations for their rule: so now I shall shew you in a few particulars, that ye all run in vain, and so do lose the prize of the high calling, the knowledge of the Man Jesus.

First, in that ye know not who he is, not where he is, that ye run to, and therefore some of you run after a God of three persons, when you have neither Scripture nor revelation for to warrant you the truth of your journey; and others of you run after a God of an infinite Spirit and two persons; and the rest of you after a God that hath no person at all, so that I say you are all out of the way, and really believes no God at all, neither can any of you say with *Paul, I know in whom I have believed;* but ye run doubtfully, not being fully perswaded that the God ye preach and pray to, is the true God, neither indeed do ye trouble your selves to know what he is, but onely speak the word Father, the word God, the word Christ Jesus, as a tradition educated by your fore-fathers, established in your Articles, Creeds, and Catechisms, exercising your disciples from them to believe as the Church believes, not having faith in any thing ye profess: As deal plainly and impartially, answer me upon your salvation, as you hope to see your God in glory, that you are fully perswaded, that your God and your devil is the way, and the truth, and no other besides it? I say not any of you can avouch it as the principle of your assurance, that the God ye profess is the true God, and yet what a rabble rout of pretended believers there is among you, that some of your members swears, God damn them they believe in God, be drunk, and believe in God; whore, and believe in God; cheat, and believe in God; bear false witness, and believe in God; tyrannize and oppress , and believe in God; nay, the land lords for a Quarters-rent will turn the poor into the streets, and yet believe in God; and the great devil Broker will usurp 30 or 40 pound in the hundred, and protest he believes in God, and a very pack-horse of the Scriptures to seal up your own damnations; as when I was among you, this was my condition, and the state of you all, in one of those evils or another; so that with admiration, against angel or man I can say, I have not run in vain, that those which in the knowledge of God I thought was before me, are all left behind zealous in their devotions to the unknown God whom ye ignorantly worship, which in all my writings I have revealed, that your God cannot be known neither to Saint or Angel, having no form or person, but an infinite eternal Spirit without a body, how do you think your nothing God should be known? nay, had *Abraham* known no other God then ye profess, he had never been tempted to slay his son, in that from such a God there had been no invitation, neither had his confidence been so far fixed, as to obey a command without a body; but he was really believing that his God was no shadow, but a personal substance, made *Abraham* so willing to offer up his onely beloved son *Isaac*. Now your faith having no foundation to pitch its confidence upon, but as in a Lottery men venture their money, so do ye in your worship venture your salvation, not really knowing at all that your preaching and praying is to a true God, onely ye hope well, yea hope the best, that you are in the truth and the right way, and that your God is the God, when I infalibly tell you he that runneth to God, or professeth God *must believe him as he is,* [O mind what you read] not as he is in your hope, and vain imagination, but as he is really in himself, a glorious personall God: and know this while you are in hope you do not believe, *for hope that is seen is not hope, for what a man seeth, why doth he yet hope for?* thou knowing God is true as thou believes, hope is swallowed up in that belief, *for the hope of the hypocrite shall perish,* but when thou canst without doubt say as *John* said, we hope not, *but we believe, and really know that we are of God, and the whole world lieth in wickedness, and we know that the Son of God is come, and hath given us an understanding, that we may know him that is true, and we are in him that is true, even in his Son Jesus Christ, this is the true God and eternal life,* once come to this, thy hope is no more hope, but becomes faith.

Which I am certain there is not any of you the seven Churches, that knowes the true God, and the right devil, the true heaven, and right hell, no without doubt I doubt I know that all your hopes, so living and so dying, that hath been acquainted with our Commission, shall eternally perish: and furthermore I know, that if ye did believe *Moses,* Christ, and the Apostles, ye would believe me, I knowing that so many of you as really believes the two former Commissions, if ye hear but our report, will as really believe in us, though I know all of you will say, ye believe in *Moses,* Christ, and the Apostles, but ye cannot believe in us: And why do ye not understand we are the last Commission, as they the first and second? even nothing but because ye know us alive; for while Christ and the Apostles was among them, they were of no more esteem than we. As to this purpose, saith *Paul, His letters [say they] are weighty and powerful, but his bodily presence is weak, and his speech contemptible,* so while any living knows our persons, for that our writings are despised; however, let me resolve you why you cannot believe our words now living, is because ye are of the seed of unbelief, reason, the devil, and take this for truth, ye do not believe *Moses,* Christ, nor the Apostles; ye hope ye do, ye say ye do, as the Jewes said of CHRIST, *We are* Moses *Disciples, we know that God spake unto* Moses, *as for this fellow we know not from whence it is.* Who would have thought but what they said, was truth; yet Christ tells them *John 5.45. Had ye believed* Moses, *ye would have believed me, for he wrote of me, but if ye believe not his writings, how should ye believe my words?* So that from the Lord of Glory I say, did ye really believe the writings of *Moses,* Christ and the Apostles, ye would believe in our words; but I know ye do not believe, but only confess and profess your own honor and advantage, which in the hour of death ye will be all at a loss what will become of your souls, for all your preaching and praying to your God on your bed of sickness, you have all your work to do, so that it is evident you are all out of the way, yea still in *Egypt* or the *Wilderness.*

Fifthly, Again ye run in vain, not knowing the Scriptures; for as they were written by men, inspired with the spirit of revelation, so none can give any true interpretation thereof, but those endued with the same spirit, and that I really believe none of you can with safety say ye are the men, I certainly knowing, that your learning is from the seed of Reason, which is the wisdom of flesh; So that it is unpossible ye should discern the plain language of Faith, or give a true interpretation of Scripture written by the seed of Faith, and therefore ye know not what Scripture is, and what not, though I acknowledge your wisdom of Reason, can translate Hebrew, Greek, and Latine into English, and this being done, ye make your ignorant disciples believe that you have interpreted the Scripture, when I know that the Scripture in its divine fence, is as a ridle not unfolded unto all the learned Rabbies of the world; furthermore I can with confidence say, that when any of you do assume an interpretation, you dare not conclude that is the true meaning thereof, and no other, and yet such of you who are of a contrary seed to the Writers of Scripture, do take upon you to be Judge of their writings, when I say, as I said before, you understand not what you are your selves, not what will become of another, neither doth the wisdom of Faith that searcheth the high things, yea the deep things of God, proceed from the learned education of Universities, so no spiritual men to judge of things concerning God, and his kingdom; O then why will ye presume to say this or that is blasphemy, when you know not what God nor his nature is, the devil or his nature is, and yet none so forward to cry down those that are truly sent, for false prophets, deluders, back-sliders, and blasphemers, when now I infallibly know that you onely are the men; as do but look back to the tru and false prophets of old, and then if you can [speak the truth] that whether the true be more in number than the false. *Elijah* saith, *[I even I] onely remain a Prophet of the Lord, but* Baals *priests are four hundred and fifty men.* And so all along in the second Commission there was a great number of false, to the small number of true: As now in our days what multitudes there is of false prophets and false teachers, to one true prophet and true Bishop? for this you must grant, that if ye all be true, then *Moses,* the Apostles and we, are false, and if so, in vain were that saying in Christ, *Strait is the gate, and narrow is the way that leadeth unto life, and few* (not multitudes) *but few there be that finde it;* which if ye were all true prophets, or true teachers, [as if any of you were, it must be the Baptist] but in that I know ye are all false, blot out that saying of our Lord, and write it thus, [wide is the gate, and broad is the way that leadeth unto life and salvation, and most of the world do finde it:] were it thus, ye might have some colour of justification that ye were all true, and our Commission onely false, then heaven would be full, and hell would be empty. But let me tell you once more, and so many as are elected will believe me, that this is the last Commission, yea the strait gate, and narrow way, yea the onely way to eternal life, so narrow that no hypocrite can enter among us, but he is discovered and condemned by us.

And then because it is written, *Beware of false Prophets which come to you in sheeps clothing, but inwardly are ravening wolves.* What a noise do ye make in your pulpits, one brother impeaching another for false Prophets, when I know no any of you can without doubt say, which of you are true, and which are false, though it is said, *By their fruits ye shall know them.* Can you tell me the fruits of a true Prophet from a false one? Sure I am ye cannot; therefore I shall tell you, how ye shall know a true from a false, [mind what you read] the fruits of a false Prophet, is to go before he be sent, yea sent by voice of words from Christ the true Ordainer of Prophets, so that ye go forth by the voice and ordination of men, so preach the doctrine of men, and that onely for your honor and preferment, this is a false Prophet, and the fruits of your prophecy, is to be chosen by your member, to fight with the sword of steel, to inrich your selves in the ruine of your disciples, to Lord it over your hearers, to teach a false God, and a false devil, to cheat and murther one another, as now ye do at this day, this all of you are guilty of, in one kind or another, and yet ye that are the onely false Prophets, say to your deluded members, these are dangerous times, take heed of false prophets; which if ye could discern truth, ye should bid them beware of you, that they pin not their salvation upon your doctrine; for the fruits thereof are as aforesaid, onely Reason philosophy and vain deceit: as if you did but obsere what you read, when you say, *not many wise men after the flesh, not many mighty, not many noble; but God hath chosen the foolish things to confound the wise, and weak things of the world to confound the mighty, and base things of the world, and things which are despised, God hath chosen; yea, and things which are not, to bring to nought things that are.* Do you believe this? what do ye say to this? are ye fools, are ye ignorant, are ye weak, are ye base, are ye despised? then you might have some plea that you are the true Churches of Christ; but you are too wise, too strong; too many, too honorable to be true Bishops and Messengers of Christ the Lord of Gory, and yet you will not believe this, but perswade your selves that the richest, the proudest, and the wisest are the onely true Believers, when I infallibly know from that Spirit of divine Faith, that ye are all the sons and daughters of *Cain,* that proud *Lucifer* your father, which ere long shall have your wages with him in flames of eternal burning, and that for ever.

6. Again, you are false, and run in vain, not discerning the two seeds how they became two where they remain, with the effects and operations since the beginning to this day; but having in the fifth chapter of my *Wonder of Wonders* spoken something of this secret, I shall forbear, and in a higher nature make manifest what hath been their effects and operations, from that to this day. As unto this, all that do not willfully shut their eyes, may read as they run, that according to the saying of God, hath ever since *been at enmity,* and that not onely in its own soul, but one man with another, otherways what need had there been of a Law given to Reason the *devil,* but that Reason oppresseth and injureth another, and so makes work for the *Lawyer,* yea ever since hath devoured and murthered one another, that Reason hath erected *Magistrates, Judges* and *Lawyers* to reconcile Reason divided against it self, or else condemn it to be executed by the *Hangman.* That you may in brief see the fruits, and influence of Faith and Reason, I shall demonstrate what their operations are, both in spirituals and temporals.

First, As unto spirituals, both Faith and Reason do motion forth to their original, from whence they had their being, and therefore Faith in the Commission of this last age, can tell what it was before it became mortal, and what it is now being mortal, and what it shall be when immortalized again, when as Reason motion out to the same, but having by its disobedience lost its purity, and now in mortality it soars, if possible, to know what it was, what it is now, and what it shall be hereafter, but cannot attain it, in that the Covenant or promise was not made to Reason but Faith onely. As do but enquire whether *Abraham* was the father of Faith or Reason, and then you shall read *he was the father of the faithful;* and upon that account the Covenant was made, with *Abraham,* as it is written, *I will establish my Covenant between thee and me, and thy seed after thee,* &c. So that *Paul* a man of his seed saith, *Now to Abraham, and his seed were the promised made,* &c. So that in all the genealogy of Faith, it hath in one measure or another, been capable of it descent, though never so clear, as now in this last witness of the spirit, for I can with confidence say, that my Faith hath motioned through the grave, yea pierced the heavens, and beheld the glorious person of our Lord Jesus, (and in that view) hath been filled full of divine revelation, that now at its pleasure can ascend and descend in full perswasion, that what by Faith I have seen in glory above, I have in part made known to you below; for my Faith hath evidenced in my soul, that what I have written as touching *God, Devil, Heaven, Hell,* with the death and resurrection of the soul, is the truth and no other, without the knowledge of which no soul can have perfect peace here, or glory hereafter; for the operations of Reason and Faith are much different, in that Reason desires things impossible: for what Faith can and will do, Reason never desires it, but is continually tempting our Lord to impossibilities, as to imagine God never created man to damn him. Now Faith knows that earth and water was eternal, and God hath a spiritual body, and the angels likewise, and that he created the angels Reason to be damned, so that what is possible to Faith, is impossible to Reason, and what Reason imagines is possible, Faith knows if possible: not but Faith can do what it pleaseth, yet will not be moved at Reasons pleasure, but what ever Faith demands, is possible for God to do, in that Faith desires nothing but what is his royal pleasure, being moved in the operation of its own seed, without doubt believing what ever Faith asketh, it shall receive not that Faith is boundless, but limited to its original, and so the effects thereof is moved to demand possibilities sutable to the tenor of its Commission, given by that divine voice of all powerful Faith, which now is all spiritual, not moved to any external miracles, as the two former were, and therefore generated Faith in all Commissions did never request Christ its Father, but what grew in its seed possible, knowing that his prerogative would no more move his divine will thereunto; now Reason not knowing the mind of our God, it cries and desires that God would send fire from heaven, and blast the proceeding of its enemies, supposing the will of God is the same now, as it was then, and that it is as possible for God to turn the intentions of their adversaries upon their own head as formerly. I acknowledge our God can do what his divine soul pleaseth, yet what he hath decreed to the contrary is unpossible, and sure I am as unto your request, *his hand is shortned,* and *his ear heavy, that he will not hear you;* for your hands are full of blood, your lips have spoken lies, nor have you done justice or equity when the power was in your hands; so that in the highest pitch of revelation I tell you, that it is a work of as great a wonder for our God to take notice of none of you, as when he did observe all the transactions of his Commissioners before you, and sure I am as unto externals he doth not hear us his least Commissioners, then how do ye think ye being sinners, our God should hear you? So that I infallibly say, our Lord will not preserve you, nor destroy you, but Reason subtilty must deliver you, as it hast delivered your enemies into your hands before you. If ye will not believe me, then believe the fruits of your own prayers, and much good may they do you. Answer to this, Reason flies unto Scripture, where it is written, *I am the Lord, I change not: and Christ is the same yesterday, to day, and for ever,* not in the least understanding the drift of those sayings, nor believing our God in every Commission hath new tearms of mercies and

Judgements, suitable to the nature of the Commission; for this know, those sayings lay in point of his eternal prerogative as unto damnation, and salvation, he is the same and changeth not: but in externals, *it repented the Lord be made man; and repented that he had made Saul King;* but he never repented that he saved Faith and damned Reason, though Reason moderate can soar high with exellent heaven-like words, if possible, with tears to move the Lord to answer his desires, yet all that Reason can do, can not change our Lords prerogative, to take off that eternal curse that was given to Reason in the womb of *Eve,* it being impossible for God to do Faith never requests it, though what lies in the account of Faith nothing is impossible; as *Luke 1.13.* the saying was spoke upon as great a work of Faith as ever was, though to Reason it is impossible that the power of the highest, which was the Father, could as swift as thought descend into the womb of *Mary,* and there dissolve into seed, and conceive himself into a mortal childe of flesh, blood, and bone, so called *Emanuel* or Jesus the Son of God, now what the royal will all Faith had decreed and promised to do, that Reason cannot believe, but what Faith hath decreed, he will not, so cannot do that Reason would have him to do, as to make of stones break, or come down from the Cross and save himself, which Christ could not do, because for that end he came to die that thereby he might not onely raise himself to glory, but all his seed that Reason murthered, to glory with him, and keep Reason under misery; and yet how highly is Reason reputed by you, and Faith slighted with you; and that because Faith revealeth that which Reason cannot comprehend, when as Reason can declare nothing as touching eternity, but Faith can fathom it, and binde Reason hand and foot in the interpretation of it; and therefore in Scripture it is written the high transcendent vertues of Faith, but no applause of Reason at all as concerning the kingdom of God: But

Secondly, As it is the Lord and Governor of this world, so the elder brother, its products in the affairs thereof are so wise, gallant, majestical, and glorious, that if Faith knew it not, it would delude the seed of eternity; for its wisdom is so great, that it dives into all the secrets of nature, which way to make it self happy in this its kingdom; and therefore out of Reasons seed hath sprung or risen the knowledge of all Arts and Sciences, men graving, carving, and framing, all gold, silver, brass, steel, iron, pewter, lead, glass, woollen, linnen, leather, and what not, into variety of forms and fashions, for its eye to behold, its back to clothe, and belly to feed, so that in brief there is nothing that the wisdom or hand of man hath invented, but it came from Reasons subtilty, without the assistance of Faith at all; for Faith is so ignorant and simple in the Arts and Sciences of this worlk, that without Reasons direction it could not make use of what Reason brings to his hand, so when Reason is moderated and well qualified, Faith hath a helpful Handmaid of Reason, but when Reason is immoderate and hypocritical, as seldom it is otherways, O what a monster it is to Faith, that it tramples innocency under foot! yea, brands it guilty of that which onely belongs to it self, and that because Faith cannot dissemble as Reason doth; nay, immoderate Reason is so proud and majestical, that it will not suffer its moderate brother to live by it, but sue it, imprison it, and beggar it. O what a changeable, desiring, unsatisfied seed is Reason, that it is never better but when it is plotting mischief, by back-biting, envying, and if possible, to murther what it hates! So that where Faith is supream, it reigns as a Kingly Prerogative over Reason, otherways Reason would not submit; for both Seeds cannot reign, but there must be divisions till one of them be silent, not but that the conquered will scout forth upon the borders of the Law, but being captivated it cannot act, it may talk and prate what it would do, but Faith being lord, it must have license from Faith before it can conceive its thought to action; so that where Reason is lord, its operations are never satisfied, no not a year, a moneth, or a day, but inventing new fashions, new delights, new mischiefs, sometimes it will be ruled over, and sometimes it will rule it self, as these late transactions will confirm what is written, so that well may the imagination thereof be compared to a bottomless pit, for indeed it knows not what it would be, nor what it would have, never long contented, but either too full or too empty, too rich or too poor, too wise or too foolish, too high or too low; but however the true nature of Reasons motion is to be rich and great in this its heaven, for I know this world was given to Reason, with all the riches and glory thereunto belonging, and therefore let not the devil think that this world will hold as long as it hath done, not that it shall enjoy its pleasure and lordly reign here, and in our kingdom on the other side of death too; for I know this is your inheritance by birth-right, and not the Saints at all, and therefore we the last Commissioners, or the Believers thereof, shall not plot or conspire against no Power then reigning, but submit to you however you deal with us; for it is none but your seed that disturbs your peace; therefore Faith will be quiet under thy reign, and pay according to our ability what is your demand, onely in spirituals it will not spare to reveal truth in obedience to eternity: and therefore we desire nothing of you but what *Moses* the first Commissioner requested of *Sihon* king of the *Amorites* in naturals, so we would have the same in spirituals; which was, that he might but onely pass thorough their land, not turning into their fields or vineyards, neither would they drink their water, or eat their bread, but what they paid for; yet the children of *Esau,* the seed of Reason, would not let the Seed of Faith pass by, for which they in their own kingdom were destroyed. So as I am the true and beloved Bishop of the Lord, we request but onely to pass quietly thorough your kingdom, as we have not, so we will not turn to the right, or to the left, to molest you, but be silent under your Government: but if ye will not let us pass, but stay us in prison, and there murther us for pretended blasphemy, as the children of *Esau* would have done to

Moses and his people for rebellion, then take notice, as sure as the *Amorites* were eternally destroyed, so shall ye be eternally damned; for to our kingdom we must go, and without death we cannot go: but if ye be made instrumental to hasten our journey, thereby you hasten your misery, and remember in the height of revelation I told ye so,

Seventhly, and lastly, ye run in vain, not knowing what the soul is, and so are ignorant what dies and therefore by authority in my revelation I shall with all brevity that may be, make it appear, that immortality cannot inhabit in mortality, but one must be swallowed up of the other; However ye cannot understand this, yet from an infallible spirit I know, that the spirit, soul, and body, is all one, though three titles, yet but one essence, the spirit mortal, the soul mortal, and the body mortal, yet not three mortals, but one mortal; none divine, but all humane; for they are so interwoven in the blood, through the whole body, as it is written, *the lust of the flesh is in the blood,* so not two but one; that if you hang one, you must hang both. As now you that supposeth the soul cannot die, and were spectators of those that were hanged, drawn, and Quatered, deal plainly and tell me, when you saw their bodies by a halter stifled, and by the Executioner opened, what did you see? Was there any thing whipt out when the hang man came? Certain I am, if the soul were immortal and could not be killed, you would have seen it fly some whither: And this know, if the soul could not die, it would not suffer its body to die, but take it along with it, in that the soul cannot live without the body, no more than the body can live without the soul. O blinde Reason! that you should imagine you saw any thing but their souls murthered and burned in the fire; for if the soul be in the blood, (then minde) in letting out the blood, you pour out the soul, as when by the spear there came out water and blood, then was the soul of our Lord poured forth, as it is written, *he hath poured out his soul unto death.* Now without a Scripture you will not believe that the soul is in the blood, and in spilling the blood you spill the soul, then read *Jer. 2.34.* and there you shall finde, *In thy skirts is found the blood of the souls of the poor innocents;* so that without you kill the soul, you cannot kill the body, for as long as the soul is alive, the body is not dead, but when the soul, that is the life, is killed, then the body is killed likewise. But then how shall we do with that saying *Fear not them which kill the body, but are not able to kill the soul, &c.* the true meaning is, why the body is said to be killed and not the soul, in that the soul shall rise again, and not the body: the soul by death is but changed to new life, when as the body is killed to an everlasting death; so that in relation to eternity, the body is said to be killed, and not the soul, in that the soul shall quickly rise to life again, and bring with it a body suitable to its nature, as it is written, *and to every seed its own body;* concerning this you may finde more at large in the ninth chapter of my *Dialogue.*

But then you will query, *If the soul and body be one, so but one life, and that life in the blood, then it is the soul is afflicted with pain, sorrow, and grief, nay it is the soul that is faint, weary, hungry, and suffers cold.*

Answ. Were ye not of the contrary seed, I should not need to trouble my pen any further, but answer you in plain tearms, that it is the soul that eats and drinks, and that is capable of any pain, sorrow, or joy; nay I infallibly say, that when you get a childe you get a soul, as it is written, And all the soules they had gotten, she bare unto Jacob, *sixteen souls,* and all the souls went with Jacob *into Egypt. And what soul soever eateth any maner of blood: And she was in bitterness of soul: his soul within him shall mourn: and my soul is heavy unto death.* Now these souls that were got, and upon their feet did go, and eat, and drink &c. were they not men and women? judge ye; So that now let any sober man judge, whether that any thing but life is capable of death. O how senceless it is to think that death must die, and that mortal life can get to immortal life without death! for death is the way to a new life. O then remember when you see a man dead, you see a soul dead, and that not verbally, but really; for as darkness is as real as the light, so death is as real a being as life, though death is not to be understood but by life, and so to be owned by every true Believer.

FINIS.

An Epistle left upon Record for the Believers of this Commission in *London*.

Brethren, you are not ignorant that I was as one born without a *Mother,* and like a prodigal run from his *Father,* yet when I was in the height of my rebellion, my *Father* remembred me, and spread the skirts of his love over me, yea as a brand out of the fire delivered me, and in due time, by his great beloved and last Commissioner, was ordained, and in the Authority of his Commission, often related what a glorious instrument I should be, to illustrate and beautifie his Commission, the like never should come after me, with many infallible expressions uttered to our beloved *Frances* concerning me, all which was done when I was in my infancy, yet according to his revelation have proved true, as is now upon record in publick by me: O what love was bestowed upon me, that I, yea I, that was the greatest of sinners, should have the first and last fruits of his ordination, who had the voice of God, yea was spoken unto mouth to mouth by God, which none now living never had, nor never shall have like unto *John Reeve,* but onely visions, dreames, and dark speeches, which is nothing in comparison of him, yet by this the greatest Prophet that ever shall be, was I made worthy to be a fellow laborer in the work of the Lord with him, who hath not been slothful, but improved my talent beyond all now living, or that shall come after me, in discerning of hypocrites from sound hearts, and finding out the lost sheep of this last age, yet in all this I glory not, but rejoyce that in my knowledge I am not puffed up, but humble as a servant in obedience to it, for which I slighted a good name, with the prosperity of this world, and do stand with my life in my hand, against all spiritual Principalities and Powers of the devil: am I not ready to offer the death of my soul, to what Reason shall demand, that by my revelation you may hold out to the end, and raign in glory with me, though suffer nothing like unto me. O then can you look abroad, and see at home? can you be true, if I be false? can you be happy, and I perish? Is Christ divided, that you are at enmity? Then in vain is your Faith, have I not labored to beget ye Sons in the truth, though not all of you here, yet most of you elsewhere have been the travel of my soul, to leave a Legacy behind me, for the comfort of believers after me, which then will be prized, though not as it ought by you regarded. If I complain, it is because of you, that useth the freedom of a Commission in the abuse of it, I therefore intreat you, if ye believe it, and truly know it, be wise, yet innocent in this your profession, and walk worthy of it, for I am pressed in my spirit as a refiner to try you, and sift you as corn is sifted in a sieve, and who shall deliver you, or feed you with fancies that shall perish with you? O brethren, let me leave this in charge with you, and forget not what I say in mortality, lest ye be forgotten in immortality, that you accuse not another of that you are guilty of your selves, but first examine at home, and then you may the better discern abroad, for from the highest to the lowest, while in mortality there will be infirmities; O then be silent, and cover each others nakedness, and in love strengthen one another, (you are but few) and have many enemies, therefore be friendly among your selves, be kind, comfort, and that not grudgingly, but willingly refresh one another, and grieve not the heart of him that hath rejoiced yours, whose soul doth mourn in love to this Commission. Are ye saints? Then banish spiritual pride, partiality, and vain-glory. Are ye believers, then revile not when reviled, see and not see, hear and not hear, do not say and unsay, fend and prove, backbite, and sowe dissentions, for Faith that worketh by love, cannot quivocate nor dissemble, but doth bear and forbear; Faith that worketh by love doth abase it self, and exalt another, yea suffereth all things. O thou *Kent* and *Cambridgeshire* there is much beauty in thee, and mercy flows from thee, as also some in *London* is not behind thee, for where truth is grounded in love, it doth walk suitable to a God of love, and who is contrary minded from such turn away: now the royal seed-spring within you preserve you that ye may live in love and unity as our Lord hat practiced before you, then you will not fall out by the way, but like *Abraham,* take the left or right to preserve peace here, and glory hereafter.

Farewel.